AND JUSTICE FOR ALL

This edition was prepared
especially for the Japanese
American Citizens League.

JUSTICE FOR ALL

An Oral History of the Japanese American Detention Camps

John Tateishi

RANDOM HOUSE
NEW YORK

All rights reserved under International and Pan-American Copyright
Conventions. Published in the United States by Random House, Inc.,
New York, and simultaneously in Canada by Random House of Canada Limited,
Toronto.

Library of Congress Cataloging in Publication Data
Main entry under title:

And justice for all.

1. Japanese Americans—Evacuation and relocation,
1942-1945. 2. World War, 1939-1945—Personal narratives,
American. I. Tateishi, John, 1939-
D769.8.A6.A67   1984   940.54'72'73   82-42823
ISBN 0-394-53982-6

Manufactured in the United States of America
98765432
First Edition

To the memory of my father

Preface

Until recently, one of the least known episodes in the history of the United States was the forced exclusion and detention during World War II of over 120,000 Japanese American civilians who resided on the West Coast at the outbreak of the conflict. These civilians were forced by armed military guards to abandon their homes and jobs, and denied their constitutional rights, they were herded into detention camps, which had all the trappings of prisons. This was not one of the prouder moments in our collective past, and those who were victimized by that experience would not, and in many ways could not, even much later, publicly talk about their years as prisoners of their own government. Although unfairly stigmatized by accusations of disloyalty, they could not find the voice within themselves to tell others, often even their own children, about what happened to them personally. And so the victims exiled themselves to a silence that lasted forty years.

This book makes no attempt to be a definitive academic history of Japanese American internment. Rather, it tries to present for the first time in human and personal terms the experience of the only group of American citizens ever to be confined in concentration camps in the United States. Taken from recorded interviews, the personal accounts presented here are those of only a few of the thousands who suffered the trauma of false imprisonment. Nevertheless, I think they exemplify what we all went through behind barbed wire during those war years. Emerging from accounts of our common experience are a number of unique stories as well, some of pain and hardship, some bittersweet, some with touches of humor, many with an extraordinary dedication to American ideals. But underlying all of the accounts is a sense of personal tragedy for having experienced a nation's betrayal of a people's loyalty and faith.

Up to now, painful memories have kept Japanese Americans unwilling and unable to talk. But they are silent no more.

John Tateishi
San Francisco

Acknowledgments

An oral history, of course, cannot be the result of only one person's efforts. Many have to contribute, and I am unable here to name and thank all of those who contributed to this one. I wish, however, to express special thanks to a few people who so generously provided me with their time, skill, and emotional support.

Bill Yoshino of Chicago was involved in this work from its inception and labored with me through the difficult task of editing a preliminary manuscript. He also not only put me up, but put up with me as well during my stopovers in Chicago. Without his assistance and wisdom this book would not have been possible.

Minoru Yasui of Denver generously gave of his time to help me with two of the interviews included in this book, and his wife True painstakingly transcribed those interviews.

Grant Ujifusa, editor at Random House, provided invaluable guidance in shaping this book. His moral commitment to the project and his honest appraisal of the Japanese American exclusion and internment experience have inspired me throughout this enterprise. In fact, the idea of an oral history first occurred to Grant.

Carole Hayashino, my colleague in San Francisco, in typical fashion provided whatever assistance and resources I needed in putting this book together. Her help was, as usual, both inestimable and invaluable.

I would be remiss if I did not publicly thank my wife, Carol, and my children, Stephen and Sarah, for their many sacrifices during the course of this project. As a family, they gave up more than just evenings, weekends, and holidays while I worked on the book; they have been tremendously supportive throughout the two years I have labored with this project.

I also wish to thank my transcribers. Tsune Nakayama of Berkeley worked on some of the more difficult interview tapes and, I know, relived a painful past in doing so; Lois Tateishi of Los Angeles also generously and efficiently transcribed many of the interviews; Yuki Fuchigami of San Francisco cheerfully contributed her time in this effort; and Sandra Jerger of Chicago provided superbly professional and accurate transcriptions of most of the taped interviews, and so made my job much easier.

And finally, I am grateful to all those who were interviewed, some of whose stories do not appear in this book, for graciously allowing me to share their personal stories and pain.

Contents

Introduction

The dropping of Japanese bombs on the naval base at Pearl Harbor on December 7, 1941, triggered a series of events on the West Coast of the United States that culminated in one of the most extraordinary episodes in the history of this country: the establishment of concentration camps in America. There were ten such camps built in remote wastelands in the country's interior: Manzanar and Tule Lake in California; Poston and Gila River in Arizona; Minidoka in Idaho; Topaz in Utah; Heart Mountain in Wyoming; Amache in Colorado; and Jerome and Rohwer in Arkansas. These were not the death camps of Europe, but they were complete with barbed-wire fences, guard towers, searchlights, and armed military guards. The enclosures were the consequence of the forced exclusion of United States citizens and resident aliens of Japanese ancestry from the West Coast.

The desolate compounds were designed to imprison civilians— men, women, children, the old, the infirm, even newborn infants. None of these people was ever charged with any crime, and no evidence of wrongdoing was brought against any of them. Most incarcerated—about 77,000 out of the 120,000—were United States citizens, born and raised in this country, but some were resident aliens, known as Issei. These people were first-generation immigrants who had chosen to live in the United States for over a half century, but unlike their European counterparts, they had been denied naturalization rights by federal statutes. The entire West Coast ethnic Japanese population of 120,000 were ordered from their homes by soldiers bearing rifles and bayonets and were placed into military detention. Denied fundamental rights, Japanese Americans became prisoners of their own country.

The government's policy was based on the incredible notion that this group of people, solely on the basis of ancestry, had to be regarded as inherently disloyal to the United States. They were simply presumed to be a racial nest of spies and saboteurs, there being no individual review whatever.

By releasing only selected information concerning the situation, the federal government made it appear that the internment policy was a direct and necessary result of the attack on Pearl Harbor. The government asserted that it was forced to take the extreme measure because there was no other recourse, given the fear and hysteria on the West Coast and the presumed difficulties in determining the loyalty of any individual Japanese American. The latter position was bitterly ironic in a nation founded on the principle of personal justice.

The fact is that the exclusion and incarceration of Japanese Americans during World War II successfully accomplished what local pressure groups on the West Coast had been unable themselves to achieve for half a century: the complete removal of the entire ethnic Japanese population from the coastal states. It was an act of racism and had nothing to do with establishing security measures of any sort in the coastal regions.

Behind the exclusion was a long history of anti-Japanese and anti-Chinese agitation on the West Coast. In California, where over 80 percent of the ethnic Japanese population resided, many politicians had long been exploiting the Yellow Peril issue and fear of the Japanese menace. The jingoism was whipped up by special-interest and white-supremacy groups, such as the Native Sons of the Golden West, the California Grange Association, the American Legion, the Japanese Exclusion League, and the American Federation of Labor in California. Also beating the drums heavily were the Hearst and McClatchy newspapers. These groups got their way.

What instead should have guided the federal government's policy toward Japanese Americans were the reports of various intelligence agencies, whose direct responsibility it was to maintain internal security for the country. The President and his Secretary of War, Henry Stimson, were well aware of the real situation on the West Coast prior to December 7, 1941, through reports provided by the Office of Naval Intelligence and the Federal Bureau of Investigation, both of which had conducted extensive investigations on the West Coast over a number of years and had identified anyone who might have been considered a possible security risk. Based on this information, FBI agents swept through the Japanese communities along the West Coast within hours of the attack at Pearl Harbor and rounded up any aliens who were language-school teachers, Buddhist priests, community leaders, newspapermen—anyone who had been singled out by the intelligence agencies. This in itself imposed great injustice on a group of people overwhelmingly, often touchingly, loyal. Satisfied that the quick action of the FBI had secured the West Coast from any threat of potential fifth column activity on the part of either whites or Japanese, FBI Director J. Edgar Hoover assured the White House that the West Coast had been made secure and that, beyond surveillance of the Japanese communities, no further security measures were necessary.

West Coast politicians and pressure groups, in the absence of legitimate grounds for demanding the mass eviction of Japanese Americans, turned to racial attacks that inpugned the loyalty of the entire Japanese American community. These groups also spread false rumors about sabotage, creating fear in the public mind, especially in the early months of the war as reports from the Pacific brought news of American military defeats to a seemingly invincible enemy. The California congressional delegation wrote to President Franklin Roosevelt urging the removal of the entire Japanese population from the coastal states, and both the Military Commander for the Western Command, Lieutenant General John L. DeWitt, and California State Attorney General Earl Warren, then an exceedingly ambitious politician, went on record as backing some of the most farfetched arguments for a policy of mass exclusion. DeWitt, who was not the most clearheaded of military men, stated that "The very fact that no sabotage has taken place to date is a disturbing and confirming indication that such action will be taken." Warren elaborated DeWitt's argument before a congressional committee in late February 1942, saying that to believe the absence of sabotage by the Japanese population was proof of loyalty was "simply to live in a fool's paradise." He viewed the absence of sabotage to that point as an "ominous sign" that "the fifth column activities that we are to get are timed just like Pearl Harbor was timed." It was a damned-if-you-do-and-damned-if-you-don't argument: the loyalty demonstrated by Japanese Americans was proof that they would be disloyal. As incredible as this logic was, the argument served as a justification for the mass exclusion and subsequent internment.

Meanwhile, the press on the West Coast began an openly racist campaign, led by the Hearst and McClatchy newspapers, which ran inflammatory editorials and news columns that produced a sense of outrage among white Californians against their Japanese American neighbors. Somehow these people became responsible for the attack on Pearl Harbor. Henry McLemore wrote in his syndicated column: "I am for immediate removal of every Japanese . . . to a point deep in the interior. I don't mean a nice part of the interior either. Herd 'em up, pack 'em off and give 'em the inside room in the badlands. Let 'em be pinched, hurt, hungry and dead up against it. . . . Personally I hate the Japanese. And that goes for all of them." Although a few courageous commentators urged fair treatment and defended the rights of Japanese Americans, a wave of racism and hysteria pervaded the press and radio, which included such respected voices as Walter Lippmann. The federal government, in order to appease the public, found an easy scapegoat in the Japanese American population, and its acquiescence to regional pressure resulted in what former Senator Sam J. Ervin has called "the single most blatant violation of the Constitution in our history."

As I see the politics of the issue, the moment Franklin Roosevelt chose to have the War Department handle it, the matter was settled. The War Department under Secretary of War Henry Stimson and his assistant John J. McCloy had been involved in the plans for exclusion, and FDR knew that the War Department would be receptive to the demands of military people in the field and to local politicians. Roosevelt could have intervened to prevent the policy of mass exclusion from being implemented, had he chosen to expend some presidential political capital, but he chose not to, perhaps fearing advantages that might accrue to Earl Warren. Warren was later elected governor of California in 1944 and was nominated as the Republican candidate for Vice President in 1948 before becoming a notable Chief Justice of the Supreme

Court. In short, the two principal players here were Roosevelt in Washington and Warren in California, with the buck stopping in the Oval Office. The victims were Japanese Americans and the Constitution.

The announced basis for the government policy was "military necessity," which meant that Japanese Americans were considered a security risk because there was no way to determine their loyalty to this country. DeWitt asserted without a shred of supporting evidence that because ethnic ties to Japan among Japanese Americans were stronger than their sense of loyalty to the United States, the complete removal of all persons of Japanese ancestry from the coastal regions was a "military necessity." Ironically, the Army commander in Hawaii found that the same "necessity" required the presence on the islands of the Japanese American population, not only because they constituted a major part of the labor force, but also because they were needed to serve in critical defense capacities. Hawaii, three thousand miles closer to the enemy and the very point of the devastating attack, did not share the West Coast's racial sentiments and therefore based its policies toward Japanese Americans on reasonable and rational grounds.

If the West Coast policies had been similarly governed by the completely reasonable intelligence agency reports, the mass exclusion would not have occurred. Instead, the federal government suppressed pertinent intelligence information and did little to ease the rising anxiety of the coastal populace. The fears on the West Coast were exacerbated when Secretary of the Navy Frank Knox returned from an inspection of Pearl Harbor on December 15 and was quoted by the press as saying that "the most effective Fifth Column work of the entire war was done in Hawaii with the possible exception of Norway." This did nothing to promote justice for Japanese Americans living on the West Coast. Knox's statement was later proven to be completely untrue, but it effectively impugned the loyalty of Japanese Americans and suggested that the attack at Pearl Harbor would not have succeeded without assistance from the ethnic Japanese residents in Hawaii. It further sharpened the fears of a West Coast invasion and prompted even greater pressures in California for an exclusion policy.

And so on February 19, 1942, President Franklin D. Roosevelt signed Executive Order 9066, the key governmental document that paved the way for a massive eviction and subsequent imprisonment of Japanese Americans. On March 21, 1942, Congress passed legislation that made it a criminal offense to violate military restrictions. Despite warnings by the U.S. Attorney General, Francis Biddle, that the forced removal of American citizens was unconstitutional, Roosevelt signed 9066 with the clear intent of excluding citizens and aliens alike. The intent of the order, however, virtually left untouched aliens of German and Italian ancestry, except those who had been specifically and individually identified by the intelligence agencies as security risks.

On February 25, six days after the issuance of Executive Order 9066, General DeWitt ordered the eviction of the Japanese population of two thousand from Terminal Island in Los Angeles, giving the residents twenty-four hours to vacate and sell their homes and businesses. Fred Fujikawa, whose story appears in this book, was among those forced out of Terminal Island. And on March 2, in issuing the first of over a hundred military proclamations, DeWitt declared the western half of California, Oregon, and Washington as military zones with specific areas of exclusion. It was also under Military Proclamation No. 1 that all Japanese Americans and their alien parents were told that they could "voluntarily evacuate" their homes and move out of the exclusion areas. But knowing they were unwelcome in the interior and hearing stories of violence against the few who had attempted to resettle outside the restricted zones, the majority remained where they were. The Nisei, second generation Japanese Americans born and educated in this country, believed that the government would provide fair treatment for them because they were citizens. Although they were very worried about their parents, they were convinced that they themselves would not be affected by any exclusion orders and therefore felt no need to leave their homes and businesses.

On March 24, DeWitt issued Military Proclamation No. 3, which established a nighttime curfew and a five-mile travel restriction imposed only on persons of Japanese ancestry. On the same day, the first Civilian Exclusion Order was issued on Bainbridge Island in the state of Washington, ordering the Japanese American population off the island within twenty-four hours. Three days later DeWitt issued orders prohibiting further "voluntary" movement from the exclusion zones. By then, with the evictions from Terminal and Bainbridge islands, Japanese Americans sensed that the entire ethnic Japanese population would be evicted from their homes and that the rights of citizens would be ignored. But because they were under a five-mile travel restriction, they were unable to leave the military zones to seek new homes elsewhere. Only a handful, like Paul Shinoda, whose account appears here, dared to defy the military orders, and the majority awaited what they knew by then to be the inevitable.

By early April 1942, exclusion orders began to appear on telephone poles in all the Japanese communities, ordering all persons of Japanese ancestry, "aliens and nonaliens alike," to report to assembly points on specified days. In typical fashion, the government once again avoided the constitutional question of infringing on the rights of citizens by semantically designating them as nonaliens. While people in some areas were allowed only days to settle their affairs, most were given up to two weeks to sell homes and businesses prior to vacating the West Coast. The story, included here, of Theresa Takayoshi typifies the way in which neighbors, like scavengers, swooped down on the Japanese communities and offered outrageously low prices for homes, businesses, cars, and other personal property, knowing that because Japanese Americans were being forced to leave on such short notice, they could not get market value for whatever they owned. Caught in that situation, Japanese Americans salvaged what little they could and, as a community, suffered enormous economic losses.

Mary Tsukamoto recalls how Japanese farmers, to assist in the U.S. war effort, had planted their crops at the request of government agencies and clung to the hope that they would be allowed to harvest them before leaving their farms, but they soon began to realize that they would have to leave it all behind. They were required to vacate within weeks and even days of the spring harvest, reaping none of the profits and incurring all of the debts. The forced sales caused all but a handful of Japanese Americans to be completely disenfranchised by the exclusion process. The few who were lucky enough to hold on to their property returned to varying circumstances: some found their homes and farms in shambles, but a rare few who had trusted white friends to care for their property returned to homes that were well kept. The majority of Japanese Americans, however, lost everything they had at the time they were forced to leave the West Coast.

On June 2, DeWitt designated all of California, Oregon, and Washington, and the western half of Arizona as military zones and exclusion areas. The small number of families and individuals, Iwato Itow among them, who had earlier left homes to resettle in places outside the exclusion areas now suddenly found themselves caught in the same web of restrictions in the newly designated exclusion areas. No one of Japanese ancestry living in the states of California, Oregon, and Washington, whether citizen or alien, enjoyed freedom in America by June 1942.

It is significant that on June 2, 1942, the day that General De-Witt declared the entire West Coast as exclusion areas, the Battle of Midway was taking place in the Pacific. It was at Midway that the Japanese naval fleet was virtually destroyed. Shortly after the naval battle, U.S. Naval Intelligence sent reports to Washington that the Japanese fleet was defeated, dismissing any further threat of a West Coast invasion. If in fact the exclusion and detention policy was based on "military necessity" and the potential threat of invasion (as the government stated), such a threat no longer existed and the exclusion policy should have been lifted. By the beginning of June 1942, only 17,000 Japanese Americans had been moved to the permanent camps. The exclusion policy continued, and an additional 93,000 Japanese Americans were placed in the permanent detention camps in subsequent months. Military necessity clearly became a rationale for what was from the beginning a questionable government policy.

Contrary to the popular belief that Japanese Americans quietly acquiesced to their eviction, over one hundred individuals defied government restrictions and orders. Those arrested were convicted by the courts, but with the eviction near and without financial resources to appeal their cases, they were unable to continue their challenge in the courts. However, three Japanese Americans did establish test cases on the constitutionality of what they viewed as the government's discriminatory measures. Minoru Yasui, an attorney in Portland, Oregon, whose story appears in this book, was the first to challenge the legality of instituting a curfew in the absence of martial law and as a restriction directed at a group of citizens based solely on ancestry. Shortly thereafter, Gordon Hirabayashi, a student at the University of Washington in Seattle, similarly violated the curfew and, like Yasui, also refused to obey orders to leave his home. In San Leandro, across the bay from San Francisco, Fred Korematsu disobeyed the military orders and refused to evacuate. All three were arrested and convicted by the federal district courts.

Their cases were appealed to the United States Supreme Court, which accepted the argument based on military necessity, and without examination of the evidence, it rendered the decision that the forced exclusion and detention of American citizens, without cause and based solely on ancestry, was constitutional. Justice Robert Jackson, dissenting, stated that "the Court for all time has validated the principle of racial discrimination in criminal procedure," and "the principle then lies about like a loaded weapon ready for the hand of any authority that can bring forward a plausible claim of an urgent need." The judgments in these three cases have been criticized by constitutional experts over the last forty years as some of the worst decisions ever made by the Supreme Court.

The Japanese American incarceration began in April 1942. Having been ordered from their homes and allowed to take only what they could carry, they were placed under detention in what the government euphemistically called Assembly Centers, temporary camps which were hastily converted racetracks and fairgrounds where entire families were housed in either horse stalls or crudely built barracks. Emi Somekawa tells what life was like living in the stench of the horse stalls while others, such as Violet de Cristoforo and Miyo Senzaki, describe typical living conditions in the barracks. The encampments were ringed with barbed-wire fences and armed military guards to prevent escape. There were fifteen such "centers," with all but three in California. Japanese Americans arrived at these camps by the thousands daily. The group from Bainbridge Island and people from some parts of Los Angeles were sent directly to Manzanar Relocation Center, the first of the ten concentration camps to be opened.

So severe was the government's policy that orphaned children living in Alaska, then a territory of the United States, were shipped to the mainland and interned if they had so much as one-sixteenth Japanese blood. Helen Murao tells her especially poignant story of being an orphaned sixteen-year-old girl with two young brothers, forced into the Portland detention center. Caucasian women married to Japanese men found their husbands and children interned, and most chose to follow their families into detention. By

August 1942 the exclusion process had been completed, and persons of Japanese ancestry were no longer to be found in the cities, towns, and farms of the West Coast states which they had previously inhabited. The relatively few who had escaped the government's restrictive policies and left their homes early had moved far into the interior of the country, but the vast majority were prisoners of their own government.

Japanese Americans remained in the temporary camps for up to six months, just long enough to adjust to their makeshift detention, at which point they were boarded onto antiquated railway cars with shades drawn and under military guard and sent to destinations unknown to them, arriving at the permanent camps—the so-called relocation centers—situated in the barren wastelands of the interior. They were greeted by dust storms and once again faced compounds enclosed by barbed-wire fences and surrounded by guard towers and searchlights. This was to be their home for the next two to three years.

Japanese Americans interned in the camps found their own means of making life bearable, but having come from the milder climates near the Pacific Ocean, they found the weather harsh and unrelenting. There was little protection from the winter storms and scorching summers in the crudely built barracks that housed them. With ten thousand to eighteen thousand men, women, and children crowded into the camps, privacy was not possible, and family life began to disintegrate.

There was violence at some of the camps: at Santa Anita Assembly Center, the famous racetrack converted into a temporary detention center, a minor riot broke out because of a food shortage; at Tule Lake, a pro-American element fought with a smaller dissident group, and both were subdued by military guards; and at Manzanar, a riot occurred when residents discovered that a food shortage in the camp resulted from guards and authorities selling food on the black market. Harry Ueno, considered the leader of the so-called Manzanar riot, gives insight into the event. These were incidents isolated from each other.

But the first major outbreak occurred in all ten permanent camps when the War Relocation Authority (WRA), the civilian agency created to administer the camps, issued a leave clearance form to all adult men and women over the age of seventeen. The form, which came to be known by camp residents as the "loyalty questionnaire," contained two questions which caused great emotional upheaval. The infamous questions 27 and 28 asked, first, if the respondent was "willing to serve in the armed forces of the United States in combat duty," and second, if, after swearing allegiance to the United States, he or she would "foreswear any form of allegiance or obedience to the Japanese emperor" or any other foreign government. While many may have been willing to answer yes to question 27, question 28, as preposterous as it was, created a sense of outrage among a very large number of camp residents. To answer yes to this question would imply former allegiance to the emperor of Japan which was inapplicable for the American-born Nisei; but to answer no would implicate them as disloyal to the United States. And for the Issei, who had been denied the right of citizenship in the United States, to answer yes to question 28 could leave them stateless in a situation where their futures were at best unknown and precarious.

Questions 27 and 28 split the camp communities into the "yes-yes" and "no-no" groups, and the latter group came to be known as the no-no boys. There was no middle position that could be taken on the questions, and often families were torn apart over the issue, separating fathers from sons, brothers from brothers. It left strong bitterness within families, as is described in the account of Ben Takeshita. It was the most volatile of all the issues to arise among the excluded, for it also raised the question of whether young men in the camps should accept voluntary military service or eligibility for the draft. Indignant that they were being asked such questions while denied their rights as citizens, many answered no to both questions and were soon thereafter taken from the various camps and sent to the Tule Lake center in California, which was designated by the government as a segregation camp designed to isolate the so-called troublemakers and the disloyal. The treatment at Tule Lake was often harsh, especially for those who were singled out by the guards, as in the case of Morgan Yamanaka, who provides his account. The no-no boys—Jack Tono among them—maintained throughout that if they were given their freedom, like any other American citizen, they would more than willingly serve the country in uniform, but they protested their treatment, using the questionnaire to express themselves. This was risky. Some people who answered no-no were being deported to Japan as late as 1946. So deep-seated became the conflict over the issue that after four decades, questions 27 and 28 still divide the Japanese American community.

Among those advocating the yes-yes position was an organization called the Japanese American Citizens League (JACL), a young Nisei organization, which from the very beginning of the exclusion and internment program counseled loyalty and cooperation. Because it had an established network throughout the Japanese American community prior to the war, the JACL was chosen by the government to serve as a communication link with the West Coast Japanese community. But the JACL leadership soon found itself thrust into the role of chief negotiator for Japanese Americans. The Nisei of the JACL were in their mid-twenties and less than experienced in the world; they were often dazzled by the government's negotiating tactics and found themselves confused when trying to advise their fellow Japanese Americans. Government authorities themselves were also often confused and issued contradicting orders. Sensing that the forced eviction of their entire ethnic group from the West Coast was inevitable, the JACL encouraged Japanese Americans to cooperate with the government. The organization argued that only by working with what they knew to be an insensitive Army command could they avoid violence and bloodshed. The JACL also felt that cooperating would be a genuine demonstration of Japanese American loyalty to the country. This position was harshly criticized by many people in the Japanese American community, just as was the group's later yes-yes position on the loyalty questionnaire.

The JACL went one step further in its attempt to demonstrate the loyalty of Japanese Americans. The organization asked for the creation of a segregated unit in the Army. Taking again an extreme position, the JACL suggested that Japanese Americans would be willing to serve in what was really proposed as a suicide unit to fight against the Japanese enemy in the Pacific. This, the JACL believed, would serve as an ultimate testimony of the loyalty of the Nisei and the entire ethnic Japanese population in America. The War Department agreed instead to the creation of a separate unit, the all-Nisei 442nd Regimental Combat Team, which, when joined by the Japanese-Hawaiian 100th Battalion, became the most highly decorated United States military unit during World War II and the most highly decorated unit of comparable size in United States military history. Over thirty-three thousand Nisei served in the 442nd and 100th, many of them coming from the camps where their parents, wives, and children were interned, as in the cases of Wilson Makabe, John Kanda, and Tom Kawaguchi, described in this book. The 100th Battalion, known as the Purple Heart Battalion because of its heavy casualties, fought in Africa and Italy, and finally joined with the newly arrived 442nd in France. Together, they fought with extraordinary courage and skill in some of the bloodiest and fiercest campaigns in Europe.

One of the costliest campaigns was the rescue of the Texas Lost Battalion in the Vosges Mountains in France, where the 442nd fought for six days to reach the Lost Battalion nine miles away. A detailed account of this is given by Shig Doi. They saved 211 men from the Texas Battalion but at a cost of 800 casualties, suffering more losses than the number of men saved. No less significant was the battle of the Gothic Line, where, from the time of their assault, the 442nd broke the German line of resistance in thirty-two minutes. With 4,000 men the 442nd accomplished in a half-hour's assault what two divisions with a total of 40,000 men failed to achieve in five months of fighting. The achievements of the 442nd and 100th were unparalleled during the war and demonstrated an incredible loyalty to a nation that had sorely misjudged them.

Further testimony of their loyalty was evidenced by the Nisei contributions in the Pacific. The Military Intelligence Service (MIS) recruited some 6,000 Japanese Americans from both the Nisei and Kibei. The latter were Japanese Americans who were born in the United States and were therefore American citizens but who had received part or all of their education in Japan. Volunteering for special assignment, the Japanese American MIS soldiers served as interpreters and interrogators in the Pacific against the Japanese, dispelling the belief that the Nisei and even the Kibei, "whose natural affinities are with the Japanese enemy," in the words of General DeWitt, would prove disloyal to the United States if given the opportunity. Because their operation was highly classified, there was little recognition of the MIS, but their contributions to the American war effort proved extremely significant. Major General Charles Willoughby, intelligence chief for Douglas MacArthur, stated that the Japanese American MIS soldiers "saved a million lives and shortened the war by two years."

On the home front, in the waning days of the war, the government prepared to close the detention camps. While earlier the loyalty questionnaire had caused divisions within the camps, it nevertheless did establish from the government's point of view a determination of loyalty and rightfully should have led to an end to the exclusion policy and forced detention. In light of the clear evidence that the basis for the exclusion was not really legitimate in the first place, the government could no longer justify its continued enforcement on the grounds of military necessity and on the grounds that no way existed to distinguish between the loyal and potentially disloyal. The War Department and the military leadership in Washington acknowledged this by early 1943, but Roosevelt ignored their conclusions, and the policy remained in effect until December 16, 1944, when the War Department finally announced the revocation of the exclusion policy. On December 17, the WRA officially declared that the camps were to close, an announcement which curiously came the day before the Supreme Court handed down its decision in the Mitsuye Endo case (*ex parte* Endo). Endo had challenged the government's right to detain indefinitely any citizen about whom a determination of loyalty had been made. The court ruled in Endo's favor the day after the WRA announced the closure of the camps.

Since there was no longer any justification for the exclusion according to the War Department's own determination, Roosevelt's motives must be questioned. Why did he wait a full eighteen months before revoking the exclusion order? A study issued by a congressional commission in February 1983 suggests strongly that a significant factor was the election of 1944 in which Roosevelt ran for an unprecedented fourth term. Also, Roosevelt continued to get pressure from West Coast politicians and interest groups to invoke a permanent exclusion of the Japanese population from that region of the country.

Nevertheless, the gates to the camps were finally opened, and Japanese Americans began to return to the West Coast, thus bringing to an end one of the darkest episodes in our nation's constitutional history.

The Japanese American internment was an experience unparalleled in the history of the United States. A group of American citizens and their alien parents became the innocent victims of a racist policy that ignored all the protections of individual rights which are intrinsic and essential to the very principles of constitutional government. But in that time of national crisis, emotion, political expediency, and economic greed prevailed, and the Constitution was grossly violated. All three branches—the executive, legislative, and judicial—failed the trust reposed in them and embraced West Coast prejudices that were infused with racist assumptions. The exclusion and internment of Japanese Americans during World War II was an injustice felt at the deepest personal level by those who experienced it, but for all Americans, it remains a betrayal of the principles upon which this nation was founded.

AND
JUSTICE
FOR
ALL

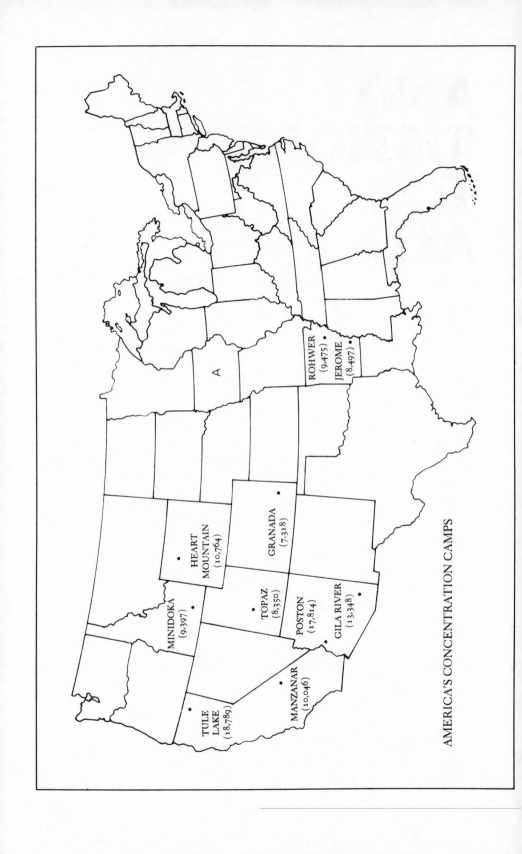

TULE
LAKE
(18,789)

MINIDOKA
(9,397)

MANZANAR
(10,046)

HEART
MOUNTAIN
(10,764)

TOPAZ
(8,350)

POSTON
(17,814)

GRANADA
(7,318)

GILA RIVER
(13,348)

A

ROHWER
(9,475)

JEROME
(8,497)

AMERICA'S CONCENTRATION CAMPS

MARY TSUKAMOTO

Jerome

I was born in San Francisco. My parents came from Okinawa and had the Capitol Laundry on Geary Street, where I lived when I was very little. Then my father moved to Turlock. When I was ten, he moved his family to Florin to raise strawberries, and became one of the bigger strawberry farmers there. From ten on I grew up in Florin, where I had the shock of attending the Florin Elementary School, because a few years before we arrived, the school was segregated. Until then we hadn't really encountered that kind of prejudice. Everyone whispered, and you felt kind of ashamed and afraid, and it made you kind of tighten up your body.

When Al and I were married, we became members of the Florin JACL which was organized in 1935. In 1939 we decided we wanted to do something for the community. So we wondered if we couldn't ask the school trustees and the county superintendent if the school might be integrated. Surprisingly, the superintendent didn't object, and the trustees and the principal were agreeable. So the segregated school lasted about fifteen years, from 1923 to 1939.

We went to Elk Grove High School, which was not segregated, but it was an experience to come out of a school where there were only Japanese children and then go on to Elk Grove High School. It was a traumatic experience for many of us who were very sensitive during those teenage years. I remember how we meekly walked around and we huddled together, and very reluctantly responded to invitations to various activities. But as we developed, amazingly, the boys who were athletic got involved, and they were more popular. But the kids who weren't very athletic often got beat up. The Manchurian crisis was in the news then and caused many of the kids to get into fights. Some of the teachers were trying to help us develop better feeling among the students, but it wasn't very easy because the community went along with a strong Native Sons and Daughters of the Golden West organization. Everyone was affected by their propaganda.

I remember we had an annual oratorical contest sponsored by the Native Sons and Daughters, and I ended up one of the nine qualifying competitors. Then the principal and the teacher called me in and told me that I couldn't be in it because of my ancestry. I was relieved I didn't have to do another oration, but the teacher didn't let me forget. She was upset and so discouraged that the Native Sons wouldn't change their position. She was really angry because it was a whole class assignment, given to every one of the children who took public speaking. That they would discriminate made her very angry, but she couldn't do anything about it. She was the one that was responsible in getting me to college because of that experience—to the College of the Pacific. I graduated from high school in 1933. That teacher was poor herself, but before my dad knew anything about it, she had arranged to get me a $150 scholarship. She even had to go and ask Dad if he would let me go and not help at home because every child was needed for the strawberries at that time. Every child and everybody in the family worked together to eke out a living. My dad was so deeply touched, of course, he let me go.

But there were other things he had learned about this country too. He was chased out of Turlock, where there was a great deal of anti-Japanese sentiment. He had always had a difficult time because he didn't know the language. There was a time when the Japanese farmers lost a lot of money because they couldn't even write contracts, and they lost a lot of money by verbal agreements. And all of this was part of what he remembered, but also he remembered this wonderful teacher who got me to college. That's how I ended up being a schoolteacher, and for that I feel very grateful.

Florin was an unusual community because more than 60 percent were Japanese people who were farming. There were also a lot of Japanese townspeople working in the basket factory or cover factory.

They would work out in the fields as laborers during the harvest season but lived in the town of Florin the rest of the time. Altogether there were 2,500 Japanese people making a living here, depending on each other. We raised strawberries, and then in the fall we harvested grapes.

Way back in 1892, when Grandpa Tsukamoto, Al's father, came to Florin for the first time, he already found Mr. Nakayama growing strawberries. He had figured out a way of making the patches just so wide so he could also nurture the new young grapevines. They realized that it took four or five years for the grapes to start producing. But in the meantime they were able to harvest strawberries to make a living, and so, by combining the two crops, they managed to survive.

Anyway, because grape growing was a very profitable way of making a living, the white owners were very happy to have the Japanese farmers come into this area. This is how Florin grew, and by 1942 we had a very large Japanese colony. It was sort of a mistake beyond our control. There were too many Japanese compared to the Caucasian people. I found out that sociologists said it was a mistake to overpopulate with a foreign group that should be in the minority if we were to work together happily. But that wasn't so here. We had no control over it, because we were encouraged to come, and we were welcomed by the landowners. But some people around us didn't quite like what was happening. They were afraid and spoke out. The Native Sons and Daughters and the American Legion and the California Federation of Labor and the Hearst papers and the McClatchy papers all claimed that the Japanese were going to own all of California, that we were going to take over the land. So, many people decided that they wanted to try to get us out. Publicity would periodically appear in the papers, and the campaign seemed to hit us every election year. Prejudice was deliberately manufactured, and people had to work hard to create and stir it up. We were innocent victims, but we have to understand this background if we are to understand what happened when the war broke out.

I remember some of the boys. We just knew when we were walking home from school that they would throw stones at us and call us Japs, but we just couldn't do anything back. The thing is, when the legislature was working on the alien land law in Sacramento, a small group of white landowners who were very kind and friends to Japanese were alarmed at what was going to happen. They tried to go to protest, but they weren't given an opportunity to speak in favor of the Japanese. It just wasn't the popular thing to do. They were very disappointed that they weren't given a chance to be heard and tried to get it into the papers. But, of course, with McClatchy and Hearst, they just didn't have a chance.

I do remember Pearl Harbor day. I was about twenty-seven, and we were in church. It was a December Sunday, so we were getting ready for our Christmas program. We were rehearsing and having Sunday School class, and I always played the piano for the adult Issei service. Of course, because there were so many Japanese, all of it was in Japanese; the minister was a Japanese, and he preached in Japanese. But after the service started, my husband ran in. He had been home that day and heard on the radio. We just couldn't believe it, but he told us that Japan attacked Pearl Harbor. I remember how stunned we were. And suddenly the whole world turned dark. We started to speak in whispers, and because of our experience in Florin, we immediately sensed something terrible was going to happen. We just prayed that it wouldn't, but we sensed the things would be very difficult. The minister and all of the leaders discussed matters, and we knew that we needed to be prepared for the worst.

Then, of course, within a day or two, we heard that the FBI had taken Mr. Tanigawa and Mr. Tsuji. I suppose the FBI had them on their list, and it wasn't long before many of them were taken. We had no idea what they were going through. We should have been more aware. One Issei, Mr. Iwasa, committed suicide. So all of these reports and the anguish and the sorrow made the whole world very dark. Then rumors had it that we were supposed to turn in our cameras and our guns, and they were called in. Every day there was something else about other people being taken by the FBI. Then gradually we just couldn't believe the newspapers and what people were saying. And then there was talk about sending us away, and we just couldn't believe that they would do such a thing. It would be a situation where the whole community would be uprooted. But soon enough we were reading reports of other communities being evacuated from San Pedro and from Puget Sound. After a while we became aware that maybe things weren't going to just stop but would continue to get worse and worse.

We read about President Roosevelt's Executive Order 9066. I remember the JACL people had a convention in San Francisco in

March. We realized that we needed to be able to rise to the occasion to help in whatever way we could in our community. We came home trying to figure out just how we could do that. We had many meetings at night and the FBI was always lurking around. We were told we couldn't stay out after eight o'clock in the evening.

Meanwhile, Hakujin [white] neighbors were watching us and reporting to the FBI that we were having secret meetings. We were not supposed to meet after eight o'clock, but often we couldn't cut off our JACL meeting at eight o'clock, and so we would have tea or coffee and keep talking. We would be reported, and the police would come. There were so many people making life miserable for us. Then we heard that we had been restricted to traveling five miles from our homes; it was nine miles to Sacramento, and at that time everything was in Sacramento, like doctors, banks, and grocery stores. So it just was a terrible, fearful experience. Every time we went anywhere more than five miles away, we were supposed to go to the WCCA office in Sacramento, nine miles away, to get a permit. It was ridiculous.

A lot of little things just nagged at us and harassed us, and we were frightened, but even in that atmosphere I remember we frantically wanted to do what was American. We were Americans and loyal citizens, and we wanted to do what Americans should be doing. So we were wrapping Red Cross bandages and trying to do what we could to help our country. By May 1942, more than a hundred of our boys were already drafted. We worried about them, and they were worried about what was going to happen to their families. We knew what we wanted to do. We started to buy war bonds, and we took first aid classes with the rest of the Hakujin people in the community. We went out at night to go to these classes, but we worried about being out after eight o'clock. It was a frightening time. Every little rule and regulation was imposed only on the Japanese people. There were Italian and German people in the community, but it was just us that had travel restrictions and a curfew.

And we were still trying to think about how we could serve the community. I finally opened a JACL office near the end of March, and I was running in and out of the Wartime Civilian Control Administration (WCCA) office. They finally decided to send some people out to work with me to advise me and the welfare office and the Federal Reserve Bank and the Farm Security Agency. They were to help the people who were asking questions and trying to get ready for this terrible ordeal that was ahead of them. Not knowing for sure, many of them kept hoping and wishing that we would not have to go, that somehow things would change and we wouldn't have to leave.

We tried to get everybody instructions, and the WCCA would tell me one thing one day, and I would then tell everybody this is what we're going to need to do, and then the next week the whole regulation was changed, and we just ended up being liars right and left. It was such a state of confusion and anger, everyone being so upset at what was happening. I remember I was crying inside and I just felt like I was put through a hamburger machine. I was human and worried and scared for myself too, but worried about everybody else and trying to help people.

I remember Ida Onga. Her husband was taken by the FBI, and she came in here so big; she was going to have a baby in a month or so. She cried because she was supposed to go and see the doctor, and she didn't know that she had to have a traveler's permit. She had come from Folsom and had traveled more than five miles. I needed to get her into town so she could get to the doctor, and so I took her to the WCCA office for a travel permit. There we found out that Mrs. Tsuji's husband was taken away by the FBI. But nobody thought about the family left behind needing food and money. We finally arranged for the WCCA welfare office to provide food, and she cried because Japanese people are proud and they weren't willing to accept handouts. They never had been on welfare before, and she felt terrible because here she ended up receiving food. But we told her this was different, because her husband was taken and because it's what you have to do. She had three children. These things were happening.

I remember Mrs. Kuima, whose son was thirty-two years old and retarded. She took care of him. They had five other boys, but she took care of this boy at home. The welfare office said No, she couldn't take him, that the families have to institutionalize a child like that. It was a very tragic thing for me to have to tell her, and I remember going out to the field—she was hoeing strawberries— and I told her what they told us, that you can't take your son with you. And so she cried, and I cried with her. A few days before they were evacuated they came to take him away to an institution. It was very hard for me to face that family. I felt as though I was the messenger that carried such tragic news for them. It was only about a month after we got to Fresno Assembly Center that they sent us a wire saying he died. All these years she loved him and took care of him, he only knew Japanese and ate Japanese food. I was thinking of the family; they got over it quietly; they endured it. I just felt guilty, you know, just for having been involved.

I had anxieties for Grandpa and Grandma. They were old and had farmed all their lives, and after more than fifty years here, the thought of uprooting these people and taking them away from their farm and the things they loved was terrible. Grandpa growing tea and vegetables, and Grandma growing her flowers. It was a cruel thing to do to them in their twilight years. But we had to get them ready to leave, anxious for their health and their safety. And my daughter, who was five, had to be ready to go to school. Al had had a hemorrhage that winter, so we all had our personal grief as well.

The Farm Security Administration (FSA) told us that we should work until the very last moment. Yet we had to worry about selling our car and our refrigerator and about what we should do with our chickens and our pets. And we worried about trying to buy the right kind of things to get ready for a place we knew nothing about. We thought about camping. They said "camp," so we thought about going up in the mountains somewhere. I even bought boots thinking we would be up in the mountains where there might be snakes. Just ridiculous all the funny things we thought about!

In those days women didn't wear slacks much, but we all bought them, and we were running around trying to get ourselves ready. I was busy almost to the last day at the JACL office, sending the weekly bulletins and handling the personal problems of everybody. And I wrote to the President of the United States and the principal of the high school and the newspaper editors thanking them for whatever they did for us. I don't know if I was crazy to do this, but I felt that history was happening, and I felt that it was important to say good-bye in a proper way, speaking for the people who were leaving and trying to tell our friends that we were loyal Americans and that we were sorry that this was happening. We needed to say something, and that's what I did.

We left early in the morning on May 29. Two days earlier we sold our car for eight hundred dollars, which was just about giving it away. We also had to sell our refrigerator. But some wonderful friends came to ask if they could take care of some things we couldn't store. Mr. Lernard, a principal of a high school, took my piano, and his daughter took our dining table set, which was a wedding gift. They did that for us. Other things we had to sell, and still other things we had to crate. The Japanese community hall was declared the "federal reserve bank," a warehouse, and some of our things were stored there as well as in the Buddhist Church gymnasium. So people were bringing their stuff, crating it, stacking it up, and storing it. Some were working until the very last minute.

A few days earlier signs had been nailed to the telephone poles saying that we were to report to various spots. They told us to register as families. We had to report to the Elk Grove Masonic Building where we were given our family number, No. 2076. In the family I was *B* and my husband was *A*, and we were registered. We found out we were going to the Fresno Assembly Center.

It happened so suddenly to our community. You know, we grew up together, we went through the hardships of the Depression, and then finally things were picking up. People who had mortgages on their land were beginning to be able to make payments back to the bank. They were going to own the land that they had worked so hard to have. Then we had to evacuate. So there were still some people who owed some money on their property, and they lost the property because, of course, they couldn't make mortgage payments.

These were our people, and we loved them. We wept with them at their funerals and laughed with them and rejoiced at their weddings. And suddenly we found out that the community was going to be split up. The railroad track was one dividing line, and Florin Road the other dividing line. We were going to Fresno; the ones on the other side went to Manzanar; and the ones on the west side went to Tule. The ones on the west and north went to Pinedale and Poston. We never dreamed we would be separated—relatives and close friends, a community. The village people, we were just like brothers and sisters. We endured so much together and never dreamed we would be separated. Suddenly we found out we wouldn't be going to the same place. That was a traumatic disappointment and a great sadness for us. We were just tied up in knots, trying to cope with all of this happening at once and so fast. I can't understand why they had to do this. I don't know why they had to split us up.

We'll never forget the shock and grief and the sorrow on top of everything else that was happening to us. You know, every day we were supposed to pick berries, and that was important, because in those days we were barely making a living. We had to borrow ahead from companies and stores, and we had to borrow to buy groceries until we had our crop, and then we paid them. This is how we managed with the produce-shipping companies too. They loaned us money ahead, advanced it. So every day the berries being harvested and turned in was important to us so that we could get out from under a debt. We all tried very hard to pay our debts. If New Year's time came and we welcomed the new year with debts, it was a shame. That was an inherent part of the culture.

At the JACL office, we handled all kinds of problems. Let's say a big family came in. You can't split that family up. So we'd ask some smaller family that had signed up earlier for a different camp if they would be willing to go to Manzanar instead. Everybody got angry about things like that. We urged them to go somewhere else, and some of them didn't want to, because they were going to be separated from their friends and relatives. That was a tragic thing, and some of us were blamed for people being shipped to Manzanar. A lot of terrible things were said, and we were at each other's throats. The Japanese people were blaming me and the JACL for sending people every which way and keeping our personal friends together.

I don't know, we had been a very happy family. When we left, we swept our house and left it clean, because that's the way Japanese feel like leaving a place. I can just imagine everyone's emotions of grief and anger when they had to leave, when the military police (MPs) came and told them, "Get ready right now. You've got two hours to get ready to catch this train."

Early in the morning, Margaret and George File came after us in their car because we no longer had one to move our things. We had taken our luggage the day before on the pickup. We were very fortunate. Al had a very dear friend, Bob Fletcher, who was going to stay at our place and run our farm, our neighbor's farm, and Al's cousin's farm. So these three adjoining farms would be taken care of, at least the grape vineyards would be. Bob would stay at our place, and we left our dog with him. Nobody could take pets, and this was a sad thing for my daughter. There were tears everywhere; Grandma couldn't leave her flowers, and Grandpa looked at his grape vineyard. We urged him to get into the car and leave. I remember that sad morning when we realized suddenly that we wouldn't be free. It was such a clear, beautiful day, and I remember as we were driving, our tears. We saw the snow-clad Sierra Nevada mountains that we had loved to see so often, and I thought about God and about the prayer that we often prayed.

I remember one scene very clearly: on the train, we were told not to look out the window, but people were peeking out. After a long time on the train somebody said, "Oh, there's some Japanese standing over there." So we all took a peek, and we saw this dust, and rows and rows of barracks, and all these tan, brown Japanese people with their hair all bleached. They were all standing in a huddle looking at us, looking at this train going by. Then somebody on the train said, "Gee, that must be Japanese people in a camp." We didn't realize who they were before, but I saw how terrible it looked: the dust, no trees—just barracks and a bunch of people standing against the fence, looking out. Some children were hanging onto the fence like animals, and that was my first sight of the assembly center. I was so sad and discouraged looking at that, knowing that, before long, we would be inside too.

As we arrived, there were all these people, peeking out from behind the fence, wondering what group would be coming next, and, of course, looking for their friends too. Suddenly you realized that human beings were being put behind fences just like on the farm where we had horses and pigs in corrals.

It was hot, and everybody was perspiring. We were tired from the train trip, and here they were just staring at us. It is humiliating to be stared at like that. These were Nihonjin ("Japanese") people staring at us, Nihonjin people. We came in dragging suitcases and luggage and all our clothing. We felt so self-conscious to be stared at, but of course I looked right back to see if I recognized anybody. My father and mother and my cousins had gone a day or two ahead of us. I was looking for them, and they came looking for us. There were joyous greetings and gladness of reunion.

Then we began to realize what it meant to stand in line—long hours standing for eating in the mess hall, standing in line in front of the latrine, standing in line for our bath. That was a shock, but I guess the Army's latrine is the same everywhere. For us women and children, this was something which we just couldn't . . . it was just a shock. I remember we got sick . . . we couldn't go . . . we didn't want to go. It was smelly, and it was dirty. In the shower, the water was poured over you, and there were no partitions, and it was so cramped that we almost touched each other. It was very humiliating. It sure helped when the kids had a variety show. Many were quite talented, and one night they made us all laugh, and we cried with laughter because it was so funny. There were five or six boys standing in a row, dramatizing the time when we go to the latrine.

I guess we needed to laugh it off like that, and soon we learned to cope, and we managed to enjoy whatever we could and got busy. I taught English to Isseis, which was a delightful experience. I also taught public speaking. This was thrilling to me, because I found out that the Isseis really wanted to learn something that they never had the opportunity to learn before. Some dear old ladies and old men who could hardly hear, hardly see, hardly hold a pencil, realized that this was a chance to learn English. One mother said, "I want to be able to write my son a letter. I'm always asking other people to write for me. When he's in the service and worried, I want him to know I'm all right. I want him to understand from my own letters that I care for him and that I am okay."

We used unfinished buildings for temporary classrooms, and we hastily tried to keep everybody busy. Soon surprising things began to happen. The Issei ladies were making crepe-paper flowers. They were taking classes from old Mrs. Nagao, who was a farmer's wife, brown and tanned and wrinkled. All I knew was that she was a strawberry grower's wife, and I knew that she could pick strawberries. Here she was a teacher of this crepe paper flower making class.

Other hidden talents began to emerge. Everett Sasaki was in charge of the victory garden. He was one of the JACL people in Florin. Quiet little old Everett was directing that project and planting all kinds of vegetables. Soon they were producing more than we could use at Fresno. There were a lot of other things going on. Baseball games. Obachan ("grandmother") loved baseball, and they got busy going to baseball games, watching baseball games. My mother and father and uncle and aunt got busy playing Chinese checkers and things like that.

We would be just so angered because we had to wash the sheets, and we had to borrow old-fashioned washboards to do it. But within a few weeks somebody had already planted a garden. Soon somebody would give us a little cucumber or one tomato. Before we left in October, the whole camp was transformed. Who but Nihonjins would leave a place like that in beauty? It was an inspiring sight. I felt proud that the Nihonjins who had coped through the heat of the summer had faith enough to plant a garden. We left it beautiful. Of course, it was probably torn down quickly because it was a Fresno fairground.

That's the way we drove out of the camp. I remember seeing the morning-glory vines covering the tar-paper barracks. And the sight of just so many beautiful flowers and vegetables, so lush and green. And we drove away knowing that even a place like that could become a part of us, our home, because our loved ones were there.

I remember another thing. We had our Fourth of July program. Because we couldn't think of anything to do, we decided to recite the Gettysburg Address as a verse choir. We had an artist draw a big picture of Abraham Lincoln with an American flag behind him. Some people had tears in their eyes; some people shook their heads and said it was so ridiculous to have that kind of thing recited in a camp. It didn't make sense, but it was our hearts' cry. We wanted so much to believe that this was a government by the people and for the people and that there was freedom and justice. So we did things like that to entertain each other, to inspire each other, to hang on to things that made sense and were right.

We were finally moved from Fresno in October 1942 to the Jerome relocation camp in Arkansas. After we were there awhile, all of a sudden cold weather arrived, and they didn't have enough wood to heat the rooms. We were on the edge of the Mississippi River, the swamplands of Arkansas. We had to go into the woods to chop wood. All the men stopped everything; school, everything, was closed and the young people were told to go out and work. They brought the wood in, and the women helped to saw it. Then, of course, we can stoop so low as human beings; we get so greedy and selfish. People started to hoard wood. There wouldn't be enough for some people. I felt sorry for the block manager who had to go in and check every apartment. When we're unhappy and miserable, our sense of values and our behavior change. We can become hateful people.

In Fresno, I remember, we heard language from over the partitions, language I didn't want my daughter to grow up hearing. There was talking back to parents, young people shouting, fathers shouting and angry. All of that made me hate people, and I was ashamed of being a part of a group of people who would be so hateful to each other. But after a while, we all got on each other's nerves. It was a terrible, terrible time of adjustment when we were in Fresno.

I remember Dr. Allen Hunter, who spoke to us. Some of us asked him to teach us how to pray. I said we feel like hating everybody; we just can't stand so many people all around us. Wherever we go we're with everybody, and there is no privacy. He said, tomorrow morning when you get up, you just know that every single person in that camp, 5,600 people, every one of them has a halo over his head. Each one is trying to grow tall enough to fit under that halo. He said that each one of us is trying his very best to be a good person, and I never forgot that.

After all I had gone through and when I had an opportunity to speak, when people asked me to tell them the story, why didn't I have the courage to tell the truth? I realized that I needed to be angry not just for myself personally, but for what happened to our people. And also for our country because I really believe it wasn't just Japanese Americans that were betrayed, but America itself. I'm saying that for the kids—for the Yonsei ("fourth generation") kids and for their children and their friends and all the generations that are coming. For their sakes, we need to be angry enough to do something about it so that it will never happen again. It's not anger because I'm bitter or disappointed that it happened to me. I'm disappointed for America that it had to happen, and I want the record to be straight.

I remember my daughter was five, and she cried for a whole week —she cried and cried and cried. She was so upset, because she wanted to go home; she wanted to get away from camp. Adults felt the same way, but we weren't children and so could not dare to cry. I remember I always felt like I was dangling and crying deep inside, and I was hurt.

I know many Niseis who say, That was all so long ago. Let's forget it and leave well enough alone. But I just say, we were the ones that went through it—the tears and the shame and the shock. We need to leave our legacy to our children. And also our legacy to America, from our tears, what we learned.

EDDIE SAKAMOTO

Manzanar

I was born in Japan in 1904. I came to the United States in 1921; my parents were here already. I had two brothers, George and Dick, at that time also here. After I arrived in the United States, I went to school about eight years total. I went to UCLA for two years, but the Depression came, and got worse and worse. So I stopped going to college.

I used to help my folks in their fruit stand. When I quit going to school, I opened my own market at Brentwood. I quit the fruit-stand business 1936 and became a gardener. Then on December 7, 1941—that was a Sunday, and I was working—a Caucasian fellow said that Hawaii was bombed by Japanese. The war started, he said. I couldn't believe it. I didn't have too much feeling about Japan. I was in school in Japan quite a few years, but I also was in a school here, so I felt I should be loyal to America, the United States. I have two brothers born here, and my parents live in the United States. So even though America is my second country, when the war is started, I feel that Japan shouldn't do that against America.

That same night my father was taken; he was taken without any explaining. He was taken right away. The man from FBI or police station came, and he was watching my father to come back—he was out somewhere—and as soon as he was in the house, they told my father to get the suitcase and toothbrush and so forth. He didn't understand why he had to do that, but anyway without any reason, he was taken to I think it was Montana.

When notices were posted and we were told we had to evacuate, I thought I have to do whatever the government said. This is the war, and we can't do anything, you know. We just have to follow the government order. By that time, I was married and have three little kids, and I am responsible for kids to grow and not get hurt.

The day of evacuation was April 28, 1942, and that morning was light rain—rain drizzling—and we have to get in buses. We went straight to Manzanar.

Everything was new, and before we went to Manzanar, lots of people talk about Manzanar like a different country—like they have mosquitoes big as flies, big flies, or something like that. That made us scared a little bit.

When we got to Manzanar, we saw lots of buildings lined up at the foot of Mount Williamson, and, I don't know, I don't feel much about it. When we get out the bus the officers are checking everything. You know, inside of the suitcase. They look for knives or flashlights—such things we cannot take. And if we don't have that, it's okay. But if we have it we have troubles.

At the beginning there, I felt like a prisoner because they had four watchtowers, and the soldiers with their guns, you know, was watching from on top of the tower. And anybody try to go out, not escaping, but try to go out, they shoot you, without giving any warning.

In camp, the future is uncertain. You can't predict what's going to happen. I'm not against American government. The government, we're trusting that they won't do any harmful decision; we trusting that American government will treat us maybe fair, you know.

WILLIAM HOSOKAWA

Heart Mountain

I was born in Seattle, Washington, January 30, 1915, and educated in Seattle public schools and the University of Washington, class of 1937. After graduation, the first thing that I had to do was look for a job, and things were pretty rough in those days. We had both the effects of the Depression and the virulent anti-Orientalism on the West Coast. Those were times, when, if Bill Hosokawa and John Smith with equal qualifications went to the same place to look for a job, it was a foregone conclusion that John Smith would get it. I had an offer to go to Los Angeles to work on the English section of a Japanese American paper, but that was a pretty risky thing, so I took a job as an English secretary at the Japanese Consulate in Seattle.

I worked at the consulate for about a year, and then I went to the Far East to work as a newspaperman. I got married, and my wife and I went to Singapore in the fall of 1938. I worked on the English-language Singapore *Herald* for about a year and a half, and then I went up to Shanghai and worked about a year there writing for the Shanghai *Times*, which was a daily English-language paper owned by British interests. I was also doing part-time work for a magazine called the *Far Eastern Review*, which was American-owned.

I tried to get back to the States in July of 1941, which was a very precarious time. It was evident that there was going to be some kind of collision between the United States and Japan. The American

Consulate in Shanghai had been telling nonessential Americans to get out of China, to go on home, and so in July of 1941 I decided it was time to get out. I started from Shanghai and got as far as Tokyo when the United States abrogated the Treaty of Friendship and Commerce, or whatever. This meant all shipping across the Pacific between the United States and Japan was suspended.

I waited in Tokyo about two or three weeks to see if anything would happen, but it became apparent that this was going to be a long drawn out thing. So I sent a cable to my former employer in Shanghai and asked him to put me on the waiting list of an American ship. Then I flew back to Shanghai and I was there until about early in October of 1941. I finally got space on the *Cleveland*, an American mail-line ship, and I left Shanghai. I landed in San Francisco late in October of 1941, and the war came just five weeks later.

We were evacuated to a WCCA camp which was at the fairgrounds at Puyallup, Washington—euphemistically named Camp Harmony, where there was very little harmony.

In fact, it was a miserable place. Because the Puyallup fairgrounds were not large enough to accommodate the seven thousand people from Seattle, the authorities divided the camp into four areas. The main one was in the fairgrounds proper, with others set up in parking lots around the fairgrounds. Each area was surrounded by barbed wire and military guards. There was very little access between the various areas so that you could not go to see your friend in another area without going through a lot of red tape.

There were two kinds of buildings: one was clapboard, the other just plain board. They looked like chicken coops, a long row of them, and inside they were divided into cubicles. There were no ceilings, so that if a baby cried 150 feet down on the other end of this long line of cubicles, the crying could be heard throughout the entire building. Of course, there was no running water, so that for water, you had to go to the central washroom. There were other units in the central fairgrounds that were under the fairground stands. They had concrete floors and were very cold and dank. These, again, were partitioned into cubicles.

We had been there from May until the early part of September, when it was announced that the people in the camp—who were almost entirely from Seattle—would go to Minidoka, Idaho. But I got a summons one day to the office of the camp director. He said,

"You have four hours to get ready because you are going to be sent to Heart Mountain, Wyoming." And I said, "Just me?" And he said, "No, you and your family—your wife and your son." "Why am I being sent to Wyoming, when everybody else is going to Minidoka?" And he said, "I don't know, these are just the orders I have."

I couldn't understand it. Then I got some other information. There were several others who were being separated from the main group of Seattleites, but I had never had any conversations with them. After a while, it occurred to me that whoever it was who was in authority figured that we were potential disrupting elements.

I was working with Jimmie Sakamoto in coordinating the activities of the camp in cooperation with the Caucasian "overlord," and I was not shy about bitching if something went wrong and criticizing things that I thought were unfair, and I presumed that although my loyalty to the United States was unquestioned, someone figured that I might cause problems by being so outspoken.

So we had a few hours to get ready, and my wife and I and my infant son were escorted by guard onto a train, and we were sent off to Heart Mountain, Wyoming.

We were very fortunate on this train trip because the guard was a decent fellow, and a Pullman berth was provided for my wife and child, and I sat up in the coach. But this was on a regular train. The guard was supposed to keep us in sight all the time, and he sat across from where we were sitting. Apparently because he realized that I wasn't going to try to blow up the train or do anything rash, he gave us a good deal of freedom. We had an individual guard who escorted us all the way. The people who were moved en masse had special trains, and the only people who got berths were invalids, pregnant mothers—people like that. We were lucky.

The guard delivered us to Heart Mountain where he turned us over to somebody on the WRA staff. Still under construction, Heart Mountain was a desolate place. There were workers everywhere putting up military-type barracks, about 125 feet long, six living units per barrack. They were made out of wood and covered with black tar paper. The natural cover of the desolate countryside—the sagebrush and the buffalo grass—had been torn up by the construction workers in bulldozers and trucks, and so the least little bit of wind would raise the dust—a very fine, alkaline dust.

I spent the next fourteen months at Heart Mountain. One of the things that concerned me when I was separated from the Seattle group was that I was being blackballed in some way, and that I would not be given the same opportunities that other people would be given to do something meaningful. Most of the residents at Heart Mountain were from Southern California, around the Los Angeles area. There were some from San Jose. A few came from the Yakima, Washington, area.

One of the first fellows I met at Heart Mountain was Vaughn Mechau. He was a newspaperman, and he was what was called the "reports officer." He recognized my background in professional newspapering, and he wanted me to go to work for him. And we decided early on that it was permissible and desirable to have a camp newspaper.

It was necessary to get information out to the residents. Very soon they were coming into the camp at the rate of five hundred to six hundred every two or three days—a trainload every two or three days—and they had to be assigned barracks and mess halls, and it was essential to get out information to these people. So we began to issue a series of bulletins—newsletters to the newcomers—telling them about the camp, what the regulations were, giving them a little background. That was the start of the information program. Eventually we started a weekly newspaper, the Heart Mountain Sentinel. I became editor of the paper, and I enjoyed that kind of work, as much as one can enjoy anything working behind barbed wire.

There was a big story early in 1943 when the War Department decided to call for volunteers for military service and when the questionnaires were passed out. Questions 27 and 28 caused a great uproar, and we reported all this as objectively and as completely as we could. I should point out that there was no overt "censorship" of what we were doing. There was a certain amount of staff censorship. But we tried to be very objective in the way we covered the news, and we tried to confine our opinions to the editorials of the paper, and these were generally supportive of the government program.

This was late winter and early spring of 1943. There was a great deal of tension in the camps. The largest group of people were fairly noncommital, and there were the very strongly pro-American group —young men who felt it was their obligation to volunteer and go into service and do what they could to demonstrate that they were indeed loyal, and the government was wrong in putting them into camps. They felt that they could demonstrate this by showing their pro-Americanism. There were others who said, Sure, I'm American, but I'll be damned if I'm going to risk my life for a country that doesn't believe in me and has stuck me behind barbed wire. And then there was a very large group who just kept quiet.

And then there was a very articulate and small group who were looked upon as being pro-Japan. They really weren't pro-Japan, and they really weren't anti-American. They were just fed up and angry at the treatment they received and felt that they should not cooperate with the government in any way as long as they were kept behind barbed wire. And these various elements were all stuck together. They had to eat in the same mess halls. There was a lot of time to sit around and think and argue and complain, so that there was an enormous amount of tension in the camps.

The whole affair was an unfortunate thing. It's necessary only to look at the experience in Hawaii were there was no mass internment. The War Department had expected to get 1,500 volunteers for military service out of Hawaii, and more than 10,000 showed up, because they were American citizens, they believed in America, and they had nothing to be mad at the government about.

But on the mainland, three thousand miles farther from the front, the government in its lack of wisdom, lack of understanding, had picked up these people on a strictly racial basis and interned them and suspended their civil rights. It was natural and understandable that many of them should be resentful. And I think the marvelous thing out of all this is that so many of them did volunteer to give their lives for their country, and so many others retained their loyalty and affection for their country.

YURI TATEISHI

Manzanar

I was born in Riverside, California, in December 1913. I went to Luzinger High School in Lawndale. My parents farmed strawberries and vegetables in Lawndale and later moved to what is now Torrance. I was married in 1934 and was living with my husband in West Los Angeles when the war broke out.

On Pearl Harbor day the whole family was planning to go downtown, but when we heard the news we didn't know whether to go out or not. We didn't know what the reactions of the people were, but we decided we would go anyway. Of course, when people were staring at us, we weren't very comfortable, but I recall people didn't say anything. The reaction you got was, "Oh, these people," and it wasn't a very comfortable feeling.

We just stayed within our own neighborhood, and the immediate neighbors were not bad, but we heard there were other people that were harassed. Our neighbors were good to us. In fact, they felt sorry for us when they heard about the evacuation.

When we were to be evacuated, there were some people that wanted to go east to Colorado or Utah, but of course we knew no one back there, and so my husband went to Colorado to see if he could meet with any Japanese people to see if there were any chance of moving out there to get something started. But it was quite difficult, and then while he was back there the curfew went into effect, so he had to rush back and we were worried that he wouldn't be allowed to come back.

When the evacuation came, we were renting a home and had four kids. It was terrible because you had to sell everything. We were just limited to what we could take with us, and so everything was just sold for whatever we could get. Our furniture was rather new at that time because we had just bought a living-room and dining-room set. I just finished paying for a refrigerator when I had to sell that. Of course, we got nothing for it, because we had such a limited time. I don't remember how much notice we got, but it seems it was two weeks or something because we had to rush to sell everything. I don't remember how much time we had, but it wasn't very long. Otherwise, we wouldn't be selling at such low prices.

The day of the evacuation was April 26. The day before, we had to sleep on the floor because all the furniture was gone. We all slept on the floor, ate on the floor, and cooked what we could with what few utensils we had. I recall we had to get up very early in the morning, and I think we all walked to the Japanese school because no one had a car then. And everybody was just all over the place, the whole Japanese community was there, the West L.A. community. The Westwood Methodist Church had some hot coffee and doughnuts for us that morning, which helped a lot, and we were loaded in a bus.

Just about the time we were ready to load, my youngest son broke out with measles that morning, and I had him covered up, and then a nurse came up to me and said, "May I see your baby?" He was almost three, but I was carrying him, and she said, "I'm sorry but I'm going to have to take him away." Of course, I thought, he would be sleeping at that time so he wouldn't know, but I thought also that he would wake up in a strange place, he wouldn't know anybody; and he probably would just cry all day or all night. But the neighbors said that they would go and check him, so that kind of relieved me. If he were awake, maybe we would have been able to tell him something, but he was asleep. It was easier for me because he was asleep. I don't know. But when I thought about how he might wake up and be in a strange place, with strange people, I just really broke down and cried. I cried all morning over it, but there was nothing we could do but leave him. He stayed at the general hospital and joined us at Manzanar in three weeks.

When we got to Manzanar, it was getting dark and we were given numbers first. We went to the mess hall, and I remember the first meal we were given in those tin plates and tin cups. It was canned weiners and canned spinach. It was all the food we had, and then after finishing that we were taken to our barracks. It was dark and trenches were here and there. You'd fall in and get up and finally got to the barracks. The floors were boarded, but they were about a quarter to a half inch apart, and the next morning you could see the ground below. What hurt most I think was seeing those hay mattresses. We were used to a regular home atmosphere, and seeing those hay mattresses—so makeshift, with hay sticking out—a barren room with nothing but those hay mattresses. It was depressing, such a primitive feeling. We were given army blankets and army cots. Our family was large enough that we didn't have to share our barrack with another family but all seven of us were in one room.

The next morning was very cold. I went out to brush my teeth. There was a faucet at the front of each building, and it was so cold, so painful it was so cold. You felt like a prisoner. You know, you have to stay inside and you have a certain amount of freedom within the camp I suppose, but, I don't know, it's not a comfortable feeling. You had to stay within the confines of that camp, not in the sense that you're in a jail or anything, but you're kept inside a barbed-wire fence, and you know you can't go out.

And you don't know what your future is, going into a camp with four children. You just have to trust God that you will be taken care of somehow. It's scary—not in the sense that you would be hurt or anything but not knowing what your future will be. You don't know what the education for the children will be or what type of housing or anything like that. Of course, you don't know how you're going to be able to raise the children.

After we had been in Manzanar for about a year, as I understood it, someone by the name of Mr. Ueno was treated unfairly and was taken out of the camp to jail, and some of the men felt that they should try to get him released. They didn't think it was right that they should take him, and a few men were chosen. My husband was one of them, and these men went to the administration to negotiate this man's release, but while they were negotiating a crowd gathered, and it got larger and larger and it just got out of control. The men came out of the meeting and told the crowd to quiet down and go home, but they just wouldn't listen, and that's when the trouble started outside. Well, somebody got shot. The people that were negotiating were taken. They were kept at the jail in Independence, and then after that they were transferred to Lone Pine and then sent to Utah. They stayed there quite a while, and then they were transferred from one place to another.

When my husband was arrested, someone came and told me, but I didn't try to go see him because there was no chance of seeing him. They had already taken him. I didn't think I'd have a chance; I don't think they ever would have given me the chance. It wasn't that kind of a situation. I hoped that he would be released soon but, again, you really didn't know what was going to happen. It occurred to me that I might not ever see him again. He wrote letters, but they were all censored. He came back, I think eight months later.

When I think back on the evacuation, that's something you'd like to erase if you can, but it's a fact; we went through it. I'm unhappy about it, but I don't think I was really bitter. You feel like you can't do anything against the government. They tell you, You go or else. You just had to go.

You hurt. You give up everything that you worked for that far, and I think everybody was at the point of just having gotten out of the Depression and was just getting on his feet. And then all that happens! You have to throw everything away. You feel you were betrayed.

HARUKO NIWA

Manzanar

My birthplace is Japan. I was born in 1906 in the city of Ueda. I graduated high school there, and then I went to Tokyo. I came here to the United States in 1923.

After I graduate from two years in business college in Tokyo, my father, who was in San Francisco with my brother, invite me for just one year, for just visit, but I stayed instead. I liked it very much. I liked San Francisco and the United States and living in United States. It's very attractive. And I stayed there and went to a girl's high school in San Francisco. And then, following year, I married Mr. Niwa. Then father and brother went back to Japan, and I stayed. I married and had two children.

December 7, it was quite a shock—like thunder and lightning on top of my head. I never dreamt there could be the war between Japan and United States, you know. Because it was just like ants poking an elephant. I never dreamt about Japan against the United States. So, I was quite shocked. And then, next minute, I thought, well, here I have two sons who are citizens of United States, and whatever they have to do, I follow them. I made the decision that we have to live, and no matter what kind of difficulties comes out, to do the best for the two children.

Nobu was just finishing Emerson Junior High School, and Aki was in junior high, too. Nobu was fifteen, and Aki was thirteen and a half.

I decided before then, December 7, what we would do. My father and my brother and relatives, particularly father, wrote many letters asking us to please come back to Japan. He said the *Tatsuta Maru* will be the last boat to go back to Japan, so you don't have to bring any souvenir or anything—just pack, and whole family should come back to Japan, because some great tragedy will arise. But at that time, I prayed and prayed, and then I decided that no matter what kind of troubles come up, my two boys are United States citizens, and if we take them to Japan, it will be their tragedy. So I trust United States that they will protect our two boys, so I will stay here. I didn't want to cause any hardship for two boys. So we took a picture and sent to father along with the letter saying we're not going back to Japan with the last boat. So I have sort of set my mind that something happen. But not that bad, you know, not that big a deal as evacuation.

Mr. Niwa was a newspaper reporter for *Rafu Shimpo*, and he was working downtown. Reverend Nicholson came from Pasadena, all pale faced and asked, "How about Mr. Niwa, is he okay? A big thing happened, you know, it's going to be war." He was quite worried. And then my husband came back home from downtown. He was quite busy with a communication from downtown about putting notes on telephone posts and churches and stores.

Reverend Nicholson said this was government's order, and so the best thing is choose the camp as close as possible for your children, and we don't know how long we have to stay, but if we are within California, it's easy to come back. United States will provide the education. He suggested, if you have to go, choose Manzanar. Just stay in Los Angeles and don't go to relatives or friends.

It's wartime, and as long as government protect us, we have to obey whatever they decide to do. I decided to do the best I can. I don't even think about evacuation. I thought it will be very, very uncomfortable, and something might happen. I thought that it wouldn't be same as before the war, you know—something would happen—but I never thought about this kind of big operation of evacuation.

I was kind of bitter at first. I trust the United States so deeply, its freedom and this Constitution. We are very proud about the United States, and I trusted this country so much. My children need parents, and they can't separate the family whether citizen or not citizen. Small children need a father and mother, so it's a blessing that the family going together. But I thought about all the adults who have a business and contribute to the country and school-teachers and the government workers and all this. I was kind of bitter about it. But it all owes to wartime. I thought that no matter what, we have to obey military and government's order. But if I have to leave two kids and have to go somewheres else, well, that will be really, really something.

I bought quite a few bottles of vitamins for children. I don't know what's going to happen in the camp either, so I bought a ledger and the books that they have to read. We don't know when school starts or when they'll be able to go to school.

When time to go, we gathered at the Japanese school, and all the church federations of this area provide the breakfast, serve us coffee and milk and cocoa and doughnuts and things like that. Then we got on the buses and left right after breakfast.

I was happy all the West Los Angeles church people and the friends and residents, all go together, all this area that we're familiar with.

I told Nobu and Aki that from now on you kids have to be really strong and pray every minute, because whatever happen, you have to decide yourself. I cannot watch you constantly and we don't know from now on what kind of living we going to have. We don't know we can continue family unity. Maybe everybody have to go to same place, or maybe it's just like a big camp or dormitory. We cannot protect you, so you have to stand up and protect yourself and decide what is wrong and what is right, because Mommy and Daddy can't follow all over, because we don't know what's going to be. We have to be closer than before, because we're going to have strange different living. That's what I told the two boys, you know.

The next morning, the first morning in Manzanar, when I woke up and saw what Manzanar looked like, I just cried. And then I saw the mountain, the high Sierra Mountain, just like my native country's mountain, and I just cried, that's all. I couldn't think about anything.

I thought, well, we just have to accept this situation and do the best we can. But Aki was sitting on the front entrance step, and he was crying with a drop of the tear like a marble. I know he missed the school in Westwood. He enjoyed so much school activities that I know he missed that—all the friends in school and all that—and thinking about what is going to be his education and future. Oh, he had the marble-size tear rolling down from his eyes, you know. And Nobu was quiet sitting in the corner of the barracks. He was just sitting, just staring from the corner at nothing. I know he was deeply hurt too. But they never talk against the United States. They never say anything, but as the days passed, day by day they're just saying that Dad and Mom, we are not going to stay here forever. We have to go out, no matter what, we're going out, we're going out.

Nobu graduated June 1944, and then he went out to Milwaukee, Wisconsin. Father and Nobu went out first. Aki graduated the next year; then we joined the family.

I kind of tighten my nerves because we are going to strange city. I have never been outside of California, so I was sort of not scared to death, but sort of strong challenge, facing new world, and it's still wartime too.

But when we took the train toward Wisconsin, the soldiers are packed in train too, but they are very sweet and gracious and nice to us. Next to my seat was a soldier and he offered coffee, and whenever the train stop and he hop out for lunch or something he say, "May I get you sandwich or something?"—you know—he offer something.

Aki worked in a tire recapping company with Mr. Niwa and went to college. Then I was working in the resettlement association as the director in Milwaukee. And when we were in Wisconsin, my husband gets up with the stars and goes home with the stars and moon. But after a long time he wants to go back to West Los Angeles. He was really missing the good old town of West Los Angeles more than anybody, so it's really big decision to go out, but we did for our children's education. And it was very hard first year because two boys went to college. Then Aki got the notice from the Army while we were in Milwaukee, so he volunteered to the Navy.

August 15, I was riding a bus from downtown coming home, and then all the church bells rang, and whistles and firecrackers and all that, and all the ladies in the seats in the bus kiss me and hug me. Oh, we were very happy that the war was ended. We just kept crying. It was happy for all of us, and my husband hustle and bustle for going back to West Los Angeles. Day and night he was making a box and putting everything in. We knew we were coming home.

At that time my situation wasn't terribly disastrous or tragic, be-

cause if I have a farm or big business and then have to evacuate—
that kind of situation—it would be real tragedy.

At first, when we have to evacuate, I was kind of hurt, you know.
I was hurt, but I thought about it: It's wartime, so I thought, do the
best we can whatever situation arise. We thought we do the best
for the children. I decided to stay here. I turned down my father's
request and all that, so I chose United States. I will obey the law of
United States and everything. Even with the hardship and bitterness and how we were treated by United States, all these Japanese
American citizens of United States obeyed the law and went to
camp with the family and do the best of living in difficult time.
They still show the loyalty and volunteered and served for the
United States in the battlefield. The 442nd and 100th Battalion
showed loyalty by doing that.

We have to be grateful no matter what kind of difficulty, what
kind of bitterness and anger and all that, but when the Nisei decide
to join the 442nd and do the righteousness, well, God gives us award
of such effort by them. But we never again; this is my country, but
we never again.

DONALD NAKAHATA

Topaz

At the time of the evacuation I was twelve years old, and when I came out of camp, in 1945, I was fifteen. We were living here in San Francisco at 2092 Pine Street. The house is still there. Pine, between Buchanan and Laguna.

We lived in my grandfather's household, and in 1941 it consisted of my grandfather, my Aunt Faith, my mother, my father, my sister, and me. Maybe after the war started, my grandfather's niece from San Diego, because she was a widow, came to live with us also. My dad had had a stroke in 1937, and he was trying to rehabilitate himself, working for one of the Japanese newspapers here in town. In fact, Howard Imazaki and Duncan Shimizu used to work for my dad at one point.

So my father was a part-time newspaperman. He was also part time at the *nihonjin-kai* ("Japanese Community Association"), which is probably the precursor of the *nichibei-kai* ("Japanese American Association"), doing that as rehabilitation. Prior to that, he had quit a job in Los Angeles, where he was secretary of the Japanese association. I guess he'd been manager of a farmer's co-op that eventually shut down, partly as a result of the alien land laws. The last thing he did in agriculture was in Brawley in the Imperial Valley. And then he came up here. The story I was told was that he got mad and quit one day. He was making pretty good money during the Depression. And he just up and left. He had a Model A Ford that was given to him as a wedding present by the farmers' co-op. So he was doing all right. Up here he had worked as a newspaperman many, many years before. So he came back to it, and I grew up here in San Francisco. But as a newspaperman, my father was a prime target of the FBI.

Before Pearl Harbor, we knew something was afoot, even though parents do a marvelous job of shielding children from a lot of anxieties like that. So I was just a kid until evacuation.

My father was arrested either December 7 or December 8. He was working for the Japanese association of San Francisco and San Jose. After Pearl Harbor he figured that in San Francisco there would be enough community leaders, so that somebody needed to cover the Japanese community in San Jose. So he decided to go there. And I walked him to the bus stop. We went down Pine Street down to Fillmore to the number 22 streetcar, and he took the 22 streetcar and went to the SP (Southern Pacific) and took the train to San Jose. And that was the last time I saw him.

And I guess that was probably the last time that anybody saw him in our family. Finally, word came through the grapevine somehow that the FBI had picked him up, and he was now being held at a detention station on Silver Avenue someplace in San Francisco. So my aunt and my mother got some clothes together, and they went out to visit him. And when they got there, there were these busses lined up, and they never did get to see him, because they were ready to be moved someplace else. But somebody took the bundle of clothes which I assume he got.

We were poor and struggling, and with my father gone, every day was a fearful day. But we all coped with it, and I remember little things. I can visualize 2092 Pine Street. There's a ground level, there's a lower flat, and then we had the third and fourth stories. You go up some stairs to the entrance, and then you go up more stairs to our flat, and you look down dark stairs. And I can see the bright sunlight outside. But I had this fear of being left behind—you have to be on time or you're going to be punished somehow. That's one of the few things I remember, the fear of being left behind.

I also remember that we were going to be evacuated and that we were going to the desert someplace. And I wanted a pair of cowboy boots because we were going to go to the desert. And that's about it. I also remember the last day at school. They gave all us Japanese kids a little book of American birds or something like that, and the teacher inscribed it. And I think I still have the book.

We were first sent to Tanforan. We lived in the barracks there and didn't have to stay in the stables, because my grandpa was a Christian minister, and we were in his household, and he was about eighty-three at the time. You know, this is really a very interesting situation; I've never really tried to remember. That's a tremendous period in the life of a child, from age twelve to fifteen. My mother died fourteen months ago, and I really wonder how camp affected our relationship. I'm not sure, and I guess with the loss of a parent you always feel a certain guilt. But, about camp, I sit here and can't remember feelings. I remember getting beat up by some kids and not wanting to go to school. I remember going to swim in the irrigation ditch. I remember going out working in the chicken ranch, poultry ranch. So for a long time I couldn't eat eggs and chicken, but I learned to drive a tractor. I remember going with the poultry ranch people out to look for trilobites.

Dad was gone, and we just heard from him a little. We have a few letters from him. And you know, I have no feeling if I look at them now. He apparently suffered several more strokes in various camps. But I know he was in Fort Sill, Oklahoma, and Camp Livingston, Louisiana, and I think he died in Bismarck, North Dakota. It's really kind of sad if you think about it, that I don't know where he died. And I think he was in Santa Fe, New Mexico, at one time. Occasionally we'd get a letter, and there'd be sections that would be cut out or blanked out. Where the FBI questioned him about certain activities, those things would be cut out of the letter. And he never really said anything much about his health. But later some other people who'd been in the same camps said he was in the hospital in such and such a camp. And somebody, I don't remember who it was anymore, came back and told us about the funeral that they had for him.

We got a telegram one night after dinner saying that he'd died and that we should advise the authorities by eight o'clock the following morning as to the disposition of the remains, or they would simply bury him in the cemetery there. So my aunt, who worked for the welfare department in camp in Topaz, went and beat on her supervisor's door and managed to get them to send a wire saying they should send the remains back. And that way our family was able to verify the fact that he had died.

He was cremated in Delta, Utah, and my mother carried his remains around for a long time, and he's buried now in a Japanese cemetery in San Bruno.

My mother, as I learned after she died, had been a missionary in Japan, and she was really a very devout Christian. And that's how she made it.

After Tanforan, we were sent to Topaz—that was in September 1942—and in August 1945 we got out and went to Rochester, New York. We took the train—it's amazing, you know, that I can remember all this. My sister was going to the University of Rochester. My aunt Faith, Mrs. Nakamura, my great-aunt and second cousin maybe, and my mother and me, we all went to Laramie, Wyoming. We got off the train there, and my uncle and aunt had driven up from Brighton, Colorado. We went to visit them for a while. And then we got back on the train and went to Chicago, and the layover between trains we spent with some people that Mrs. Nakamura had known from San Diego. And we went from there to Cleveland, because we had some distant relatives in Cleveland, and we visited them overnight, and then we got to Rochester, New York.

We decided to go there because the church people said, for a family that consisted of just women and a young child, it was not the proper time to come back to the West Coast. And so they arranged for us to go to Rochester, New York. We stayed with one family for a while, and I started high school. Then my aunt got a job as a domestic, working for a guy who was president of Stromberg-Carlson. And so she and my great-aunt stayed there. My mother worked as a domestic for a physician, and so she and I stayed in the attic of this house. It's really incredible when you think about it. We lived there for a year, and then she got a job also with the same Anglo family that owned Stromberg-Carlson.

The Anglos were really nice people, and so they let us stay there, and my mother earned our keep essentially. We stayed until I graduated from high school, and I couldn't afford to go to college in the East, so we came back to California.

I can look back now, you know; it's almost emotionless, yet I can intellectualize that we really got the shaft. We were boat people in our own country. If you figure people like my dad helped establish

California agribusiness, and that's what we got. . . . I guess I'd never really confronted all of that before. You know, it had happened, and I guess I'm the kind of guy that just, like my son Pete, responds and makes the best of what's going on.

As I've talked to people about this, I realized, if nothing else, we really have to set that record straight. It's a matter of honor. You know, we really got shafted, and we really have to have people know; but for ourselves, we have to set that record straight. It matters because we went through it. And simply to forget it and sweep it under the rug dishonors all those people whose lives were changed by it. Sure, war changes everybody's lives, but we weren't asked to take our lumps along with everyone else. We were singled out to take our own special kind of lumps. That wasn't right. Simply to have had all of that happen to us, and to me, and to our families, done by our government, my government, your government, our American government, and to simply forget it as the vicissitudes of war just isn't right.

The fact is that in 1942 our government didn't look at us as people, didn't look at us as any different from the government of Japan, and didn't look at us as Americans, which is sometimes the problem today. People will approach you and say, "You speak English well; how long have you been in this country?" And now that I'm fifty-two years old, I know damn well that I've been in this country longer than a lot of those people who ask that question. But they still ask it because we don't look white American. That's why we have to make it part of the American consciousness, that you don't have to look like a genuine American to be one.

I remember during World War II they used to laugh at things Japanese and say, those dumb Japs, they talk about loss of face. But the concept of loss of face or loss of image or the impairment of image is something that's accepted now, and we use that phrase constantly today in talking about politicians or ourselves. I think maybe some of that sense of honor comes from part of a forgotten samurai code that may seem a cultural anachronism. But that again is still image—it's the consciousness of your own self. And that consciousness or that concept was dishonored or violated by the evacuation.

I may have my own bastardized version of honor, but I also have an Anglo-Saxon desire to go out and screw the guy who did it, or let him know that it wasn't right. Or maybe if you want to put it in that idiom, the forty-seven *ronin* ("a masterless samurai") were dis-honored. They didn't sit back, and they did something about it. But my mother, in various things I used to do, would sometimes take me aside and say, now, that's okay, you shouldn't protest about this issue, argue about that, just let it go. And she would quote this Japanese saying that says, *deru kugi utareru*, which means, "the nail that sticks up the farthest takes the most pounding."

And as I look back over forty years, I think a lot of times I took the way that wouldn't stick out, not wanting to or being afraid to, yes. Maybe I have a defective chromosome or something. Or maybe, I sometimes think, we kept—and keep—a low profile, because we were afraid to take a risk. People didn't want to stick out and tried to be as American as possible. I remember being in Rochester, New York. I was uncomfortable because my mother and my aunt would speak Japanese in public. And my aunt, who was pretty outspoken, used to get very mad. She would say, well, the Italians speak Italian, the Germans speak German, why the hell shouldn't we speak Japa-nese in public? But, of course, she didn't swear.

How did we survive it? For the same reason that Japan is an economic power today. We were Meiji people, disciplined and used to getting along on less, and conditioned for the knocks, I guess. We just kept our heads down, and then came a time for economic ex-pansion for the United States. People who worked hard and had some skills in a relatively accepting political climate could make a strong comeback. Of course, if you take the men who were in their thirties and forties, they never made it back. And the Japanese busi-ness community was destroyed. All those young men starting those businesses, most of them never restarted them, but they ended up working as gardeners and domestics. But their children made it.

The thing is, have you ever walked away from a fight that you knew you couldn't win? And what did you feel like? You know, I asked Yas Abiko what he felt like, and he never really answered. I guess he thought, we went along with it because we knew we were second-class citizens. I would assume that's what he thought. As much as you can control your own destiny, they no longer had that control.

It was an emasculation. That's why nobody would talk about it. It was rape. That's why we have to be able to leave a marker in American history. It's to reclaim honor for those people, for our people. That's the honor that I'm talking about.

HELEN MURAO

Minidoka

I was born in Portland, Oregon, in 1926, which makes me fifty-six
years old. I had gotten through my sophomore year in high school
when evacuation came about. I did a year of high school, such as
it was, in camp and then finished up in Madison, Wisconsin.

My parents died within three years of each other in the mid-
thirties, my mother dying first. I was still in grammar school when
that happened, and we became wards of the state. I had an older
sister, Mary, who died after this, but she was not at home, so I
was the oldest of the three of us, me and my two younger brothers.
The Japanese community was very fearful and very reluctant to
take us into their homes because Mary had had tuberculosis, and
there was nothing more fearful to them than that disease. So
they did not offer their homes to us—even our very close family
friends. It was with Caucasian people that we made our homes. My
two brothers were with Japanese families at the time of evacuation,
but they were Japanese who were not friends of my parents. They
had been asked by the members of the church, so they were doing
it as a charitable thing, the Christian thing to do. It was not out of
friendship. During those years it was very hard for me to come to
grips with the realization that the Japanese people forsook us.
They just didn't want to have anything to do with us. Just out of
fear for their health.

At the time that my father died, our next-door neighbors were a very young Caucasian couple, who had come from Nebraska and had never seen Orientals in their life. My dad had helped them when they came by giving them fuel for the furnace and kind of helping them out. So that when my dad died very unexpectedly, this couple, without a moment's thought, took the three of us into their home. And they couldn't afford it—they didn't have room or anything. But they did it just as an act of kindness. And we lived with them for the better part of a year in a two-bedroom house, until their younger child got pneumonia, and they just couldn't do it anymore. I was to have stayed with them, and the two boys were to go to other homes.

A Japanese man, who had been my father's close friend, was the executor of the estate and sort of our guardian. He insisted that we all go to Japan to be with our relatives. My sister, at the hospital, did not want this to happen, and she worked very hard for us not to be sent to Japan. We had to find a home for the three of us together, and a Caucasian high-school teacher and his family took us. But we were very unhappy there. We were then in various homes until it was apparent that no family could handle three children. I mean, it was very difficult. People were just coming out of the Depression, and nobody could afford it, though we were wards of the state, and the state was paying for our care. We were welfare kids —not a happy situation and a very humiliating one for me. But that was the way it was. After we tried different homes that just didn't work out, I went back to live with the Caucasian family, and the two boys went elsewhere. They lived in a lot of places, too, but at the time of Pearl Harbor, they were with Japanese families.

During the late thirties my sister was living in a hospital, but she was pronounced cured and came back to Portland. She had been in the hospital for about four years. Part of that time was because she had no home to go to, because none of us really had one. When she got out, it was very important to her not to let anybody know that she had been in a tuberculosis sanitarium, because it was such a great stigma. So she lived in a residence for young women, and we were told not to say where she came from. Then right after Pearl Harbor she had a relapse and had to go back to the hospital.

Well, my sister died April 24, which was like a week before evacuation. We were evacuated from Portland May 5, 1942. Before she died, when she was still out of the hospital, the plan was for her to go with the boys. She was going to take the two boys, and I was going to stay with this Caucasian family. I was very attached to this family because . . . I don't know, I think there was an affection or a show of affection or a sense of belonging that I just hadn't had. It was very important for me to keep this. I think Mary sensed this, and so she said, "You stay there," and she would evacuate with the two boys. And then she had her relapse and went to the hospital, and . . . she died. So, within a week's time, I had to make a very serious decision. That was, to go in my sister's place. When we had to go on the fifth of May, I evacuated with my two brothers.

After all these years it's still very hard for me to talk about it. I was fifteen and she was about twenty. I'm not fully aware of how she died, but she had tuberculosis, and when she had her relapse, she went back to the hospital in Salem, and—as she wrote to my younger brother—in order to get well faster so that she could go to evacuate with them, she was going to take what was called a gas treatment. I may be inaccurate, but this involved collapsing a lung and letting it rest and then letting it inflate after a period of time. Now whether this is medically sound or not I don't know.

She was so anxious to have this done. Now remember, she was twenty years old, so she may not have been terribly informed in her thinking. Her doctor was out of town, and somebody consented to letting her have this gas treament, and it was a risky kind of thing, but somebody consented to let her take it. The morning that she took it she wrote a letter to my younger brother, which incidentally I kept all these years until this last spring when I gave it to him, and in that letter she wrote that she was going to get well quickly so that she could take the two boys to camp. And she had just gotten her hair cut and shampooed and she had fixed her fingernails and she was writing this letter to him, and then she was going to walk over to have this gas treatment. Well, that was a Friday, and by six o'clock that afternoon she was dead. So she went very quickly from being a well person to being gone.

At that time, there was a curfew for all Japanese in Portland. We had to be in from eight at night until six in the morning, I think it was, and we could not travel outside of a radius of five miles from our homes. Very early in the day I got a telephone call from Salem saying that Mary was seriously ill and could I come. It happened that in my foster family there was going to be a wedding. So my foster mother was at the hairdresser's, and everybody was all excited about the wedding the next day. But somehow I realized that this was something very serious, and I said, "Yes, I'll come right away," knowing that it took, in those days, a good hour and a half or so to get there. It's fifty miles away, but it took a long time to get there.

I went immediately downtown to the Western Defense Command or whatever office it was, I don't even remember, because I knew I had to get permission to go outside the five-mile radius. I had called my sister's boyfriend, who was maybe twenty-one or twenty-two, and told him what the problem was. I said I would go and get Roy and Harry, my two brothers, and we should go right away. It was the middle of a workday for him, and it wasn't convenient, but he somehow realized that it was very serious too, and so we met at the office, this Western Defense Command office, and started getting permission to leave.

This involved a telephone call to Salem to find out that this was in fact an emergency. The people at the office talked to doctors and nurses who swore that, yes, she was ill and, yes, the family should come immediately. And then they hung up and they talked about it for a while and decided that if we couldn't travel at night, maybe we should have a place to stay overnight. So then they called the hospital back again. This was a state tuberculosis sanitarium, and they didn't have facilities for guests. So after much conversation, it was settled that the four of us would drive up, and, yes, someplace in the hospital they would find some kind of accommodation to keep us off the road.

I can't remember how many other people they had to call, but even as a teenager, I thought, my God, this is what they call government red tape. It was just interminable, and I was getting more and more upset. It was three or four hours minimum that we sat there on telephones, waiting and waiting. They finally let us go, and we didn't take overnight clothes with us because it just didn't occur to me.

We just left, drove to Salem, and by the time we got there, she was dead. Her room was empty. Her name was still on the bed, so I knew we were in the right room. She was not there; the body was not there. In fact I didn't know she was dead, because I couldn't find her. I couldn't find anybody who could tell me anything about her. Somebody, I don't remember who, but somebody told us, yes, that patient had died. But they didn't know where the body was, and they didn't have any other information. I never did speak to a doctor or anybody who was connected with it who could give me any kind of information. I was so young then, but I felt so grown-up, because I was, you know, used to being independent. I certainly didn't perceive of myself as being a child. But I didn't think the treatment I got was right. I'm not sure whether it was because I was a child or what that we were treated in such a cavalier manner. It was, yes, the patient has died, and they didn't know where the body was. No official confirmation, no nothing.

I turned to George, who was my sister's boyfriend, and said, "I'm not staying here." And he said, "But we have to, the Army said we have to." And I said, "Not me. We're going to go home"; and with George in tow—he was the chauffeur—and my two younger brothers, we took off without telling anybody. It was as if the hospital, I mean everybody, had gone home for the day. I felt that nobody was there to talk to us. And I had no desire to see my sister's body once I knew she was dead. And I've often thought, why didn't I want to see her? But it was not important to me then.

All I knew was that she was dead, and "they" had done it. And I can't identify even now who I felt "they" were. It was just, you know, me against everybody, and everybody else had done it to me, or to us, and so I had no feeling of need to see the body at that point. All I wanted to do was get out of there, and I was very upset that nobody accorded us any kind of sympathy or any kind of human courtesy at all. There was such a feeling of abandonment there that I really wanted to leave that place.

So we drove home to Portland immediately, and I remember my two brothers, who were eleven and thirteen—they were just young children, really—pushing and shoving and playing in the backseat of the car. I turned around and said, "You know, now I'm the head of the family, and I'm telling you that Mary just died, and out of respect you should not play." Which was ridiculous, but that was my way of letting them know that I was in charge, and they were not to be acting normal.

When we were back home, I called a girl who had been a friend of my sister's. She came over, and we started to plan the funeral. I don't know why, but there are lots of things I don't remember about those next few days. I don't remember that the body was returned to Portland. I do remember the funeral. She had been a very active member of a certain church, and I wanted her funeral to be there. I remember that a lot of people from the Japanese community came. I felt that what people were saying then was, you know, another member of that family has died—as if we were kind of stigmatized. Because in a very short time my father, my mother, and now my sister had died. And several years prior to that, a brother had died. And I can remember thinking, this is not the way that it's supposed to be at all.

But I had no control over it, and all these Japanese people were there. And I really felt very bitter and angry, because in the years after my father died—my mother died first and then my father— the Japanese community was not friendly to us. They certainly did the opposite of rallying around. They were unwilling to help us children when we sorely needed it. Maybe this is unjust, but I felt that they had ignored us and abandoned us, when as kids we needed so much and they gave us nothing. So that when my sister died, I was terribly bitter, and I was angry, and I let it be known to that Japanese community the way I felt. She died the twenty-fourth, and her funeral was maybe two or three days later, and then it was a week later we were evacuated. This happened so quickly that I really don't remember details, only this feeling: terrible bitterness and anger.

I made my own decision. Nobody even approached me about it. I made my decision to go into camp with the two boys. At that point, as loving as my foster parents were, I did not think that they were good for me, and I think it's a good thing that I did not continue living with them. But I didn't know it at the time. They took me to the Portland Assembly Center and said good-bye to me. My foster mother had helped me pack, and we packed camp clothes, summer-camp clothes. You know how you pack shorts and tennis shoes and things like this. And I packed for maybe three weeks and thought this is only for a while, I'll be back. So I left school clothes, good clothes, cold-weather clothes and things like this, and books. I just took enough necessities for three weeks, thinking I surely would be back. She let me feel this way; she let me believe this way and let me prepare this way and took me to camp.

This was the first experience I'd ever had with living among Japanese people. Our home had been in the north part of Portland where we were the only Japanese family. So that, as children, we went to school as the only Japanese family in school, and our peer associations were not with Japanese people at all, so this was my first experience among Japanese people.

There was an overwhelming, confusing feeling, and it was just all negative—all bad feelings that I had. Not only the country having done this—causing us to have to be evacuated—but the Japanese people having done this to us. So I really was a very unhappy, bitter child, and I really entertained, at fleeting moments, some feelings that maybe I'd be better off if, you know, I tried to . . . I felt it might be a solution if I just did away with my brothers' and my own life. I thought that. I entertained that as a possibility, as a solution, and then abandoned it. But I thought this because it was so black for me at one point, you know. If your country is doing this to you, and if your people are doing this to you . . . I just couldn't see a way out of a big black hole. But I gave that idea up, obviously.

We spent the summer, through the end of August 1942 when we were evacuated into Idaho, in the Portland Assembly Center, which had been where they had stock shows. I remembered that from the time my parents took us to things like county fairs and stock shows. This was the county-fair grounds. All the places were very familiar to me as a child, and I recognized the place where we were assigned as the pavilion where they kept animals. They had these one by six's or one by nine's, however large those boards are, with big knotholes, just over the pens. It was a huge pavilion with twelve-foot-high plywood walls and with curtains as doors. Row after row after row of these. My two brothers and I were assigned to one of these. We had cots, and a curtain to cover the door, and our belongings. You've heard it all before. We ate in the community mess hall. We were given salt tablets because the weather was so hot.

I didn't know a soul. I knew a few kids, peers; but I didn't know them well, because I didn't live in the community. I was just beginning to feel like a teenager, and, you know, this is the time when peer relationships begin to be very important. Boy-girl relationships begin to be very important. It was a very brief period, but there was a nice feeling that I had when I first started to meet the kids. With them I was a social equal.

You probably have not experienced this yourself, but in the

late thirties and forties in my neighborhood where I grew up with Caucasian kids, we were all just one big family. But as we approached our teen years, you know, sex started to become important, and boys and girls started to pair off. While I was just great as a neighbor and a friend, all of a sudden I wasn't right to be dated.

So, I had very strange feelings. I discovered that among the Japanese people I was really kind of an oddity, because I had lived among Caucasians, and I was a novelty. When the guys started really coming around, I was thinking, Boy, this is terrific. I was getting offers for dates and stuff like that, and I thought that this was just going to be great. It was this racial thing that I was just beginning to become aware of, and I was trying to sort that out in my mind. And I discovered that among the Nisei people I was an equal, that I could compete with the other girls for the boys' attention, and I could be very successful at it.

When I went into camp I was just overwhelmed with the numbers of Nisei boys and girls and everybody. But also I would remember taking walks with my sister's boyfriend and telling him how I felt about how angry I was at the Japanese people, at the world, people in general, the country in general, the war, the everything. And that I wanted to have nothing to do with the Japanese people. And he would say, yes, but so-and-so wants a date with you. And I'd say, that's terrific, but I don't want to have anything to do with him, not at all. And he would say, now you think about it. You may feel different, but you aren't different. You're one of us. Like it or not, you are here. You chose to come here. Face it and live with it.

That summer I had this sorting out and coming to terms with my own self and my own life. It was not an easy time. When my brothers and I got to the Portland Assembly Center there were no persons, no agency, no group there to counsel not only me but anybody. No social workers, no social-service agency of any kind. There was an infirmary for cuts and bruises, but nothing else. I know, because I went seeking help one day when I can't tell you how low I felt. If a kid fifteen years old could even consider suicide, you know that she's got to be awfully unhappy. I went seeking some help and was directed by someone in charge to the infirmary. That's not what I needed.

There was nobody to give me any kind of emotional support of any sort—no Caucasians or Japanese personnel. I guess that this probably was the worst experience of my life, the hardest period of my life. I somehow got it all in my mind that it was the United States government, and it was this country, and it was the Japanese people—everybody was really out to do this to us. At that point, even if it hadn't been for the war, I might have felt this way. But I think that evacuation just heightened it all because it was just heaping one indignity after another onto me. It was just almost more than I could handle, it really was.

By Labor Day 1942, when we were to be moved inland to Idaho, I guess I was beginning to feel that I had no choice. I had to quit being so angry and to quit being so hateful. I had a job to do with my brothers, and I ran them like a drill sergeant, and people who met me in those years smile and laugh and talk about it now; they say, "Helen ran those boys like she was a drill sergeant." I wouldn't let them be out after nine o'clock, I made them go to school, I made them study, I made them . . . you know. I had them help me scrub their clothes so that they would be clean. Then somewhere during that time I came to feel, well, we're going to show these people. We're going to show the world. They are not going to do this to me; nobody is going to make me feel this miserable. The United States government may have made me leave my home, but they're going to be sorry. You know what I mean; I came around to feeling that nobody's going to do this to me. *I'm going to prevail, my will is going to prevail, my own life will prevail.* I'm not going to kill myself, I'm going to prevail.

I made up my mind that my two brothers and I would show everybody. We were orphans, yes; we had come from an unhealthy family, a tubercular family, and we were like pariahs, but I made up my mind, and I told my brothers that we will excel, and we will be better than anybody so that they'll be sorry. Not that they would be proud of us, but they would be sorry, the whole world would be sorry that they did this to us. It was not a healthy attitude on my part.

At Idaho's Minidoka we were assigned our barracks. Well, the end rooms of the barracks were the small rooms, quite small, the smallest. We were given one of those. It was usually for two people, but since we were kids and we didn't take up so much space, three of us were put in one of those end barracks. But I do remember managing to get a bed by using feminine wiles because the guys in camp were teenagers, and they were running up and down the block saying, "There's one over there," and "There's a good one over here." They were pegging the families that were coming in that had—you know—good-looking girls. They came running up to me, ran in and looked, and they saw that it was me, that there were no parents around. They asked how many beds? The camp was giving out pillow ticking that you filled with straw, and cots. The old and the infirm got beds with mattresses, and the younger people got cots and pillow ticking. I managed to finagle a real bed with a real mattress from these guys. I thought that was pretty neat. That's all we had, that's absolutely all we had.

I had no skills, and I did not want to work as a waitress. So, I lied and said I could type, and I worked in a steno pool. Well, the fellow watched me and he knew damned well I couldn't type. I couldn't. But, again, I used whatever I could muster up and batted by eyelashes and said I would be a hard worker. He let me stay, but not because of any typing expertise, he just let me do that. So I had a job for which I was paid. A stenographic job was sixteen dollars a month, and I was part-time, so I got eight dollars a month.

I was still in high school, so I had to go to class. My two brothers had to go too, and I lied a lot because I didn't want to go. I would stay at home, because the hot water in the mess hall and in the laundry rooms was available in the morning. I would scrub my brothers' blue jeans and their clothes on a washboard and try to wring them out and also launder our sheets in the morning. Then I would write a note saying, "Please excuse Helen for being absent, she was busy." And then I'd sign it, and the teacher would accept it. I still managed to get good grades. But I never, never, was in class. I insisted that my two brothers and I eat together in the mess hall as a family unit. I insisted that we have grace before meals. And I insisted that they be in our room at eight o'clock at night. Not because I wanted to see them but because I thought that's what we should do as a family unit—we should be together, spend our time together, and live as a family group—and I tried in all the really childish ways to maintain us that way. It's incredible, as I think about it now, how we did it; but we lived as a family unit. I don't know what gave me the strength to do it, but I can't help but feel that those early years with my parents must have given it to me. It must have been that, because that year and a half from evacuation until the time when I left camp were terribly hard times. Not only for me emotionally, but just keeping body and soul together. And that whole time we had absolutely no money, absolutely no financial support. No emotional support either. No adult nurturing of any kind. The people were so wrapped up in their own misery in camp, in their own unhappiness, in their own problems, which is only to be expected, that nobody had anything to give to anybody else. It didn't occur to them that maybe we were needy in other ways.

We got out of camp because we had a sponsor. It was in August 1943. The same woman who helped me plan my sister's funeral worked for the Baptist Home Mission Society. I wrote to her, and I said it was imperative that I get out immediately. I said, "Will you find me a place?" And, again, there's something that's marvelous about being young and ignorant; you just ask and somehow things materalize. She had access to homes throughout the country willing to take students. She sent me a list of several, and one of them was a family, a Presbyterian minister and his family, in Madison, Wisconsin. They wanted an evacuee. I didn't stop to think whether that was going to be all right or not; it just meant getting out. So I went. They were a terrific family. When I came out of camp, they gave me the support that I really sorely needed, and they have been friends ever since.

I felt wonderful the day I left camp. We took a bus to the railroad siding and then stopped someplace to transfer, and I went in and bought a Coke, a nickel Coke. It wasn't the Coke, but what it represented—that I was free to buy it, that feeling was so intense. You can get maudlin, sentimental about freedom; but if you've been deprived of it, it's very significant. When I ran in there as a teenager to buy that Coke, it was the freedom to buy it, the freedom to run out and do it.

Something my parents did for me provided the glue that held me together from age fifteen through seventeen. In my adult years the experience made me a very strong person, very strong. My two brothers—one is an M.D. and one is a Ph.D.—are very successful professionally. I have a master's degree. We all did this on our own. Nobody helped us.

Before my brother graduated from college, he said, "You know, I sort of would like to go to med school; what do you think?" And I said, "I think that's just terrific." And he said, "Well, how about money?" And I said, "Well, we don't have any. We just don't have any." All the time I went through college I went part-time, and I worked part-time. All of us went to school, but we worked part-time. We pooled our money. And so I said to Harry, "If that is your wish, then we'll do it. I don't know how, but we'll do it." And we did. There were no such things as student loans then. We got a few scholarships. When I couldn't help with money, I could help by providing. I took an apartment, and I gave them board and room. So that was some kind of help.

There were unseen hands, though, that helped. There just had to be. When I went to Madison, I finished high school, and somewhere a scholarship materialized for me to go to the Madison Business College. Now that is a private secretarial school, and nobody gets scholarships to go there, but what did I know? There was this fully paid scholarship to go. Who gave it to me? I don't know. But in typical sixteen-year-old fashion I said, "Oh, no thank you." I also got a scholarship to start at the University of Wisconsin. I thought about this, and I said, "No, thank you, I can't do that now." I had to get myself into a position where I could get some skills to get a job to earn some money. So I decided, instead of the University of Wisconsin scholarship, I would take that scholarship to the Madison Business College which was ludicrous. But somehow those unseen hands made things possible.

It was during the war years, and they let us go at our own pace. There were so few students, and instead of a three-year course or a two-year course, or whatever, you could go at your own pace. Well, I went at my own pace, and I was out in something like six months and got a job. Then I decided that if I could get a job, I could call my brothers out of camp, which I did. We got an apartment. My starting salary was ninety dollars a month full-time. I took an apartment. Because housing there was at a premium, this apartment that was share-the-bath, share-the-kitchen, one bedroom, and a ten-by-twelve living room was $160. I rented it and then I went to the Office of Price Stabilization (OPS), Rent Control, and I asked them to come and inspect the apartment. I said, "I don't think it's a correct rent." They came, and they said, "You are right, it should go down to $90 a month." So I said, "Thank you very much." The landlady was going to evict me but she couldn't, and she was very upset. But that was absolutely critically important to us that the OPS do this. So the rent was the same as my gross income was. The brother who had just come from camp got a job delivering milk. We didn't have a whole lot of extra money, but we made it.

Camp wasn't a dreadful place, it wasn't a wretched place, but I think the most significant thing for me was our loss of freedom. I did have some good times in camp. As I said, I met a lot of kids and learned how to interact with my peer group, the Japanese peer group. But the overriding feeling that I had, without even being conscious of it at that time, was the deprivation of freedom, and that is a very traumatic thing. You don't appreciate it until you don't have it. As I said, you can flag-wave and you hear all these people who make it seem so trite, but it isn't. I guess that the camp experience, the evacuation experience, as bad as it was, was never life-threatening. I never felt it was life-threatening. But it made even a young child, as I was then, value things that I didn't understand or appreciate even then as it was happening. See, when I left camp and bought the Coke, it was a wonderful feeling and I was exhilarated.

I couldn't articulate then what was in my mind. It's only since then that I can define those feelings. But I think that experience probably was a good one for me. Who needed it, though? I think that I'm a better person for it, a stronger person certainly. Maybe even a better human being for it. But did it have to be that bad for me to have this feeling?

So, you know, we never forget, but I'm all through being upset and angry. That's not productive, you know. My overriding feeling, and I've told my children, is don't let anybody else do something to you that you don't want to have happen to you. Don't let anybody control you. I have not wanted anybody to control me. My first reaction was, I'll show you. Well, I did show them. So I guess I proved something, but I don't want anything to control my life. Hatred and bitterness can control you too, right? I think I've resolved it.

PAUL SHINODA

"volunteer" evacuee, Grand Junction, Colorado

My father was from a farm family in Japan, and my mother's father was a school superintendent. My dad came to the United States—Hawaii, first. He worked about a year, and then he came to California in 1905. And he made *shoyu* ("soy sauce") for about one year here, and then he couldn't get the barrels. In the barrels they found some insect or bug, and they put an embargo on them. So then he had no containers to sell his shoyu in. Well, maybe they could have made them here, but he didn't know where you could have them made, so he went out of the shoyu business. A friend of his said, "Shinoda, you ought to go into the flower business," and he said, "I don't know anything about it." The friend said, "I do, I'm working for a flower grower."

So they made a verbal agreement that he would quit the other job and come and work for him on a semipartnership basis. My dad would put up the money for the lease, a least on the greenhouses. Well, he put his money up, and about the time he got ready to occupy, this fellow backed out. So my dad was on his own, and that's how K. Shinoda and Sons was born.

At that time, of the nine children, five were born in Japan and four here, and I'm the seventh in line. I was born in 1913. My dad sent all of us through college, except the two oldest. My oldest brother didn't go to college, and my oldest sister didn't go, but my second oldest brother, who is a Nishimura, went. See, my dad was born a Nishimura, and he went to his uncle, a Shinoda, and became an adopted son to carry on the Shinoda name.

After World War I, in 1918, there was the big flu epidemic, and flowers were in demand for funerals. My father made enough money to buy this sixty-acre farm, I think it was. He dug nine holes and the holes were dry, and that broke him—no water. So then he borrowed money on my brother's life insurance and his life insurance and my mother's life insurance and bought the original five acres in San Lorenzo. That was 1921 or so, because I remember the first car he bought in San Lorenzo was a Model T. You had to crank it, no self-starter on it. And I think the self-starter was about 1922 or 1923. Before that I think you had to crank them—no self-starter on the Model T.

My dad bought this place in San Lorenzo from a fellow called Tamimune, who went to Japan with the money and spent quite a bit of it. He came back and was growing sweet peas outside in southern California in Dominguez Hills. My dad couldn't make the payments, so he took a train to ask Tamimune if he could prolong the payments. In doing so, he visited the flower market in Los Angeles and found that they had no roses, or they had lousy roses. So then Dad went back to San Lorenzo and tore out all the carnations and built more houses. He doubled his volume, and started growing roses. Everyone said Shinoda has gone crazy; he's already in debt up to his eyeballs. Well, then he started prospering with the roses by selling in Los Angeles. They were shipped down by Railway Express every day to my brother, Kiyoshi, who was down in Los Angeles selling the flowers.

Mom and Dad were both converted by a missionary by the name of Blackstone from England, and that's why they decided to come to the United States, because they couldn't see raising five children under the predominant atmosphere of Buddhism. So that's why he left Japan and never went back. All the years he lived, he never went back, not once, and neither did my mom.

My father had a philosophy about when you're in America: this is your country, you're growing up here. Don't speak *Nihongo* ("Japanese"). He was against Japanese schools. He says you go to the school your neighbor does, and what they play, you play. So he said, if you want to learn Japanese and you think you need it, when you get out of college, you go spend a year there.

I went to Oregon State and had reserved a room at Buck Hall

dorm. There's three dorms for men, and Buck Hall was the one we had our name in for, for ten dollars. Art Kodani and I waited, and the housemother came and said, "Just wait a minute now," and we sat in the lobby. In the meantime a Hakujin came in, and the housemother took him up and assigned him a room. And another fellow would come in. Art and I just sat there—we're both Japanese, you know. Finally the dean came, Dean Duwak, a real nice guy, and explained to us that they don't allow Japanese in this dorm. This was 1931, the fall of 1931, and it was late in the afternoon already, so he said come and stay with us, Mrs. Duwak and I, and tomorrow we'll look for a place, and he found us a rooming house.

I was seventeen, a young freshman, and lonesome, and I didn't go to socials. It started to rain when we got there and didn't quit until we left, and in southern California you're not very much at home in the rain. Everything social was with women, and I didn't have the guts to ask Hakujin gals for a date.

I went to Oregon State for a year and a half, and after I was there awhile I called my dad up and told him it was anti-Japanese. I said I wanted to go to the University of Illinois, because they had the only school of horticulture in the United States. So he said to go to Illinois: "Mother says you can go next year, but if they're so bad, and there's so much anti-Japanese feeling, go ahead and go now." But I waited until the next fall to go to Illinois. Then my brother, Kiyoshi, died. He died in July of 1933. I was in Illinois for a year and finished up at Berkeley in 1935.

The family bought a place in Monrovia, and I went down and started it. There was no future in it. So I wanted to go back to the greenhouses, and we found property and bought it in Torrance. We started out there in spring of 1939, so I must have bought the property in about January of 1939. I built the nursery in Torrance from scratch—all the greenhouses. It was just flat ground. We bought five acres the first year, five acres the next year, and then after the war we bought more land and ended up with 19½ acres.

On December 7, I felt, Holy smoke! What's going to happen? But I was confident that nothing would happen to me, because I believed in American fair play—being an American citizen and learning this at school. And I associated with Hakujins most of my life in various phases of business. Of course, there was nothing social for us, because organizations such as Kiwanis were not open to Japanese then. So there was little socializing. It was just business and so forth, but I figured . . . well, I didn't know what to figure. In those days we'd work on Sunday and not on Saturday, and I came home for lunch and heard it on the radio. I was shocked and didn't believe it.

This evacuation came up, and then they put the curfew on, and I stayed in Gardena. But then it turned out Japanese people from Gardena couldn't go across Western Avenue anymore. So I couldn't go to the nursery anymore. I lived east of Western Avenue—I couldn't go west—so the next day we packed up and left. I figured as long as I got out to the eastern zone by six, I'd be all right. In the meantime I traded my car in and bought a pickup and rode with the three kids and all our earthly goods in the pickup and took off to West Del Rey. I knew about evacuation, but Hakujins didn't know. Even the cops, everyday cops didn't know much about it. So as long as I behaved myself and didn't drive recklessly or anything and just drove normally up the ridge route, nobody would bother me. Nobody asked me questions; they never did. Just because war broke out, I didn't think these guys would change that much—you know Americans can't change overnight. Like in Russia they're always asking questions, but not in the United States.

So, by the time I got to Dey Rey at eight at night, my family was in shock. My family knew that I was coming up. Joe was up there, and Pete was there already. They said, "What are you guys doing, it's after six—come on in, get in," and all that stuff. But we didn't even discuss what was happening—Mom and I never discussed it.

But when we first heard about evacuation I was just sure I wasn't going to be a ward of the government in any camp or anything, I could take care of my family, and my wife and I could get a job and my family wouldn't worry about starving. I wasn't going to be any ward of the government. I didn't even discuss it with my wife, but she figured it the other way—she just figured we're going to discuss it, because we're going to camp. Finally I couldn't go across the street. I couldn't go across Western Avenue. So I just packed up to go. And my wife asked where we were going, and I said Del Rey. And that's the first time she heard of it. That shows how much I felt that I wasn't going to be a ward of the government.

We owned our house but we sold it to a guy named Benboon. He got a job at the shipyard, but he didn't have any dough, so he agreed to pay so much a month. Every time I needed more money I asked him to make an advance payment, and he did it. I think altogether it was $3,500 and he owed about $2,500 on it. We only lived there about a year and a half before we sold it. We couldn't pack up all the stoves and refrigerators and stuff like that. We stored them away in the nursery—our stove, our kids' toys, and some of our furniture. Some truck driver took our stove and never paid for it. When we got back from camp we had nothing—even the toys were all gone. Everything we had was what we brought back from Colorado, which was very meager. We had to buy all new furniture when we got back.

At the time of the evacuation I was president of the Gardena JACL, and I kind of thought we were going too much like sheep. We should have sat still and been taken one by one with bayonets instead of going along like sheep. I felt that we were sold down the river. They hauled a lot of Issei away, but not the Germans and Italians; but, unlike us, the Italians and the Germans didn't have anybody to get up there and say, okay, we'll go; I'm the leader and they'll all follow me. That got my goat more than anything. That's how I felt at that time, and I still feel that.

The evacuation order came, and that night, Johnny, Pete, and I sat down and discussed it and decided, let's leave. I had a pickup, Pete had a car, and John had a car, and we were going to buy gasoline, and I was going to carry it in the pickup. We'd go from there to Independence and to Nevada, but they chickened out. We talked about it until eleven o'clock at night. We wanted to go the next morning and get the stuff together and go the following night. I think it was about an hour or two hours after we discussed this as a group—Pete, Yoshiko, John, June, Mom, and me—the six adults discussed it, and we had all the things ironed out and ready to go, and the plan was already started. Early that night, about an hour after we disbanded to get some sleep, Pete came by and said he didn't think he was going to go—he didn't want to take a chance. And Johnny came back a half an hour later and he didn't want to go, and I didn't want to go alone.

There was a company recruiting sugar-beet workers, and this was in June and they let us go out that way. They gave us a flowery talk saying we would get to go on the train and we would get meals and accommodations. But it turned out to be like a cattle car, and the one meal we got was in Salt Lake City. You had to jump off when the train was stopped, and go buy something—whatever you could. We ended up in Blackfoot, Idaho, and they lined us up. And the farmer got to choose us. There must have been several cars, about 130 or so people and 40 in a car and three or four cars, and that was hard. It was traumatic, lining us up like slaves at the market. They did everything but open your mouth and look at your teeth and feel your muscles. They picked you out of the crowd, and we didn't get picked. We had three little kids, and they would have had to give us housing. Dan had my mother and dad with him, and they didn't pick him either.

We went to an FSA camp, and finally I found a job at the Parkers'—for ninety dollars a month. We had a house, and we had a potbellied stove and running water, with a bucket under the sink to catch the water—the sink didn't have a drain—and we had an outhouse. My mind just shut it out. They had a victory garden and we could help ourselves to vegetables. Little Paul, Jr., was about five and a half in 1942. He started school in Grand Junction, and David was about three, and Annie would have been about a year old. We lived across the street from a grammar school, and Paul started school there.

I was a farmhand and cut hay. It was already too late for planting sugar beets. So the first maybe three weeks to a month, I rebuilt the old Parker house for my family, put a finished roof on. And Parker built a new house across the street but he didn't know how to hang the garage door. Well, I made it and hung it for him, and he was surprised I could do it. Next I was doing chores every morning and every night. The house I lived in used to have a lean-to. We wanted to make more use out of it, so I did that for him, made one ridge, and I put new shingles on it and a whole new roof.

By that time it got time to start haying, cut the hay and alfalfa, and that was a lousy job. You had to cut the hay with a horse. I never drove a horse before in my life, and when you go around the corner you've got to raise the bar. It was a wonder I didn't fall off that damn thing; and if you did, it would have cut your legs off. The sickle bar would come up and you've got to put a lot of power in that to raise it for leverage. Yeah, and then the horses. You used to change horses twice a day and one team in the morning and one team in the afternoon. They had to go so fast to make that sickle bar cut because it was traction that moved the cutting bar. Parker worked hard too, and then after that, it got to be grain-harvest time.

We had to trade work, and I had to work at the other farmer's place. We helped in threshing, and that was a tough job. It hurt my back permanently.

Then came potato harvest. Jack Parker would take the tractor and dig the potatoes and lay them on top of the ground with the machine. Then the guys on piecework would pick them up and put them in gunnysacks of about sixty-five or seventy pounds. Dusty, dirty, and heavy work, and I got ninety dollars a month, and the ones picking the potatoes were making fifty dollars or twenty dollars a day. That was part of the deal until the season was over and there's no more work, when the field is dormant. The following spring we went to Colorado.

My father died at Grand Junction, Colorado, December of 1944. He had a stroke so he was pretty much a vegetable for many, many months—for a year or two. About the time he died he was just skin and bones. I don't know if he understood us saying that we were going to get to go back to California. In December we knew, and he died December 22, just before Christmas. Nobody had any flowers, and Joe went down to Watson's flower shop in town and asked them if we could use the facilities to make funeral sprays if we had our own flowers. We'd pay rent for it and for whatever supplies we used. We got Johnny to come and do the floral work for us. Was that guy from Watson's surprised when roses came and carnations came all from our nursery—red roses right before Christmas. So we had a nice big funeral for my dad. But this guy from Watson's couldn't believe his eyeballs. He wanted to know where we got them, because he couldn't.

We have pictures that my wife took of Annie and the three kids when they went ice skating on the Gunnison River. We have savored memories of that. My wife took them ice skating. But a man came and said, "Sorry, but we have to take you to jail." There was this ore processing plant nearby. So he took them in, and they were scared to death, the three kids and my wife. And this is a security guard, not a public appointed sheriff or anything. I got home, and I went there and asked the guy where my camera was. He took it. I asked, "What right do you have to take my camera?" I said, "You have no right," and I took this big clocklike thing on the desk, and all I said was "Until you give me that, I'm taking this. I've got just as much right to take this as you've got the right to take my wife's camera. Now if you don't believe me, watch me," and I took it and left. I said, "When you bring my camera back with the film in it, I'll give this back to you." He wouldn't let my wife and kids go, and finally he brought it back, and there was no evidence that my wife took pictures of the plant or anything. It was just the kids skating.

I lost about five years—I just lost them. If I'd gone into the Army, I'd have lost about the same, though. The sad part of it is, there's no glory in being evacuated, you can't say I'm an evacuee—veteran of the evacuation.

It was a lousy, lousy deal they gave us. I didn't think they'd do it, because I thought American fair play was there, the Constitution too. And we had the right to the pursuit of happiness. Going to camp and being evacuated didn't fit that. I don't think it shook my faith. The basic thing is I didn't know anything else, this was the only country I knew. But if they picked just the Japanese for an evacuation again, I'd raise holy hell, and I'd sit here until they pretty well shot me before I'd move. I wouldn't go because someone told me to go or agreed with General so-and-so that he'd get the Japanese to go. I'd tell the whole bunch, the hell with them. Because another thing, I'm older and I don't have too much more to go. So they kill me, so what? Maybe it's because I'm different now, I don't know. America is still a nice place to live. I've been all over, and it's been a good place to live. But I think we ought to be compensated for it, and what I'd do with it I don't know. But that's the only way they are going to know that they did an injustice to us. Make them pay for it. That's the way the Americans are—if you do something wrong, you have to pay for it in dollars. You don't have to go to jail and pay for it, but if it's anything civil you've got to pay for it in dollars.

The person who lived next to us in Gardena, for instance, knew that the Japanese were patriotic; those that took time to be with us knew, but those bastards that didn't know anything about us made the decision. Well, I guess that's how the United States is: all the decisions are made by a few guys who don't know what it's all about. There was once someone, I don't know what his name was, who had kids about our kids' ages, and he went and told them not to play with ours anymore. The kid came over and said, "I can't play anymore because my mother told me not to." But if you went to these people and asked them had we done anything unpatriotic, they couldn't say anything. They didn't see us do anything wrong, because we didn't do anything wrong. We lived just like they did, and we went to work every day and came home. And Mom stayed home and took care of the kids, and we went to church on Sunday. They knew it; they could see us as well as we could see them. But nobody came out, and nobody went to the trouble to ask—nobody went to the trouble.

MITSUYE ENDO

Topaz

I was born in Sacramento, California, in 1920. My father worked in a grocery store. My mother was a housewife, and there were four of us children—myself, one brother and two sisters. My brother was in the Army, drafted in 1941 before Pearl Harbor. My father came to the United States in 1916, went back to marry, and then came back again in 1918 and never returned to Japan after that. I went to elementary school and high school and then went to work for the state of California as a typist. Because there was so much discrimination against the Japanese Americans, the only position we could get was with the state, unless we worked for a Japanese firm.

In 1942 we were dismissed from working for the state of California because we were of Japanese ancestry. We were given a piece of paper saying we were suspended because we were of Japanese ancestry. We were accused of something, but I can't even remember any of the allegations. Some of the state of California employees were members of the JACL, and through them we got the service of an attorney in San Francisco, Mr. James Purcell, in order to answer these allegations. While this was going on, we were evacuated from the Coast. We went to Walarga Assembly Center near Sacramento for about a month, and then we went to Tule Lake. While we were there, a representative of the attorney came into camp and wanted to select three or four of us, and they started off with me because they thought I had the best background: my brother was in the Army, and my parents never went back to Japan. They felt that I represented a symbolic, "loyal" American, and I think it was in July of 1942 when the case was up before the district court.

I never talked to Purcell—never met the man. I was very young, and I was very shy, so it was awfully hard to have this thing happen to me. In fact, when they came and asked me about it, I said, well, can't you have someone else do it first. It was awfully hard for me. I agreed to do it at that moment, because they said it's for the good of everybody, and so I said, well if that's it, I'll go ahead and do it. I never imagined it would go to the Supreme Court. In fact I thought it might be thrown out of court because of all that bad sentiment toward us. While all this was going on, it seemed like a dream. It just didn't seem like it was happening to me.

During that time in camp, I was anxious to have my case settled because most of my friends had already gone out, been relocated, and I was anxious to get out too. But I was told to remain there until I got a notice from our attorney that I could leave. We had been at Tule Lake one year and then Topaz. I was in Topaz for two years. I came out to Chicago in June of 1945. I could have left earlier, but Purcell needed me to be in camp.

When I think about it now—that my case went to the United States Supreme Court—I'm awed by it. I never believed it, that I would be the one. It doesn't seem like it's me that I'm looking at when I see it in print, it was so long ago. Actually I didn't do too much. It was all my attorney's effort. It was through the state of California employees and the JACL that we got together on this thing. This is right after we went into camp, to Tule Lake, in 1942. When we got the allegations, Tom Hayashi was one of the state of California employees. I'm sure he must have been instrumental in getting the JACL involved in this, and through them we got an attorney to represent us. I remember we became members of JACL and we went to meetings. Then, through those meetings we decided to get an attorney to represent us.

Do I have any regrets at all about the test case? No, not now, because of the way it turned out.

MINORU YASUI

Minidoka

I was born in Hood River, Oregon, on October 19, 1916, the third son of Masuo and Shidzuyo Yasui. The Masuo Yasui family was six boys and three girls, but my oldest brother died at age eighteen and a younger sister at age four or five. My paternal grandfather, Shinataro Yasui, had come out of the rice fields of rural Okayama, during the mid-1890s, to work on the railroads in Idaho, Montana, Washington, and Oregon. Having put aside some money from his earnings as a railroad-gang laborer, he later sent for his two older sons (my paternal uncles), who came to the U.S. before 1900, also to work on the railroads.

Grandfather Yasui returned to Japan during 1917; his eldest son (my oldest uncle) subsequently also returned to Japan to establish a textile factory in their home village in Okayama-ken.

My father, Masuo Yasui, came to the U.S. in 1903, at age sixteen. Because he was so slight that he could not physically perform the hard labor on the railroad gangs, he became a "school boy" in Portland, Oregon, doing domestic work, learning to cook, hand laundering clothes, working in the garden. He wanted to become a lawyer, but found out soon enough that the legal profession was barred to him because of his Japanese alienage. He also discovered that he could not become a U.S. citizen because he was an Oriental. He worked in Portland in a Caucasian's home as a houseboy for about three years.

My father used to tell the story that as a twenty-year-old, he heard about a place called *Shin-Shin-no-chi* (Cincinnati), which translated would mean "a new, new land." Enthralled by vague thoughts of such a place, he took a train out of Portland (he could use his father's railroad pass) and started to head East. However, in traveling up the Columbia River gorge and coming to a place called Hood River, the terrain reminded him so much of his home in Japan that he got off the train and decided to settle there—or so he told the story.

In 1906 he persuaded his older brother, Renichi Fujimoto—a *yoshi* ("adopted son to carry on the family name")—to the Fujimoto family to start a mercantile store in Hood River. By dint of inordinate hard work (Dad used to tell of sweeping out the old Butler Bank building early in the morning, so townsfolk would not see a businessman doing janitorial work!), the business slowly prospered. The Yasui Brothers Company began to acquire extensive interests in farm and orchard lands, and to assist newly arrived Japanese immigrants establish farms and orchards on the logged-over hills of Hood River valley.

In 1912 my mother, Shidzuyo Miyake, who grew up in the same village of Nanokaichi, Okayama-ken, Japan, came to the United States through the port of Tacoma, Washington, to marry my father. Both my father and mother were Methodists at the time of their marriage, and my father insisted that all of his children would be Americans but without forgetting their Japanese lineage. My mother was a college educated woman (which was rare in those days) and had been a teacher in a women's school in Japan, before she immigrated to this country in 1912. She was able to teach other Japanese immigrant women about *cha-no-yu* ("tea ceremony"), *ikebana* ("flower arranging"), koto, and haiku, which we, as children, absorbed to some degree.

My mother's younger brother, Saburo Miyake, also later came to the United States and joined my father and uncle in one of the farms, twenty acres in Pine Grove in the Hood River valley, at the end of World War I, to grow strawberries and to raise fruit. He stayed until about the time of the Oriental Exclusion Act and the passage of antialien land laws in Oregon, which was about 1924. I have vague memories of him and his family. He returned to Japan to fulfill responsibility to the Miyake family, who were minor local officials in the village in the early Meiji years. I still remember, in 1925, my maternal grandfather with his short sword, as a symbol of his authority, when we visited Japan.

Because the Yasui Brothers Company grubstaked Japanese immigrant families to the Hood River valley, helping them with start-up capital, negotiations, and so forth, by 1940 my father and uncle had a half or a third, or some shares in probably about a thousand acres of farm and orchard lands in the valley, besides owning outright several hundreds of acres of farms. I can still remember my father pioneering, with a number of Japanese farmers, the asparagus industry at Mosier and Viento farms, shipping carloads of asparagus back East during the 1930s. By 1940, as a successful businessman and agriculturist, Masuo Yasui was a member of the local Rotary Club, a member of the board of the Apple Growers Association, a pillar of the local Methodist church, as well as founder of the local Japanese Methodist church and the local Japanese Association. He was a friend and neighbor of the local bank president, the most prominent lawyer in town, the editor of the local newspaper, and all "important" people in Hood River, Oregon.

On December 7, 1941, Masuo Yasui, in short, was a prominent member of the Hood River community. His eldest son, Ray T. Yasui, was managing one of his larger fruit farms at Willow Flats; as the next son, I was a licensed attorney in Oregon, but was in Chicago, Illinois, at the time; his oldest daughter and another son were students at the University of Oregon, with another son at the University of Michigan in engineering; his youngest son and youngest daughter were still students at the local high school. Although many of the Japanese American community leaders in Portland, Oregon, were immediately picked up by the FBI on December 7, 1941, Masuo Yasui was not arrested and taken away as an "enemy alien" until December 13, 1941. Mother, then fifty-six, and my youngest sister, did not know for weeks where they had taken my father. Meanwhile, all of the assets of Yasui Brothers Company, and personal assets of Masuo Yasui were frozen by the U.S. Treasury Department, including the mercantile store. For all Japanese American families on the West Coast, it was a bleak Christmas and New Year's season in 1941; and it was for the Yasui family in Oregon too.

I was in Chicago at the time of Pearl Harbor. I will never forget that it was about twelve o'clock noon, Sunday, December 7, 1941, when Suma Tsuboi called me when I was asleep on a couch in my apartment at the Dearborn Plaza, saying that the Japanese have bombed Pearl Harbor. I was shocked, dismayed, and at first, unbelieving. I had been out the night before with some of the Japanese Consulate people, and there had been no hint of such outbreak of war.

Upon graduation from the University of Oregon Law School in 1939, I took the Oregon state bar examination that June. During September, 1939, I was notified that I had passed the Oregon bar exams and was admitted as a practicing attorney in Oregon. During the fall of 1939, and early spring of 1940, I had accepted a retainer from the Japanese Association of Oregon to research and write a public relations piece about the contributions (mostly agricultural) of Japanese Americans to the economy of Oregon. Also, in trying to establish a law practice, I found that a number of my law school classmates had accepted positions with established law firms in Portland but were receiving minimal pay. So, rather than working for $35 less per month than a produce clerk, I accepted a position as an attaché at the consulate general of Japan in Chicago at $125 per month. My father had known Consul General Hiroshini Akino. I commenced work at the consulate on March 1, 1940.

Because my duties were not overly onerous at the consulate, I was personally engaged in running a Boy Scouts of America troop, and I participated in various community groups. I led a hyperactive social life, carousing in the bars along North Rush Street, playing poker all night, and generally running around too much. Thus it wasn't until noon that I was awakened on December 7 by the telephone call from Suma Tsuboi. I checked with friends in regard to what would be transpiring. On the next day, December 8, I resigned by letter from the consulate.

In mid-December, 1941, I received official orders to report for active duty with the United States Army at Camp Vancouver, Washington. I held a reserve commission as a second lieutenant in the U.S. Army. The instructions ordered me to report for duty on January 19, 1942. So I went down to the Union Pacific Railroad station to purchase a ticket back to Portland, Oregon. But the ticket agent wanted to know if I were a "Jap." When I foolishly answered truthfully that I was of Japanese ancestry, he responded that he could not sell transportation to a "Jap." Despite my showing him travel orders from the U.S. Army, I could not persuade him to issue me a railroad ticket. I finally had to make an appointment to see one of the attorneys in the general counsel's office for the Union Pacific Railroad in Chicago to obtain authorization for me to buy a ticket to report for active duty with the U.S. Army. I had to point to the Fourteenth Amendment to the Constitution of the United States to persuade that lawyer that I was a citizen of the United States, on the basis of my birth certificate alone.

I traveled to North Platte, Nebraska, on the first leg of my trip home to Oregon. I stopped off to see old friends and to say good-byes, because as far as I was concerned, I would be off to the wars, in the infantry, and there was no assurance that I would ever be back. While staying overnight in North Platte, the sheriff or police chief knocked on my hotel door and demanded to know who I was and what I was doing in North Platte. This plainclothes officer asked me, "You're a Jap, aren't you?" I answered, "No, I'm bog-Irish." And the guy answered, "Don't get smart with me! I'll throw your ass in jail if you fuck around with me."

"And who are you?" I asked him. He identified himself as a law enforcement officer. So I showed him my military travel orders, and he left. It shook me up as I wondered whether I had been followed out of Chicago and how could I have been spotted as a stranger in a town like North Platte, Nebraska? The next morning I boarded the train and returned to Oregon without further incident.

On January 19, 1942, I took my dad's car and drove to Portland, crossed the river, to report for active duty at Camp Vancouver. I do not remember the rank of the officer who received me, but it seems to me that it was a colonel who looked over my papers, referred to other papers in my files, looked up, and curtly told me, "We'll let you know when to report." I replied, "Okay," and left. Years later, in October 1944, I received official discharge papers from the U.S. War Department, stating that I was no longer a second lieutenant in the U.S. Army's Officers Reserve Corps. And so ended my military career in World War II. It occurred to me that was probably just as well because the outfit to which I would have been assigned was a detachment from Texas. If we had gone into any active combat situation, I'd probably have been shot in the back. Or so it seems to me now.

I went back to Hood River, Oregon. My mother had received word that a hearing would be held to determine whether Masuo

Yasui should be held as a potentially dangerous "enemy alien." The hearings were to be held during the first part of February 1942 in Fort Missoula, Montana. As a son, and as an attorney, I felt that I had to go to try to help my father at these hearings. I knew that my father was truly loyal to the ideals and high principles of this country. Also, we learned that other hearings were being conducted by the Enemy Alien Control Unit. Later I learned this unit was headed by Edward J. Ennis, but at the time I assumed that normal rules of law would apply and that unless actual conduct were shown to endanger the security of this country, the internees would be released. I knew a number of the Portland Japanese internees. I requested permission to attend the hearings of all these internees, and I talked with the wives and families of these men in Portland before leaving for Missoula, Montana, which is about eight hundred miles to the east.

With headlines screaming about the furious battles for Bataan, it was intimidating to realize that, being physically Japanese, there was no assurance of being able to get a hotel room or even being able to go to a restaurant in Missoula. In short, I was scared and alone in hostile territory. After arriving I was able to get a hotel room, and I hired a taxi to go out to Fort Missoula, to the internment center. There, surrounded by barbed wire, guarded by armed MPs, I went into the offices to try to arrange to see the various internees from Oregon.

I was permitted to visit with my father, Masuo Yasui, but denied permission to visit the others whom I had known for years. I was also granted permission to attend the hearing for my father and allowed to participate. The proceedings were a complete farce. The official for the Enemy Control Unit pointed out that my father was an influential leader in the Japanese community in Hood River, Oregon; that he had extensive property interests; that he had visited Japan for a summer vacation for three months in 1925; that he had been awarded a medal by the Emperor of Japan for promoting U.S.-Japan relations; and that he had been instrumental in obtaining a position with the consulate general of Japan in Chicago for me.

The most incredible thing was when they produced childlike drawings of the Panama Canal showing detailed drawings of how the locks worked. The hearing officer took these out and asked, "Mr. Yasui, what are these?" Dad looked at the drawings and diagrams and said, "They look like drawings of the Panama Canal." They were so labeled, with names of children. Then the officer asked my father to explain why they were in our home. "If they were in my home," my father replied, "it seems to me that they were drawings done by my children for their schoolwork." The officer then asked, "Didn't you have these maps and diagrams so you could direct the blowing up of the canal locks?" My father said, "Oh no! These are just schoolwork of my children." The officer said, "No, we think you've cleverly disguised your nefarious intent and are using your children merely as a cover. We believe you had intent to damage the Panama Canal." To which my father vehemently replied, "No, no, no!" And then the officer said pointedly, "Prove that you didn't intend to blow up the Panama Canal!" I can still remember so vividly the officer asking my father to prove that he didn't intend to blow up the Panama Canal!

Why a businessman and agriculturalist with an impeccable reputation, living in a far-off rural town like Hood River—two hundred miles from the ocean, and possibly three thousand miles from the Panama Canal—should have to prove that he had no intent to blow up the Panama Canal seemed to me then, and seems to me now, to be the height of absurdity.

It was on this kind of "evidence" that my father and thousands of others were confined to internment camps, operated by the U.S. Department of Justice and manned by the U.S. Army, and were kept for the duration, until the spring of 1946.

I went back to Oregon after the hearings, utterly repulsed by the kangaroo-court proceedings of the U.S. Department of Justice. I knew that no legal appeals would be of any use, because we were at war with Japan, and these men were Japanese nationals, and hence "enemy aliens" for whom judicial processes were not available in time of war. Never mind that U.S. laws prevented them from becoming U.S. citizens. Returning to Portland, Oregon, I made the rounds, visiting the wives of Portland internees, telling them the bad news of hearings in Missoula, based on my impressions of my father's "hearing." From there, I went to Hood River to finish application forms and reports in connection with my father's and uncle's businesses.

News from the battlefronts in the Pacific were disastrous. General Jonathan Wainwright's American and Filipino forces were being decimated on Bataan and Corregidor; Hong Kong had fallen, and

Singapore was soon to follow; Japanese expeditionary forces were entrenched on Attu and Kiska on the Aleutian chain; all of the Dutch East Indies all the way to Australia was wide open for the Japanese invaders; and news from the European theater was equally bad.

On the home front, things for Japanese Americans were deteriorating daily. In Portland, the city council gave instructions not to issue business licenses to Japanese. Business contracts with Japanese individuals, citizens or noncitizens, were being ignored, and open-and-shut cases in court were being lost when the claimant was Japanese.

Rules and regulations were being issued by the Alien Property Custodian and the U.S. Treasury Department regarding "enemy aliens." The Nisei became ensnared in tangles of red tape because of shared interests or because equitable or beneficial ownership was retained by the Issei. Normal and ordinary business transactions were becoming chaotic if you were a person of Japanese ancestry, because you had not only to prove U.S. citizenship, but to prove also that you had no beneficial interest owed by an enemy alien, that is, an Issei.

Fraud and outright cheating of rightful owners occurred in many transactions involving persons of Japanese ancestry. In such a chaotic situation, the services of lawyers were needed. Because I was the only Japanese American lawyer in the state of Oregon and the only Oregon lawyer who could speak Japanese, and particularly since we generally had to deal with the wives of internees, it seemed appropriate for me to reopen a law office in the Foster Hotel on NW Third Avenue in Portland, Oregon. I did this, and I was promptly swamped and overwhelmed. From February to the end of April 1942, my law practice was a blur of trying to do too much in too short a time. I know that I didn't do a good job of serving my clients. There were too many, too soon, and their problems were too complex for easy solutions. But I did what I could, going without sleep for days and getting no rest during the evenings and weekends.

On February 19, 1942, President Franklin Delano Roosevelt signed Executive Order 9066, but this scarcely made a ripple in public awareness, at least in Portland. On the other hand, the newspapers and radio were beginning to hammer out an incessant barrage of anti-Jap invectives. We kept hearing that the Japanese

Issei would all be interned; we heard that the Nisei would be allowed to remain at home to run the businesses and farms the Issei would have to leave behind; we heard conflicting rumors that Issei and Nisei alike would be put into work camps to labor for the war effort; we heard suggestions that all Japanese would be sterilized and, after the war, deported to Japan. We heard a hundred and one wild things, almost daily, almost hourly.

We knew that Francis Biddle, as Attorney General of the United States, had counseled that evacuation and incarceration of Japanese persons who were U.S. citizens would be unconstitutional. Nevertheless, when Walter Lippmann began his series supporting evacuation, he was shrilly echoed by Westbrook Pegler, Walter Winchell, Damon Runyan, and others, as well as by politicians of every stripe, including the now revered Earl Warren of California. The die seemed cast, particularly when it became clear that religious groups (except the Quakers) and civil rights organizations would not come to aid the Japanese Americans. This was the situation in spite of the protestations by military leaders such as General Mark Clark and Admiral Harold Stark, both of whom said that evacuation of all Japanese Americans was not necessary.

On March 21, 1942, the Congress passed a law imposing a penalty of one year in jail, a five-thousand-dollar fine, or both, for knowingly violating any military order. A penal clause is not a bad law, because there is always the question of whether a particular order, military or otherwise, is a valid order. Here, as events proved, the U.S. Supreme Court failed to make strict scrutiny of the validity of a particular order.

On March 23, 1942, as I recall, General John L. DeWitt issued his Military Proclamation No. 3, requiring all German enemy aliens, all Italian enemy aliens, and all persons of Japanese ancestry to conform to a curfew order. This extended from 8:00 P.M. until 6:00 A.M., and all affected were to remain within five miles of their usual place of abode or business, unless exempted by special military permission.

It was my feeling and belief, then and now, that no military authority has the right to subject any United States citizen to any requirement that does not equally apply to all other U.S. citizens.

Moreover, if a citizen believes that the sovereign state is committing an illegal act, it is incumbent upon that citizen to take measures to rectify such error, or so, at least, I believed. Finally, it seemed to me then and now that if the government unlawfully curtails the rights of any person, the damage is done not only to that individual person but to the whole society. If we believe in America, if we believe in equality and democracy, if we believe in law and justice, then each of us, when we see or believe errors are being made, has an obligation to make every effort to correct them.

Quixotic or idealistic as it may seem, I believed this in March 1942. And I still do today.

Consequently, at 8:00 P.M., March 28, 1942, after having asked Rae Shimojima, my assistant, to notify the FBI and the local Portland police, I started to walk the streets of Portland in deliberate violation of Military Proclamation No. 3. The principle involved was whether the military could single out a specific group of U.S. citizens on the basis of ancestry and require them to do something not required of other U.S. citizens. As a lawyer, I knew that unless legal protest is made at the time of injury, the doctrine of laches or indeed the statute of limitations would forever bar a remedy.

I was convinced, having discussed this matter in some considerable detail with a number of constitutional lawyers in Portland, that unless a legal challenge were successful, there would be no way to stop the inexorable processes of evacuation, and that unless the courts would find that the military was exercising unlawful powers, there could never be a legal claim against the United States government.

So on March 28, 1942, I began to walk the streets of Portland, up and down Third Avenue until about 11:00 P.M., and I was getting tired of walking. I stopped a Portland police officer, and I showed him a copy of Military Proclamation No. 3, prohibiting persons of Japanese ancestry from being away from their homes after 8:00 P.M.; and I pulled out my birth certificate to show him that I was a person of Japanese ancestry. When I asked him to arrest me, he replied, "Run along home, sonny boy, or you'll get in trouble." So I had to go on down to the Second Avenue police station and argue myself into jail. I pulled this thing on a Saturday and didn't get bailed out until the following Monday.

After being released I called my mother in Hood River. Dad had been interned; she was at home alone with two of her youngest children. Earlier, the Portland *Oregonian* had come out with a front-page, two-inch headline across the top of the page, trumpeting "Jap Spy Arrested." I knew that Mom would be worried. I said,

"Mom, *shimpai shiteru dessho?*" ("You are worried, aren't you?")
I wanted to reassure her that I was physically okay. Her response
was, and I shall never forget, "*Shimpai dokoro ka! Susumeru zo!*"
("Worry? Nonsense! I encourage you!") We have never given our
Issei mothers enough credit for having brought up a generation of
Nisei strong enough to endure and prevail in a hostile environment.

And so began the test case, but unfortunately, only on curfew.
I know that Gordon Kiyoshi Hirabayashi also later refused to be
evacuated; by refusing to report for evacuation and processing, and
that the federal authorities charged him with violating the curfew
as well as the exclusion orders. His case was heard by the U.S.
Supreme Court only on the issue of curfew. After starting the curfew test case, I was content to let the matter lie quietly. I was
indicted by a federal grand jury in April, but I don't remember
when my trial began. In the meanwhile, my Uncle Ren was suffering from cataracts. He needed to see specialists in Portland, and
since March was a busy season on the farms, I volunteered to take
him from Hood River to Portland. I obtained appropriate military permission for him to travel more than five miles for medical
reasons, and then I drove him 140 miles around Mount Hood to
avoid the restricted Bonneville Dam area, because I did not want
him to languish in an internment camp for violating military
orders. But in returning to Portland, I deliberately drove through
the restricted area, expecting almost every moment to be stopped
and arrested. I figured as long as they had me for curfew, I might
as well ask for a test of other aspects of military orders.

At the end of April 1942, military orders were posted for all
residents of Japanese ancestry, aliens and nonaliens (a euphemism
for citizen), calling for them to report for evacuation and processing at the North Portland Livestock Pavilion. There was about a
five-day grace period. So again, I notified the military authorities
that I had no intention of conforming or obeying what I considered
to be absolutely unconstitutional, illegal, and unenforceable military orders, and that I was going home to Hood River, some sixty
miles up the Columbia River. It was again my thought that since
I was testing the curfew, I might as well test the validity of evacuation orders too.

So before the deadline to report to the North Portland Livestock
Pavilion, I packed my files and my few belongings and left for Hood
River. I had given the military my address and invited them to

arrest me, should they want to stop me. In law, you really can't have a "preventive" arrest. After I was home for a few days, I received a call from the military offices in Portland saying that the MPs would be coming to get me on May 12, 1942, and that they would escort me to the North Portland Livestock Pavilion. I indicated that I would cooperate but would go under coercion only. Sure enough, on May 12, 1942, a sedan with a second lieutenant, a driver, and a jeep with four MPs came to our home in Hood River at the appointed time. The lieutenant said, "Let's go," and I complied in my 1935 Chevy. Molly Kageyama, a younger sister of my older brother's wife who was to be married, went with me. The entourage traveled down the Columbia Gorge highway, some sixty-six miles, and two and a half hours later, we were escorted into the North Portland Livestock Pavilion, which by then was filled with some three thousand Japanese Americans from Multnomah County.

The North Portland Livestock Pavilion consisted of a large wooden building fronting one of the sloughs of the Columbia River to the north. It was surrounded by eight-foot-high, barbed-wire fences with watchtowers on the corners. There were also searchlights, sentries, and .30-caliber, water-cooled machine guns. The main hall of the pavilion was primarily an assembly room, with the dining area on the east, where, as I recall, meals were served on tin plates in two or more shifts. My lasting impression of the dining area was that it was festooned with yellowish, spiral flypaper hung from posts and rafters. Within a short time the paper would be black with flies caught in the sticky mess. There were horseflies, manure flies, big flies, little flies, flies of all kinds. I also remember that there used to be fly-catching contests, and the winner was somebody who proudly proclaimed he killed 2,462 flies and had a gallon jug of dead flies to prove it. Flies, after all, usually inhabited livestock barns.

The sleeping quarters were of two kinds. One kind was where there had been stalls. Now the walls were calcimined and the dirt floor was asphalted over. Where a horse or cow had been kept, a Japanese American family was moved in. The other kind was in a large hall, where partitions had been put up with plywood, about eight feet high, the rest open to the ceiling. Because of the thinness of the three-ply wood, any noise—any coughing or sneezing, crying of babies, family arguments, boisterous conduct, laughing, or any shouting or yelling—could be heard throughout the hall. As I remember it, during the day and during the early part of the evening, there was a constant buzzing—conversations, talk. Then, as the evening wore on, during the still of night, things would get quiet, except for the occasional coughing, snoring, giggles. Then someone would get up to go to the bathroom. It was like a family of three thousand people camped out in a barn.

There were very few and relatively minor disturbances. One mentally unbalanced young lady would come into my cubicle and sit and stare at me for hours while I was working on papers. I was taken up for hours and hours at a time, preparing appeals and petitions on behalf of wives of internees who were first put in the Multnomah County Jail and thereafter confined at Fort Missoula, Montana. Later, we learned many of these internees were transferred to Fort Sill in Oklahoma, then to Camp Livingston in Louisiana, and eventually to Santa Fe or Lordsburg in New Mexico. Those desiring to do so were able to rejoin their families at Crystal City, Texas, provided the families wished confinement at Crystal City. The Portland people were confined there from May until towards the end of September 1942, living under wretched conditions, enduring the summer heat in stifling, confined quarters, getting wet when it rained. It is a wonder that more people didn't get sick or go crazy.

Within the barn, offices were created and manned by some government personnel. Recruitment was conducted for agricultural laborers to go out to eastern Oregon and western Idaho for farm work. Most of the farm families were happy to go, but city people simply were unequipped for such arduous work, especially families with small children or wives whose husbands were interned.

I also know that certain special privileged few were given other leaves, and this created some bitter resentment. Using the contacts made in preliminary evacuation processes, a number of Nisei were able to move out. I do not blame them even now.

My personal feeling, although I had left the Hood River valley in 1933 to go off to school, and I really had not been in and with the community for some nine years, was that I should be with my "people" to endure what they had to endure, and to experience what they had to experience. I think I tasted that to its full bitter measure. Because I had challenged the military orders, I was something of a hero to the produce-market gang, who were a rough, tough bunch of guys. Because they could not articulate their frustrations, they frequently would come to me to express their aspirations and desires in writing or verbally. As a consequence, I was also well treated by the *yogores* ("roughnecks") within the center. No one attacked me, although I spoke out strongly on behalf of patriotism and loyalty, despite what our country was doing to us. I continually counseled conformance to regulations in order to protect and benefit the population in the center while carrying on as strong a legal protest as possible.

At the North Portland Assembly Center I put in with Ronald Shiozaki and his three younger brothers who were a "family." They invited me to join them; otherwise I would have been shunted off to the bachelors' quarters, where the single men had to live dormitory-style. I also remember Benny Higashi's and Don Sugai's families. Both men were married to local Chinese American women, and both had two small children. The wives, LaLun Higashi and Pil Sugai, endured camp with us. Even though they themselves would have been exempt, their children would not, because they were half Japanese. The children, in each case, were two and four years old.

Somehow we endured the hot summer of 1942. In September 1942, trains began pulling into the siding where meat packers used to load cattle, hogs, and sheep. We were herded into what seemed to be World War I rolling stock. The grapevine had it that we were being moved to someplace in the deserts of Idaho. But no one seemed to know for sure. We were told that we were being moved into permanent camps for the duration of the war. At least it seemed better than the cattle cars loaded with Jews in Europe, being shunted off to extermination camps. But, again, who knew for sure? The Jews were told that they were going to labor camps, and six million of them died. Was the same fate in store for us? Personally, I never wavered in my belief there would be decent treatment. But among the more disillusioned and frantic there was all kinds of speculation and fear.

I remember the train stopping from time to time, mostly in Idaho, to let fast freight roll on through towards the coast. And at such stops, some MPs would allow us to buy beer or soft drinks. Mostly, I guess, I remember we were allowed to have meals in the dining car, and the black stewards would indicate their sympathy toward us as though to say, without speaking, that they empathized with us. We arrived late afternoon, at some isolated siding in the desert area, north of Twin Falls, although we did not know where we were. No houses were in sight, no trees or anything green— only scrubby sagebrush and an occasional low cactus, and mostly dry, baked earth. There was a slight rise to the north, and one could not see to the horizon.

Baggage was unloaded and piled up next to the road, and Army trucks were rolling in, kicking up huge clouds of dust. People came off the train, were lined up and loaded into the trucks, and went off into the distance. The seats were hard planks, and after riding all day on the train, most were sore and tired.

We had left the dark, dank confines of a livestock barn hoping to breathe the fresh, open air. But because the virgin desert had been bulldozed and disturbed by men and machinery, instead of fresh air, we got to breathe dust. I remember groups of women getting off the train, looking bewildered. After the lush greenness of the Willamette Valley, to see the sterile, dusty desert which was to be our home "for the duration," many sat on the baggage in the middle of nowhere and wept. As truckloads of people were delivered to Minidoka, we could see that the west end was already occupied by people from so-called Camp Harmony in Puyallup Valley in Washington, where Japanese from Seattle had been confined.

We saw again the barbed-wire fences, the watchtowers, guard houses, the MP detachments, the administration housing, ware-house areas, and block after block of black, tar-paper barracks, about 120 feet long and about 20 feet wide. I remember that at least the mess halls and kitchens were completed, and that evening we had hot meals, perhaps spam and canned vegetables. The bar-racks were supplied with army cots with metal springs, and we got padding-filled ticks and a couple of army blankets. There was a potbellied stove, and each block had a coal depot. One bare bulb hung from the center of the room. There were real composition-board ceilings, but the walls were unfinished with open two-by-four studs. The floor was wood, and single layered, so one could see the earth below, through the cracks. The smaller units for childless couples were on the end of the building, with two windows on each side, or a total of four windows. There was only one entrance to each unit. No chairs or tables were furnished; however, later the evacuees scrounged scrap lumber and built chairs, tables, bunk beds, dressers, and other things. But only those who were handy with tools could do this. The internee wives with small children were not always able to furnish their rooms comfortably. There was, however, a great deal of sharing and exchange going on.

The Minidoka camp was on a slight rise to the east, with an irrigation canal wending along its southern border. The camp proper was probably about a mile or more long and perhaps slightly less than a mile wide, with a wide street, unpaved, going up the middle of the living area. The hospital was down on lower ground, off a bit to the west and north, the administration section was centered almost due west, and the warehouse area was off to the south a bit. I am not certain where the MP unit was quartered, but it was obvious that access in and out of the camp was controlled by the military.

No sooner had I begun to settle in than I received word that I would be taken back to Portland, Oregon, for the decision of Judge James Alger Fee of the U.S. District Court. There were some delays caused, I learned later, by considerable discussion over whether I would be transported in the custody of the U.S. marshal or Army MPs. If the judge ruled against the Army orders, there was concern that I would be released to remain in Portland without supervision and under no one's control. The military suggested that if I were transported by MPs, they could physically keep me in custody, whereas a civilian U.S. marshal would have to turn me loose if the judge so ordered.

An inordinately long time was taken for the judge to arrive at his decision. We had a number of eminent constitutional law experts who had filed amicus curiae briefs, and there was some indication that the judge would find the military orders to be null and void as applied to United States citizens of Japanese ancestry. Hence, all of us would be free to come and go as we pleased.

Evidently sufficient assurances were made so that on the fourteenth of November 1942, a single U.S. marshal came to Minidoka to take me into custody and to transport me back to Portland. The marshall drove an ordinary car without any special markings and signed me out at the office of the camp director, Clarence Stafford. We got into his car and drove off. I sat in the rear seat, with no restraints or handcuffs, just like an ordinary passenger. Towards evening we stopped at Bend, Oregon, and instead of going to a restaurant for an evening meal, he delivered me to the jail where I was fed and locked up for the night. That was a shocker to me, because my interpretation of the law was that, until the judge found me guilty, I was a free man, free to return to court voluntarily.

The next day we drove into Portland, and I was delivered to the Multnomah County Jail and was placed in isolation. Knowing that Portland was in Military Zone 1, I had expected to be placed in strict confinement. The next morning, I was brought out of my cell, handcuffs were placed on my wrists, a light restraint chain placed around my waist, and I was led out of the building to the street. I found it degrading to be led around the public streets like a convicted criminal when, in fact, I had undertaken this entire matter on my own initiative and was eager to stand before the court.

Anyway, after entering the federal building I was taken to a room off the courtroom, and the chain and handcuffs were removed. After a short wait, I was taken before Judge James Alger Fee who announced his decision, giving my attorney an opportunity to indictate his intentions to appeal. Then I was led back to the Multnomah County Jail, again in handcuffs and in chains. This time it seemed appropriate, because in fact I was now a convicted criminal. The judge had found me guilty.

The judge indicated that sentence would be pronounced at a later time and that I would be given the opportunity to make a statement. I was again led into the federal court in Portland, and the judge imposed the maximum sentence on me: one year in jail and a five-thousand-dollar fine. I made a statement, expressing my fundamental faith in the United States and indicating that I believed the U.S. Supreme Court would sustain Judge James Alger Fee on the law, but would reverse his findings of fact.

Judge Fee had made an extensive analysis of constitutional law, based primarily on the old Civil War case of *ex parte* Milligan, and had ruled, in law, that the military could not impose orders against civilians in the absence of martial law, which had never been declared on the West Coast. The judge's review and analysis of the law on this point is extensive and was well reasoned. However, inexplicably, in less than two pages, Judge Fee ruled that all Japanese who were born in the United States prior to 1924, under international law were dual citizens of the United States and of Japan (how Japanese nationality laws could be held to be effective within the United States, I don't know) and had to choose which citizenship they desired upon attaining majority. He ruled that I had, by my conduct, elected to be a Japanese national. To reach his conclusion, the judge cited the facts that our family had gone to Japan for a summer vacation of three months (when I was nine years old) to visit our grandparents and that I had learned to speak the Japanese language.

Acknowledging that I had attended public schools as well as the University of Oregon, receiving both an arts degree and a law degree, he noted that I took a course in military training because it was "unquestionably compulsory," in his words. It's true that lower classmen at the University of Oregon were required to take military training for two years, but at the upperclassman level, beginning in the junior year, advanced ROTC wasn't only optional but was fairly competitive. Having been accepted into Advanced ROTC in 1935, I was sufficiently proficient that by 1937, I held the rank of cadet captain, commanding the color company.

Judge Fee noted that while I graduated with "acceptable standards"—in 1937 I was elected to Phi Beta Kappa—and received a commission as a second lieutenant in the Officers Reserve Corps and thus took an oath of allegiance to the United States, "such acts were all during minority." Since I had enrolled as a freshman at the University of Oregon in the fall of 1933 prior to my seventeenth birthday, the Army wouldn't give me my commission as a second lieutenant until after October 1937 when I was fully twenty-one years of age. My taking of the Oath of Allegiance to the United States was after I had fully attained my majority. So the judge was wrong on that point too.

The judge also referred to the facts that my father had been decorated by the Emperor of Japan for promoting better U.S.-Japanese relationships and that within a few months after I had been admitted to the Bar of the State of Oregon, I was, at the instigation of my father, employed by the consulate general of Japan in Chicago. Judge Fee ignored the salient fact that to be admitted to the Oregon state bar, one had to be a citizen of the United States. Incidentally, this occurred on December 9, 1939, when I was fully twenty-three years of age, and not during my minority as stated by Judge Fee.

As for working for the consulate general of Japan in Chicago, Judge Fee stated that I was "registered twice by the consulate general." The consulate general of Japan didn't register me with the

U.S. State Department. I sent for, obtained, and registered papers indicating that I was a U.S. citizen employed by a foreign nation. Secondly, the laws and regulations of the U.S. required that *only* U.S. citizens were required to so register, so the fact that I registered twice as an agent employed by a foreign nation is further clear evidence that I did so as a United States citizen. The bases on which Judge Fee made his ruling read: "The court thus concludes from these evidences that defendant made an election and chose allegiance to the Emperor of Japan, rather than citizenship in the United States at his majority." This of course is completely erroneous.

On appeal, first to the U.S. Circuit Court of Appeals in San Francisco, and later to the U.S. Supreme Court, attorneys for the Department of Justice didn't in any way claim that I wasn't a citizen of the U.S., and therefore, upon plea of my attorneys, the Supreme Court in June 1943 remanded my case to the U.S. District Court of Oregon with instructions to rule in accordance with the decision in Gordon Hirabayashi's case and reimpose sentence upon me.

Judge Fee sentenced me to one year in jail and a five-thousand-dollar fine. Because of his weird decision relating to my U.S. citizenship, I instructed my attorneys to appeal in order to reestablish my citizenship. Admittedly, it was tempting to let the matter stand and urge all Nisei to come back to the western reaches of Oregon, because a federal judge had declared the military orders of the Western Defense Command to be void. But I couldn't relinquish my U.S. citizenship, and so I appealed the case.

When they first brought me to the fourth floor jail complex of the Multnomah County Jail in Portland, I had a suitcase, toilet articles including a razor, and some changes of clothes. I also had some money, perhaps twenty-five or thirty dollars. Because I was a person of Japanese ancestry, and especially because the judge had ruled that I was an "enemy alien," the jailers decided to keep me in isolation. I am persuaded that in their judgment this decision was made in my best interests—to avoid any confrontations or problems.

Consequently, I was whisked past the cellblocks and led to isolation row. The floor was concrete, and they were kind enough to put me in a corner cell that had bars and a view out on two sides. The other two walls, and the ceiling, were gray painted steel.

The cell was probably about six feet wide and eight feet long. There was an uncovered toilet bowl which flushed, a washbasin with running hot and cold water, and a double-decker steel bunk. There was nothing else, except a lot of cockroaches and years of accumulated ground-in grime. When I was put into the cell, I was so keyed up for the court appearance that I don't remember whether they fed me or not, and I didn't care.

I do remember pacing back and forth, thinking of all the marvelous and eloquent things I would say in court, which I never got a chance to utter. I also remember that I could only take three steps back and forth. After the judge pronounced sentence, and after I knew that I'd be in confinement for a long time, I sat down on the edge of my bunk to take stock. I wanted my attorneys to apply for an appeal bond so I could be free pending the appeal. (They subsequently did, and it was refused.) I then thought of serving sentence at a federal work camp—at Kooskia, Idaho—but decided that serving sentence would be an admission of guilt. So I decided to sit out the appeal, still stubbornly insisting that I was right.

After the first few days in isolation, the routine of the day became fixed; I suppose one can get used to anything. It wasn't too bad, but the nights were rough, because after the lights would go out in the cells, things would become quieter and one is left alone with one's thoughts. I'd think of many things, such as what I would do after I got out of jail, where I would go, what kind of a life I'd try to lead. And always my thoughts would turn to food, and it would disgust me to be thinking about ham and eggs for breakfast, with fruit juice and toast and jam; and of shoyu, rice, and fish, or okazu ("entrée"), such as Mother used to make. Because the jail regulations allowed me paper and a pencil, I was always trying to write—poetry, letters, thoughts. At one point I was transcribing the Bible in shorthand, to occupy my mind, but gave up on names such as Nebuchadnezzar, or Jehoshaphat, and similar polysyllabic names.

Precious were the visits by Buddy and Cora Oliver, who would come around once a month. There was another devout Christian lady, whose name, regrettably. I have forgotten but who in the kindness of her heart would visit me from time to time. The hardest thing to bear was not knowing when I would be out of there; it was the uncertainty that was the hardest.

At first the guards would not let me out long enough to take a bath or to get a haircut or shave. At the end of several months, I was stinking dirty, although I tried to wash myself in the wash-basin with rags. My hair was growing long and shaggy, unkempt and tangled. My facial hair was growing in all directions, untrimmed. And my nails were growing so long that they began to curl over on themselves, both on my hands and feet. I found I could chew off my fingernails, but the nails on my toes gave me trouble. It was not until after Christmas that I was given permission to take a bath and get a haircut and shave, and that seemed like such a luxury then. Thereafter, they permitted me monthly baths and monthly hair trims.

Isolation wasn't too bad. After a while I found that the absence of people wasn't so important to one's sense of self. I knew who I was, and I knew what I was trying to do. I suppose one could say that I found peace within myself.

Then, in June 1943, my attorney advised me that we had lost the final appeal to the U.S. Supreme Court, which had sustained General John DeWitt's military orders as valid and enforceable. But because the Department of Justice attorneys did not question my U.S. citizenship, my case was being remanded to the district court in Portland for judgment and resentencing in accordance with the decision of the U.S. Supreme Court in the Hirabayashi case. There was substantial delay between the time of the Supreme Court decision and the case's remand to the district court. I was beginning to chafe a bit, because I wanted to get out of my solitary cell and to begin serving my sentence. Sometime during the end of July or the beginning of August 1943, my attorney told me that the judge had considered my time already spent in the Multnomah County Jail as sufficient punishment under the law, and he suspended the five-thousand-dollar fine imposed on me.

Finally, around the nineteenth of August 1943, a U.S. marshal came to get me at the Multnomah County Jail early in the morning and drove me straight back to the Minidoka WRA camp. It's funny, but I cannot now recall anything about that car ride from Portland, Oregon, to the Minidoka WRA. One would think release from jail . . . but I can't remember now. Obviously, I was going from one kind of imprisonment to another, but at least at the Minidoka WRA camp, there were a hundred acres in which to wander and there were people. Real live people with whom one could talk and reminisce, and plan, and share ideas and thoughts and feelings.

I came out of the Multnomah County Jail pale and pasty-faced, and a bit bloated and flabby, having been confined to a space of less than forty-eight square feet for nine months. I cannot say that I remember all of the days and nights I spent in jail. Today, it seems like an unreal blur. I do remember certain things; but overall, it's almost as though my life was suspended for nine months. And, today, I think: What a waste of time!

Clarence Stafford was still project director at the camp. I was checked in through his office, and was sternly told to behave myself or else I'd find myself back in jail again. I had had enough of jail. I did not cause any particular problems for the camp administration.

I learned that during my absence the military draft had been reopened for Nisei, and further volunteers were being sought for both the 442nd Infantry Combat Team and for the Camp Savage military intelligence school in Minnesota. Because of my infantry training, I immediately volunteered for the infantry, and many months later was advised that I had been rejected. In the meantime, in returning to Minidoka I felt that I should perform some service for the camp residents, because during my absence a group of camp residents had formed a Min Yasui Support Committee, and had raised some funds for my case. Many of them had gone out on relocation, but I felt that I owed the camp residents whatever services I could do for them.

During this period, my older brother, Ray, had taken temporary sugar beet farm work in Great Falls, Montana, and was there with his family, while my mother, my younger brother, and sisters had relocated to Denver, Colorado. My father had been transferred from Montana to Oklahoma and then Louisiana, and was now interned in Santa Fe, New Mexico. My mother had indicated by letter that it was possible to visit Dad from Denver by taking a bus during the late afternoon, riding all night, and getting there in the morning. I had not seen my father since February 1942, nor my mother and younger brother since May 1942, nor my younger sister since Christmas of 1939. I wanted to see members of the family who were in Denver, so I applied for a temporary leave from Minidoka for thirty days to visit them.

My official records at the Minidoka WRA administration evi-

dently indicated that I was not a very desirable individual. Therefore, I had extreme difficulties in getting clearance for even a
temporary leave. The records indicated that I was a headstrong
troublemaker, that I drank to excess, and that I caroused and
gambled a great deal—none of which, in my humble opinion, were
correct. A charade of a hearing was held for me, and the result
was mixed, with the civilian hearing officer recommending that
temporary leave be granted and the two military officials recommending that I be kept in custody. I offered to test this matter
by a habeas corpus proceeding, and the project director relented
by issuing me a thirty-day temporary leave in October 1943.

So, after sixty days of haggling with the Minidoka WRA administration, I was finally permitted to go into the "outside" world,
without being in custody, for the first time since May 1942.
Leaving Minidoka WRA camp by bus, I first proceeded to Salt
Lake City, Utah, to visit the national headquarters of the Japanese
American Citizens League. I met with Saburo Kido who was
national JACL president, Larry Tajiri who was editor of the
Pacific Citizen, and I believe Mike Masaoka was still around as
national executive secretary of the JACL organization. I was con-
cerned about developments in the Korematsu case, and the in re
Mitsuye Endo habeas corpus proceedings.

After several days in Salt Lake City, I drove to Denver with
some friends, and I had a happy reunion with the members of the
family. Later that day I got on the Trailways bus with my mother
and arrived at Walsenburg, Colorado, at about midnight. We
then waited for a connecting bus before going on into Santa Fe,
New Mexico, arriving probably before 8:00 A.M.

Mother had made the trip several times before, and we checked
into a hotel and took a taxi to the prison camp where my father
and several hundred other Issei were being held under armed guard.
It was an unnerving experience for me, because I had last seen my
father at the Fort Missoula prison camp in February 1942. Despite
everything, my father's health was good, his mental faculties sharp,
and his philosophical attitude was inspiring. Despite all that the
family had endured, my father was strong and firm in his belief
in America and the ideals of America. He wanted his children to
be Americans, regardless of what was happening to all of us.

Years later, through the Freedom of Information Act, we found documents indicating that during Thanksgiving 1942, after he had been transferred to Camp Livingstone in Louisiana, he received $15 from my older brother, Ray T. Yasui, who was at that time still in Tule Lake WRA camp. Records show that of the $15, $5 was paid to one of the MPs who had loaned my father money. It seems incredible that my father would be able to borrow $5 from a soldier guarding him. That indicates what manner of man he was, and there were thousands like him in these internment camps. But it galls me to think that my father, who before the war was worth possibly $500,000, was reduced to borrowing $5 from an MP.

Another scrap of paper from the archives in my father's files indicates that on Valentine's Day 1943, my youngest sister, who was then about sixteen years old, had sent my father three dollars in cash. In those days, baby-sitting in Denver paid about fifteen cents an hour. Being a sentimentalist, it raises a lump in my throat to realize that it took a month's sitting for my baby sister to send her daddy something for St. Valentine's Day, and I had frittered away more than ten thousand dollars in a quixotic quest to try to prove a point—and lost.

At any rate, Mother and I stayed in Santa Fe for three days and then took the overnight bus back to Denver. Mother made these trips monthly for a period of three years, despite her broken English and ailing body. One cannot say enough for these indomitable Issei women who held their families together despite war, separations, and hardships most people never encounter.

While in Denver, during October 1943, I met Joe Grant Masaoka, the older brother of Mike M. Masaoka. Joe Grant was the JACL representative for the Tri-State area (Colorado, Wyoming, and Nebraska). He was very concerned about Nisei refusing to register for the military draft. Many of the young Nisei men were being arrested and put into prisons. The JACL had been a prime mover in having the military draft reinstituted for Nisei—to give us an opportunity to prove our loyalty and patriotism to the United States of America. Because the JACL had in effect caused these Nisei young men to be caught in a situation where they felt they must defy the military draft orders, JACL felt a deep sense of responsibility to these young men.

There were a number of Nisei from the Granada WRA camp

imprisoned at the Federal Correctional Institution (FCI) in Engle-
wood, Colorado. Joe Grant obtained permission to visit them, to
counsel them to obey the military draft orders and the law. I
remembered going with Joe Grant to the FCI and meeting a young
Nisei who had just turned eighteen years of age, who had refused
to register and refused to conform to draft-board orders. He had
been indicted, arrested, and was being held, pending trial.

We said to him, "Son, you're ruining your life. You're still a
young man, and you'll have a criminal record that will hold you
back for the rest of your life. Please reconsider and cooperate with
your draft board."

He replied, "Why should I when the government has taken away
our rights and locked us up like a bunch of criminals anyway?"

We responded, "But, you've got to fulfill your obligations to
the government. When you fulfill your responsibilities, you'll be in
a much stronger position to demand your rights."

To which he said, "Look, the government took my father away,
and interned him someplace. My mother is alone at the Granada
camp with my younger sister who is only fourteen. If the government would take care of them here in America, I'd feel like going
out to fight for my country, but this country is treating us worse
than shit!"

We would talk in this vein for half an hour or more, cajoling,
pleading, and reasoning until tears would be rolling down his face,
and his hands gripping the bars so hard that his knuckles would
show white. It was emotionally traumatic for these young men,
and for us too, because we knew that any group of soldiers going
into combat might not ever come home again.

Joe Grant was indefatigable; we'd make trips up to the jail in
Cheyenne, Wyoming, to counsel a number of young men brought
down from the Heart Mountain WRA camp. We would confer
with the U.S. attorneys, hoping for leniency, given the impossible
situations in which these young men found themselves. We were
not at all successful in either persuading the draft protesters to reconsider or in getting the U.S. attorneys to be lenient.

Because we learned that once young people deliberately violated
the draft laws there was very little that we could do, Joe Grant
suggested that we go to the camps to talk directly with young
people before they defied their draft boards. We would also talk
with the parents to encourage them to counsel their sons, and with

the leadership still remaining in the camps to persuade them to provide the atmosphere of pride in serving these United States.

Masaoka was an idealist, and he believed that reason and rationality would prevail, despite the topsy-turvy world that we were living in during those war years.

We scheduled several trips to the Granada WRA camp in Colorado. Our reception was cool. On our second and third trips it became necessary for MPs to provide personal escorts for us as we figuratively waved the flag and exhorted camp inmates to be 200 percent American. It was a rough go. But because of Joe Grant's idealism we scheduled field trips into the Gila River WRA and the Poston WRA camps in Arizona. Thinking back, it was most foolhardly of us, but I had a deep abiding faith in American ideals and so I joined Joe Grant Masaoka on these trips.

Stum Ikeda of Mesa, Arizona, drove us across the Salt River valley, with its fields of green, past the ruins of Casa Grande. Off in the distance in the brown hills to the south, we could see the Gila River WRA camp. From a distance the settlement looked almost picturesque, because the roofs were surfaced with composition shingles of red, green, and other colors. Castor oil bean plants grew profusely, almost to the eaves of buildings, with their green stalks and leaves that were almost a bright red on the underside. However, when one entered the camp, having to be first cleared by the MPs and being surrounded by barbed-wire fences, the barracks-style buildings were just as depressing as elsewhere. Masaoka and I spoke at length at a mass gathering in the natural amphitheater between rivers and the other camp. We did not persuade anyone with our message "Have faith in America," though out of respect for our having come so far, they did listen respectfully, and no one threw rocks at us.

Several days later, the Tanita brothers of Glendale, Arizona, took us out to the Poston WRA camp. We drove seventy-five miles northwest out of Phoenix to a junction at Wickenburg, where we took a secondary road to a town called Parker, in the middle of the desert, and then drove south on a dusty gravel road along the Colorado River to Poston. Though it was late October, it was still hot for us with winter-cooled blood from Colorado. I am a native of the green, green Northwest Country and entirely unaccustomed to the harsh barrenness of the desert. It seemed to me that the Poston camps could not have been located in a more desolate, godforsaken place. The bleak, black tar-papered barracks shacks retained the heat, and the pulverized dust seemed like an extra blanket of insulation.

Our reception at Poston was hostile, and we were not permitted to speak to any large groups or any gatherings. Rather, we spoke to individuals and to some people in various mess halls, or in the "apartments" of residents. We probably accomplished even less at Poston than we did at Granada WRA, where we had to have MP protection. By the time I got back to Minidoka, it was mid-November, and nasty cold. Occasional skiffs of snow were blowing down the dirt roads. It was a bleak homecoming, and having no immediate prospects of permanent placement, I was content to winter at Minidoka. I truly reveled in the Thanksgiving dinner of turkey with all the trimmings—and especially in being with people. This, for me, was very unlike Thanksgiving in 1942.

Moreover, still being a bachelor, age twenty-seven, it was fascinating for me to meet mothers with eligible daughters who would most warmly invite me to come over to their "apartment" for coffee, because everyone knew I loved to drink coffee—which was rationed—or to sample some special *tsumami-mono* ("hors d'oeuvre"). It soon became apparent that the old Japanese custom of *mi-ai* ("matchmaking") was being practiced, and my aunt would let me know of the latest invitations. With Christmas and New Year's celebrations, things were not all that glum in Minidoka during the winter of 1943–44.

I got into the habit of bringing my portable typewriter and papers to the mess hall at night, and working late into the night. And I discovered an interesting thing: the chefs and cooks, of course, handled the food, and after midnight, after most of the rest had gone "home" and to bed, there would be steak fries or special *gochiso* ("feast") to be had. It was obviously neither fair nor proper, but I will admit that the fare past midnight was far superior to anything to be had during regular mealtimes. As spring broke, and the life in camp went on, it seemed that with so many young people and vigorous people out on relocation, only the very old or very young were left in the camps.

I prepared to leave the Minidoka WRA camp in late spring 1944, and I spent the summer in Chicago. Most members of the Yasui family were now in Denver, but I wanted to see my old friends from the Minidoka WRA camp, and since most had gone to

Chicago, I decided that I would like that city. After all, I had lived there almost two years before the war. I did not intend to make Chicago my permanent home.

It is now thirty-eight years since I came back to Denver to stay. Because I had not had five years of active law practice, I could not be admitted to the Colorado bar on motion, but had to take and pass the Colorado bar examinations. Consequently, I decided to audit law classes at the University of Denver and at the same time enroll at the downtown Westminster School of Law in order to review for the exams. I studied hard, but it was only a basic review for me, so I became involved with the operations of the Tri-State JACL office being operated by Joe Grant Masaoka in the Empire Building downtown. I participated in all the JACL activities, and I remember becoming deeply involved in the vicious campaign to enact an antialien land law in Colorado. Interestingly, in Colorado, the initial constitution of the state provided that "aliens shall have the same rights to property, real or personal, as citizens."

Because we were at war with Japan, and all the atrocity stories were coming back, there was a major effort to deny Japanese the right to own, use, or enjoy *any* property. We fought the battles in the state general assembly, and we found an ally in an amputee who had no feet because he had lost them in battle against the Japanese enemy in the Pacific. I vividly remember a state senator—young, handsome and articulate—named Arthur A. Brooks, who got up to defend the right of people to own property in Colorado. By 1944 there were probably ten thousand persons of Japanese ancestry living in Denver. We were restricted to a ghetto area near Twentieth and Larimer streets, the traditional skid row area.

But reports of the exploits of the 442nd Combat Team and the heroism of the 100th Battalion were beginning to reach people, even in Colorado. A Rev. Clark P. Garman, a Congregationalist minister, formed a Fair Play Committee and was joined by Brooks in battling the racists in the Colorado General Assembly, as well as in the general populace, unsuccessfully, and Brooks as a result lost in the 1944 elections.

So despite the best efforts of many, many people, we lost the battle, and a proposed constitutional amendment to restrict the rights of aliens to own property in Colorado was certified for a vote of the people. In the ensuing campaign I can remember a man, a Native Sons of the Golden West type, who came out of California to help enact this legislation. Many of the farm people in the Brighton, Fort Lupton, Arkansas Valley, and other farm areas were most supportive of restrictions against the Japanese, because most of the successful farmers were Japanese, most of them Issei, at that time. I remember a farmer out of Arvada leading the charge against the Japanese farmers in the state. And to our bitter chagrin, most of the Italian and Russian truck farmers were joining the attack against the "Japs." At that time the Issei could not become U.S. citizens, and if the constitutional amendment did pass, they literally could have nothing that was property.

The Native Sons type was slated to address a big public rally in Brighton, Colorado, and Joe Grant Masaoka wanted to challenge him. George Mits Kaneko had a car, and I went along with Joe Grant that evening to furnish moral support.

As the man raved on about the dirty, treacherous "Jap" and how California got rid of its "Japs," Joe Grant came out of the audience of several hundred aroused and fervent farmer types, got on the stage, and took over the microphone from him. Proudly proclaiming the wartime heroism of the Japanese Americans in the European theater of operations, Joe Grant shouted that the Japanese Americans were loyal Americans. I can still remember the rejoinder, "Who are we supposed to believe? You, damned Jap or General DeWitt?" and the roar of approval from the gathered crowd who were shouting, "Throw that goddamned Jap out!" "Kill the son-of-a-bitch Jap!" Things got awfully hairy all of a sudden, and in such a hostile, seemingly bloodthirsty crowd that could easily degenerate into a mob, it seemed best to get the hell out of there. I went up on stage to pull Joe Grant away from the mike—because he wanted to keep on talking—and some kindly soul guided us out the back way and warned us to take the back roads to Denver or else some overeager, redneck farm type might try to run us off the road or worse.

Such were the times.

I continued to study for the Colorado bar examination. In June 1945 I took the examinations and was told in September 1945 that I would not be admitted to the bar. The committee on ethics and qualifications had ruled that, because of a criminal conviction on my record, I was not considered as having high enough moral character to practice law in Colorado.

I knew, of course, that I had a criminal conviction on my record. I knew too that it was not a felony involving moral turpitude, but rather, technically, a misdemeanor of which I was guilty because of a moral principle. George Trout, who was the secretary of the examiners and a clerk of the Colorado Supreme Court, advised me that I had passed the substantive portions of the Colorado bar examination and stood first among the applicants in test results.

I was disappointed, of course, to realize that prejudices ran deep against persons of Japanese ancestry. I talked to Samuel L. Menin, an American Civil Liberties Union (ACLU) lawyer who had taken a number of cases for the no-no boys out of Heart Mountain WRA camp. He promised to take up this matter for me with the Colorado Supreme Court.

Menin was successful in persuading the Colorado Supreme Court that I was not a person of bad moral character because of my test case in 1942, and I received word that I would be admitted to the practice of law in the state of Colorado in January 1946. On January 11, 1946, I stood before the Supreme Court of the State of Colorado and was admitted to practice law in the state.

From a personal standpoint, I now felt that I could get married and raise a family, which I did. The evacuation episode for me was now over.

While I was reminiscing about evacuation recently with a long-time Nisei friend, who is urbane, polished, highly intelligent, and well educated—a "civilized" gentleman—with courtly manners and a restrained approach to life, but who had undergone the traumas of evacuation as a teenager, he remarked,

"You know, now realizing what evacuation involved—the degradation of the human spirit—if that happened again, now, you know what I would do?"

"No," I replied, "what would you do?"

"I'd get a rifle, lay in plenty of supplies and ammunition, see that my family members are safe elsewhere, and then I'd barricade myself in my home and tell them to come and get me! And there would be plenty of other younger Nisei and Sansei who would be doing the same."

"You mean that you'd actually shoot to kill," I asked, "to avoid being evacuated?"

"Yes," he replied, I'd shoot to kill. I'd kill anyone who tried to put me into one of those camps."

I pointed out that the federal government could bring in overwhelming manpower, all kinds of barricade-busting equipment, and that such individual resistance would be ruthlessly crushed.

"That's true, of course," he responded. "Certain numbers of us would be killed. But I'm not sure that the government would go so far as to kill all of us, and if they did, there would be such a feeling of revulsion, there would be the most distasteful spilling of blood that such a process would be stopped."

I wonder! Acknowledging that 1982 isn't 1942, and knowing that the fervor of civil rights and human rights reached its peak during the 1960s, nevertheless, I do wonder whether our American public has so fundamentally changed that the ruthless destruction of a few lives by the federal government would result in any sympathy for the sacrificial dead, or would that only serve to inflame the blood lust of the people?

Although such actions would have an undoubted impact upon the American people, both in terms of sympathy as well as in cries for more blood, I wonder whether there would be many other Nikkei (Japanese Americans) who would man the barricades and die, defying the government? My feeling is that there would be precious few. It certainly isn't a matter of physical courage. The Nisei men of the 442nd and the MIS (Military Intelligence Service) amply proved the heroism of Japanese Americans. Rather, it's a question of whether our deeply ingrained sense of duty and loyalty to our nation would allow us to take such drastic action. I'm personally convinced that the Nikkei in 1942 would have gone docilely to the gas chambers if ordered to do so by competent authority.

That's a terrible thing to say, but remembering the quiet obedience of the Japanese Americans in 1942, their almost pathetic eagerness to please, the lack of anger or overwhelming feelings of injustice, I'm not convinced that any large numbers of Nikkei now would take up arms to resist the U.S. government. I don't believe that Japanese Americans would fight back with violence.

And maybe that's a sad commentary on where we are today.

As for myself, I believe I would passively resist again, protesting all the way, but I cannot possibly conceive of taking the lives of other people to protect and preserve my rights. It would be far better to be killed than to kill, because the person who might kill me might just as fervently believe that he's doing his duty as I would believe it to be wrong. Two wrongs can never make it right.

Perhaps in that kind of death, rather than killing or being killed, there would be a far more principled dying.

At any rate, my good and gentle Nisei friend, in espousing violent resistance, gives us pause to think again about what we would do if this sorry sort of thing were to happen again.

Now, forty years later, we are still struggling to find means whereby this kind of thing can never happen again to any group of people. Tremendous outrages were inflicted upon us. We cannot rest, we shall not rest until we make every effort to assure that it shall never happen again—so that my good friend, a man of law and of principle, does not feel that he might have to pick up a rifle to defend his integrity as a human being.

TOM WATANABE

Manzanar

I was born in Vallejo, California, in 1919. My father settled there
after he got out of the Navy. I got my education in Los Angeles.

When evacuation came I was living in Boyle Heights, but I
moved back with my mother so that we could help each other. My
brother-in-law had five trucks because he was a trucker, hauling
tomatoes in from Laguna Beach, Santa Ana, and places like that. I
told him, you know, let's get out of here, let's just pack up his family
and my family, and let's just take Mom and go. But he was always
kind of leery, so he wouldn't go. Finally when our district was going
to be cleared out, they said if we signed up at a certain place we'd
go directly to Manzanar, so we went directly to Manzanar.

On the train to Manzanar, I was really irritated because of the
conditions—that train was old. We stopped in Bishop, and then
they transferred us into a bus and then they took us into camp.
When we got into camp it was a feeling of like, you're lost. You
don't know what the hell to do. You don't know who to communicate with. I mean it's like some guy just opened the door on a bus
and put you out on a desert highway and said, "Here it is, this is
where you're going to live." I mean you just don't know.

They assigned us to a barracks with three other families. I mean,
not families of the people that went up with us, but people I never
met in my life. Four families in one room. No partition or nothing.
The room was twenty by twenty. In that particular room there was

my wife, my two sisters, myself, the other families, almost twelve people. All we had was room enough to walk by.

Up in Manzanar it's 100 degrees during the day, but at night it's cold as hell. And we had to use our blankets for partitions, to divide off privacy for our family. And that's when I started to rebel. You know, you get so frustrated. I mean, you want to punch somebody, but there's nothing to do. My wife was pregnant when we went to camp, six or seven months pregnant when we went in. The first day we got there they told us we got to pick up our beds, which was a folding cot, army cot. Then they gave us a bag, and I couldn't believe it. It was a bag stuffed with straw, and that was our mattress.

You had the dust storm come through. You get a half an inch of dust. You either get in bed and cover yourself with a sheet or just stand out there and suffer. You couldn't even see three feet in front of you, and then by the time the dust storm was settled, you had at least a half inch of dust right on your sheet when you got under it. Used to come from underneath the floor. The floor used to have at least half an inch openings. The walls were nothing but one by sixes and tar paper. My wife and I were in the same barracks with the rest of the family and the other family until they cleared out. The system? They didn't care. It was my two sisters, my mother, my wife, and I in there with total strangers.

While we were at Manzanar, my wife came to full term, but while she was still pregnant, she went up for an examination. I went with her, and I waited, and at that time the hospital wasn't even completed. In fact, again they had to use blankets for partitions. They had the outside wall but not the inside walls and rooms and things like that. The floor wasn't—no linoleum, no nothing. You know, it was just a shed. A big shed, and when she came out she had a bottle, and they told her that since it was hot she's got to take two pills a day. The doctor told us that there was no complication, but when she started taking these pills she started to bloat. They were salt tablets. And now, you know, after all these years I find out that you don't give salt tablets to pregnant women. She took that for a couple of months and she was bloating like anything, so we stopped it and then she had the childbirth.

I was doing judo then, so one of the drivers came down and he told me that the wife just had the baby. He was an ambulance driver so he took me up there. I got to see my wife and I talked to her, and she told me that she had twins. Wanted to know what to name them and we were talking like that and it was a real hot day so I told her she better rest. I would go home and shower up and I'll come back. So I went back and I showered up and I was talking to my mother and my sister and my brother-in-law and all of them and then my mother came up to me and said you better go back there something is wrong. See, Japanese people are very superstitious and she saw that one flower by the door. She was planting a garden and one flower bloomed and in Japanese myth or mythology or whatever you call it, one flower means death. So she said you better get up there you know. So I told her well, you know, I've been up there already. She said no, get back up there something is wrong.

So I started running uphill, and then I caught a truck and went, and then I went in. And the doctors were running around, and so I went up and I was talking to her and she was hemorrhaging. And so they worked on her and then all I can remember is telling, you know, help me, help me. Through junior high school in the rough neighborhood and everything like that, I could always protect her physically; but I just stood there holding her hand you know, holding on to her, and she just drained away.

And after that I don't remember too much, and I don't remember even to this day anyone telling me about the babies. I don't know what happened to the babies. I don't know. That's the part that haunts me. Whether it was carelessness. Or that it was something that was going to happen. I know for a fact that the twins were born and the camp did not have the facilities. I know that. And they say that they all passed away at childbirth and that's a lie. I talked to her. I talked to her, and she said she knew that, you know, I wanted a boy. So I remember her asking me, she said that they were girls and was I angry? So I knew, I talked to her, so it wasn't childbirth. So like even today I do not know what happened. All I know I saw, I saw at the funeral, I saw three caskets and in fact I don't even remember the funeral. I did not even see the daughters. I didn't see even the birth certificates. I did not even see the death certificates. I don't know what they did with the bodies. Even today I don't. 'Cause like I say, I was in a state of shock and maybe a month or two later I decided I better get out.

Years later I found out one of the twins had lived twenty-four hours. The date of the time they left camp is the nineteenth. My wife died on the eighteenth. One of the girls died on the eighteenth and one of the kids, they said, left camp on the nineteenth so, therefore, she lived twenty-four hours and I didn't know that. About four or five years ago my sister-in-law in Los Angeles told me that she talked to a friend of hers who said that they knew where the children are buried. But I couldn't find the grave. Been looking and looking and looking. Whether the body was shipped from Manzanar I don't know. I don't know.

The riot from the way I understood was because food was being taken out of camp not by one carton but by the truckloads. They had the guy in the warehouse loading up trucks, and not only one semi but double semi. We don't know who was taking it. But anyway they were loading them up and going out of camp. Evidently somebody that's in the warehouse was taking down how much was going out. The white drivers coming in were stealing the food. They were coming in and the guys were loading it, and everybody figured they were taking it to another camp or something like that. So one guy was keeping a record of it and they snatched him. They grabbed him and a crowd formed and was going to go down to jail to get him released, and right away the guards came out and they lined up. They said come back that night and they would talk to us.

So that night everybody went down to the jail, and the crowd got bigger and they were marching back and forth and the guards got called out again. And they were getting pretty nervous. Anyway, I remember there was a car parked in front of the side of the jail. And the jail it was a long way back and there was a car parked there. And the guys are milling up and down in front of that and a guard along the jail. And I remember a guy having a .45-caliber machine gun, and he was saying, "Now I hope you Japs do something, you know, I'd sure like to use this on you." And the guys were taunting him, you know. And the crowd got bigger and bigger and more boisterous and all of a sudden somebody threw a tear gas and this tear gas you can't pick up. It keeps exploding. Well, out there on the desert, you know, I guess it sounded like a shot; so everybody took off. And we were going to take off too, but then a guy grabbed me and he pulled me next to the car. So four of us stayed next to the car and they opened up with everything. Finally the officer was saying cease fire and everything like that. But the damage was done.

I think three was killed and twenty-seven was wounded. And so by the time when they said cease fire, with all that tear gas, we were all choking, so we started to run for it. That night they had a meeting in Block 2 mess hall, and the Issei, you know them die-hards, they say what we should do is go against the MPs and take away the rifle and this and that. They weren't agitating but speaking their piece, and a jeep came by. Threw tear gas into the kitchen. That mess holds about maybe 150, maybe 200 people; there must have been about 500 people in that mess hall. That thing was cleared out in no time. Some guys got trampled, you know. Then the next day, light armoured tank division comes in. What are you going to do?

They had the guy from the 100th Battalion where the 442nd came down to camp and asked for volunteers. And at that particular time I had already been in camp six months. So when they told us that they wanted Niseis to volunteer, well, I told them I'd go providing they'd let me go out and live like a human being for six months, and if the government wanted to draft me I'd go like anybody else, because everybody else isn't jumping on the bandwagon and volunteering. All of them are waiting to get drafted. They're working in the aircraft plant and making money. They're waiting to get drafted, so I'll do the same thing. I'll go out and live, but don't touch me for six months. Let me live like a human, and then if you want to draft me I'll go. So they kept me in camp. That was my answer to the draft volunteer.

The way I feel is, it's supposed to be the United States Government; but if the United States Government wants to make you disappear, they can do it. This is supposed to be the people's government, but you as an individual, if they want to fry you they can fry you. It's a frightening thing. I mean, it's something that a lot of people don't even think of twice, and the reason that I think about it is for the fact that, hey, if they put 120,000 of us behind barbed wire without blinking an eye, one guy don't mean nothing. And it's a frightening thing.

Whenever I go on vacation, maybe the first day or two it's nice, and then you start thinking, you know, hey, I'm in my sixties. I go wherever I want for vacation. I buy whatever I want. My kids are all out of school. And then you know, you sort of sit back and you think, why me? This is what she wanted, but she was deprived of it; and I just . . . I just don't feel right.

You cannot put people that's been working and trying to get

ahead and trying to make a living and trying to raise a family, you can't put them in camp. It breaks them. Something snaps. That's why I had to get out of camp. You start making a living. You got married and start making a living and then getting thrown into camp and you don't know where your future is. When I went into camp we were always talking about, you know, making enough money. My wife was helping my mother in the restaurant. And if you make enough money, go to college. But when I left camp and when I looked back there and that gate closed, I said good-bye, good-bye education. You just feel like nothing. You don't feel like I'm going to leave camp, I'm going to go to this place, I'm going to start anew. Nothing. Leaves you blank.

I used to have nightmares, you know. I couldn't sleep. I had to be really exhausted to sleep. Maybe that's why I became a work-aholic. I don't know. Like I say, you know, it's still there. A certain type of music or a place, you know, you can feel it. You go all the way back forty years, maybe no, maybe yeah, you go back forty years when you're fifteen, sixteen years old, when you're dancing to Glenn Miller's music or something like that, you know, you go back. It just hits you all of a sudden. You never get rid of that. I never can. Maybe that's why I'm always on the go.

MIYO SENZAKI

Rowher

I was born in Seattle, Washington, in March 1920. I had three brothers older than me, and there were five girls. I lived in Seattle till I was nineteen years old, and then a year after I graduated we went to California. My dad and mom had an import business at that time, and things weren't working out very well there, so they decided to come to California.

The day after we moved here, Mom and Dad went down to the wholesale market, and the friends that they had who gave them the credit to buy things on consignment. They started a produce market and they eventually opened five. They stuck my oldest brother in one and my next brother in the other, and I was old enough that my father put me in one, so we all ran them. Then Mom and Dad ran another.

When we heard rumors we were going to be evacuated, that's when dad panicked and then he had to start closing his stores in so-called strategic areas. Then one by one, he had to close up the others, and then he had one left in Alhambra.

On December 7 I was already at work, Sunday morning, and people are pulling over. Then the butcher motioned to me, "Come over here, did you hear the radio?" I said, "No, what happened?" "Pearl Harbor just got bombed." I said, "What?" He said, "I have a feeling there'll be people coming and antagonizing you, or they might say something to you, so just kind of stick close by, and signal me if anybody gets funny." The impact—it didn't really hit me at the time, but then I noticed a car pulling over and one guy came up to me, and we had those old scales hanging, you know. He shoved that scale at me. I was bending over, putting the grapes up, and I looked up and he said, "Are you a Jap or are you an American?" I said, "I'm a Japanese American," so he said, "All right then, you're okay, you're not just a Jap." Then he walked away. Then I got scared. So I ran up to the butcher and I said, "Hey, that guy, I thought he was going to sock me." He said, "You just be careful today." People weren't coming in to buy; it got real quiet.

The manager called us in back and gave us our paychecks and that was it. We were terminated, and then we got scared because we were thinking, gee, we got to go home. One of the fellows that I worked with had a nursery right close by, and he said why don't all of us go over to his house and we'll kind of wait and see what happens. On the way home, I noticed they had barricades set up. Certain streets you couldn't get into; you had to sort of detour to go home. Then after that it was just a daze.

The next day, Dad got scared and started to burn all the books, Japanese books. He was panicking; he said to get everything out— all the records—and we just built a bonfire, busted everything, you know. When you panic and you don't know what's going to happen, I think you do these things without even thinking. My mother kept on saying, "No matter what happens they're not going to do anything to you because you're an American citizen." "Don't panic," she'd tell my dad. She'd say, "At least the children, they don't harm the children. They may take us away," I remember her saying, "but they won't take the kids away." So we kind of felt assured.

I got married in March of 1942. My husband used to come after me, and he found out that they were going to be evacuated. They already got their notice. That's what my husband said, "You either marry me or we just won't see each other." He already bought a ring, so I looked at him and said, "Marry you? You haven't even got a job." In order to get married to my husband, they said I would have to establish my residence using his address, because he was in a different area. So then, about a week before we were to get married, I had to move in with his family. The day we got married was the day before the old Union Church was going to close. We got married so we could go to camp together.

None of us really knew where we were going. They never really told us where, they just said to be ready. They sent us a notice, telling us to assemble at such and such a time at such and such a place. We assembled near the old Union Church, and it was walking distance for us. All the soldiers were lined up and the buses were lined up. My husband thought that we were going to go up to the desert. We ended up in Santa Anita. We thought it was going to be miles and miles away, so when we got on the bus and we got to Santa Anita, I was stunned.

The Issei felt it a lot more than I did. I was young, I had a husband, I was in love; and as long as I was going to be with him I could take it. But it was sad. I thought I'd never see my friends again, I thought I'd never see my parents again, you know. That was the sad part.

We were married on March 31, and we were at camp May 7. We were newlyweds, staying with my in-laws in the same room. Then it just really sunk in that this is what's happening, and then I got real sad and I would cry at night and my husband would say, "Aren't you happy being married," and I said, "It isn't that; I didn't think marriage was going to be like this." I said, "What are we going to do?" And then I started thinking of all these things. I said, "We don't have a home, you don't have a job, you line up to go eat three times a day," and then they sent out a notice saying that all married couples with no children have to report for some kind of work period.

I found out my folks were going to be evacuated, and somebody came and said, "You know, Miyo, your family's outside the gate, they want to talk to you." So then, right by the guard tower, they were on the other side of the barbed-wire fence and they said they came to say good-bye. Then I cried, I cried, and cried. That's when it really hit me that I'm not going to see them anymore.

One day, one of our friends came over and said there were rumors that we're going to be moving. From what I heard I was thinking, God, where are we going to go now? September came and we got on the train. The train pulled right to the side near Santa Anita. We got on, and as we traveled, I noticed that wherever we hit a town, the MPs would tell us to pull the shades down and we'd be curious, because we didn't know where we were going.

We pulled in at Rowher, Arkansas, late at night. I remember getting off the train and getting in the Army trucks and then we came to a spot and they let us off and that was the campsite. They had the barracks set up, but then everything wasn't completed. I remember one night, a friend of ours said, "Hey, you want to come along and we'll show you where a bunch of lumber is?" We were going, and all of a sudden they had these guys on horses, kind of watching, you know, so people won't steal the lumber and they said anybody caught stealing they could shoot on sight. We grabbed the lumber and ran. My husband made furniture with it because the barracks didn't have any furniture, just a cot.

Being at Rowher was just a lonely feeling that I can't explain. I thought to myself, I never ever dreamed that I would come to live here. I had this really sad feeling, never thinking you're going to be in there. You couldn't run anywhere. It was scary because there was no end to it. You could run and run and run but where are you to go? It was just nothing but water and then there were rattlesnakes. We felt like prisoners.

One day my husband came home from work and he said, "My God, I got this terrible headache. I feel like bashing my head against a wall, just cracking my head." He just went to bed, and I was panicking. I didn't know what to do, and the next morning he didn't even stir. He just went to sleep, and in the morning I looked and there was blood on his pillow. So then I said, "You'd better go see the doctor." Dr. Ikuta was the only doctor, but he was in Jerome. They had people lined up for surgery, and you just had to wait your turn. No matter how serious, you had to wait your turn.

I fretted for about a week, and then I wrote a letter to Dr. Ikuta and said that this is what you told my husband; I can't believe that you would turn him down. If it's that serious, please would you give him a chance. In about two or three weeks, I received a note from the hospital saying my husband was to report for surgery in two days. So then he went in for surgery, and that night I went to the hospital and he was under ether and he wouldn't come out of it. The nurse said there was no point in sitting there, and that they would let me know when he comes out of it. A friend of mine invited me for coffee at the barrack, so then one of the girls who happened to be a nurse, she said, "I saw this case today and you should have seen it. They removed the patient's ear bone, it was all rotted. They removed the ear bone and they found a clot, and Dr. Ikuta just laid his tool down and an Army doctor witnessing the surgery said this guy ain't gonna make it." I didn't know that this nurse was talking about my husband. Then I panicked and ran home and told my mother-in-law, then I ran to the hospital but then he eventually came out of it.

Later I said to my mother-in-law, "What am I going to do, how am I going to thank Dr. Ikuta?" My mother-in-law had twenty-five dollars she scraped up, and she said, "I don't think he'll take it, but give him this." I put a bottle of whiskey in my coat pocket and my twenty-five dollars and I sat at the administration building and waited on the bench for hours. Dr. Ikuta finally came in, so I jumped up and grabbed him and thanked him for saving my husband's life and I pulled out the whiskey and I said, "This is my worldly goods, this is all I have." I said, "Take this bottle and this twenty-five dollars," and he said, "I can't take it." I said, "Please, I would feel better. We don't have any money, nothing, but you saved his life, and if you don't take it then I'd feel bad so please take it." He said, "I can't take that money, but I'll take the drink." Then I thanked him and he said, "You know, I'm glad I did it for you, because you would have been a widow in a year."

Later, when I was pregnant with my second, that's when I flipped. I guess that's when the reality really hit me. I thought to myself, gosh, what am I doing getting pregnant. I told my husband, "This is crazy. You realize there's no future for us and what are we having kids for?" I said, "We're behind barbed-wire fence, the war could go on, what are we going to do?" I said, "It's a crime to have children, we're not doing them any favors. I'm not going to have this child in camp. I'm not going to have the second one in here, I don't know what but we're getting out of here."

Then that night it just bothered me so much, I wanted to get an abortion. I knew where a doctor lived, so then, I walked by his place. I just couldn't go in. I thought, oh my God, I can't kill this child, but then I said, if I have it, it's not fair; what am I doing? So I walked back, just could not, and I figured he was going to say no anyway. So I turned around, and then I cried and I told my husband, "Well, I'm having this one in camp, but no more kids, unless you get me out of here."

In March, he got a job, going to Minneapolis to work, doing daily contract with the Army, a tool-and-die place. Then he got a job at National Biscuit as a mixer. So then he called me in June, and my oldest one was a year and a half then, and I was expecting in December.

So then in December, I went to the hospital in Minneapolis to have my baby, and the day I was going to be released, my husband called and said, "I can't pick you up at the hospital, just take a cab and take the baby home. I'm detained at the army recruiting station; they just drafted me." Oh my God, I thought, after all this time, why now?

He had volunteered before we were married and then all his friends were being drafted so finally he said to me, "I'm going down to the draft board." So I said, "You want to go that bad?" He says, "Hell, I might as well fight for my country." I said, "Okay, if that's the way you feel." So he went down to the draft board and he came back and said, "They don't want me." They reclassified him, said that they weren't taking any more Japanese Americans. And he said, "Boy, they better not ask me again." Then of course, we got married and in camp, and another time they came to recruit, and that's when I already had my first baby, and he told them no. And when he had the questionnaire, I guess he answered every way he thought would get him out of it, and they called him back. They wanted to know why he answered these questions the way he did, and he said, hey, I volunteered and I wanted to fight and you guys didn't want me. So now I'm in camp, I had a baby, he said, the hell with you guys. He said not unless you let my parents out of here, I'm not going to fight.

Then here, the day I was going to leave the hospital, he gets drafted. I started to cry, and I thought, oh my God, I can't believe that they're taking him now. Here we were going to start life all over again and here they're taking him. So I called a cab, went home, and at eleven o'clock my husband comes home, and I looked at him and he had tears in his eyes and I said, "What's the matter?" He said, "The Army doesn't want me again." I said, "Why?" He said, "I got tuberculosis." I said, "Oh my God." Then I started crying. Then he said, "Don't cry, it just makes it harder for me." I said, "Yeah, but I can't help it." So then they ordered him to stay away from the babies. He was in a sanitarium for a year and a half and then he was released. Luckily my husband was well, but then we had to start all over again.

Deep down inside, the way I feel is that I was an American citizen; they had no right to do it. I feel betrayed, I really do. That's why I feel that we can't let it happen to somebody else again, the same thing. I wouldn't want it to happen, not to anybody.

We were young and there was no choice. There was no one really to stop it. If our leaders at the time were mature and knew the answers and had the wisdom, and if there were enough of those people, then maybe things would've been different. But there weren't enough of us. There weren't. You can just count on your hands the Nisei who tried to oppose it and who can speak eloquently. How many are there?

Life was different for us then because we took so much, in a sense. Like we really couldn't go to dances. We knew we couldn't go to certain places. We didn't have the fighting spirit. We just thought that was the way of life. We really did. So we'd go to this one place to dance every Saturday. Saturday nights you couldn't go sit on the lounge part, you had to stand outside that ring, but you know, that was the only place we could go. At least they let us in. But if you went on a weeknight, certain nights you could sit down on the lounge, because it wasn't that packed. I think to myself, I sure was stupid, I don't even know why I patronized those places, but I didn't know any better. Because the time when we were little, you know, we couldn't go to certain places, so it was just a way of life. So when the evacuation happened, my mother kept saying, oh, they're not going to take you, and I really believed her, and then when it really hit me was when I had my children. That made me open up my eyes to think what future is there, because I wanted another life for them, see.

It's funny, I don't feel that much bitterness. It's just that I feel that I don't want it to happen again. You can't turn the clock back, but I feel you can go forward and do something about it. That's the way I feel.

I would never want it to ever happen to anyone. The sadness, the trials and tribulations, especially being an American citizen, to have your rights taken away, should never happen. You learn from the time you're a child in school, from the first grade, to salute the flag; you believe in all the words that's said, you know, and all of a sudden you're in camp and you see the flag at half-mast, and you see the name of someone who volunteered for the Army. His name appears. He's dead. You think, can you salute that flag? Does it really stand for what it means? There was a time in my life when I didn't feel it stood for what it says. It was hard for me to salute that flag, and I don't feel that way now, but at the time I did have the feeling and I think that feeling should definitely never come into anyone's heart. It should stand for what it says, so you can really salute the flag and be proud of it.

I remember when we saw names of kids we went to school with who died in the 442nd. We'd run over every day and see whose name would appear. Then my friend said, "Miyo, how can you salute that flag?" and I looked at her, and I said, "I can't answer that, but I know how you feel." From the time you're in the first grade that's what you learn, and you're so proud when you do salute that flag, and then I remember going to ball games, the "Star-Spangled Banner," and there was a time when I couldn't even sing that, because I didn't feel it was right.

I remember a friend of mine who went into the service; he was killed. He was a very close friend, and one of my friends who is an artist sent us a framed picture of the flag, and I remember we had it on the wall. I used to tell my husband, "Look at the flag. To think that we were prisoners, his parents were in the camp, and he went out to fight and didn't come back." I took it off the wall. I told my husband, "I don't want it on the wall."

I want to be proud of it, when it's flowing in the sky, to be proud to salute it, because you know that it's telling you something. But you have to live what you're taught to know the meaning of it.

MABEL OTA

Poston

I was born in San Diego. I went to Calexico Elementary School, Calexico Junior High School, and graduated valedictorian from Calexico High School; and then I went to UCLA. I went out to UCLA, but I couldn't get in any of the dorms. They didn't allow Orientals in any of the dorms at UCLA, and so I ended up staying at the YWCA in Boyle Heights and commuted back and forth all those years. I got married in April 1939, graduated from UCLA in June, and then I looked for a job.

First I worked in a market as a cashier and then I took a civil service exam for the city. I passed it and got a job with the city in the Fingerprint and Identification Bureau. I had been working there for a short time when Pearl Harbor was attacked and they said it wasn't convenient to have Japanese working in that division, so I got transferred to the Jefferson Branch Library for six weeks and then I was terminated. They didn't give me a reason for it but I knew why. It was because I was Japanese.

My parents had written to me and asked my husband and me to come down to Calexico and help them sell the store, all the merchandise and so forth. We got permission to leave, and we went down there and helped my father. We advertised a closing-out sale in a local paper, and we sold everything at nominal cost and at a great loss. We had to because we didn't know what was going to happen to us or where we would be sent.

It was really sort of unbelievable. You know, when you go to college you have very high ideals of democracy, and when you have your rights taken away, it is really a shock. I kept saying all along, we're American citizens and the government couldn't possibly put us into camps. I really didn't believe it would happen until it did.

But I didn't become bitter. I guess we learn to roll with the punches. My parents were very stoic about it. You know, they never showed anger or bitterness, so I guess we sort of adopted their attitude. I guess we thought we should still be loyal and show that we are loyal by obeying. It wasn't anything that the JACL said; it was just how we felt ourselves. In El Centro we found out that we were going to be evacuated to Poston, and then they sent out a notice requesting Nisei or any Japanese Americans to volunteer to go first to help open up the camp. And so Fred and I volunteered. We thought that it would probably help us get out sooner if we showed that we would cooperate. We were already thinking of getting out of there.

They said we could go up in our own car, so I piled all kinds of things in that car. The young fellow who was a gasoline attendant in Hoytsville, who knew me because I got gas there and my family got gas there, had offered to buy our car. When we told him we had to go to Poston, he offered to drive us there. He drove us, and we had to stop at Blythe for lunch. When we went in the restaurant, they refused to serve us. He didn't buy anything either. We thought that was awful and so we walked out of that restaurant, I remember. But there was kindness from some. Like this fellow, he drove us all the way to Poston and helped us unload, and then he paid us for the car in cash and he drove the car back.

There was only one obstetrician in that camp of ten thousand people, at the beginning anyway. And many of the women there were in their child-bearing years like myself. Once a month I went in for a checkup. Then my husband, Fred, received this offer to leave to go to New York to become assistant manager of a cooperative. He left and the baby was supposed to come in May, so he said he would be back in time for the birth of the baby. But she came one month early, and when I went to the hospital, the nurse said the doctor had collapsed during the course of the previous day or night. He had delivered two babies and he had been on his feet all that time without help, so he collapsed and had gone back to the barracks to sleep.

I was in this room by myself and the nurse would come and check me every once in a while. I had a very long labor, almost twenty-eight hours. The nurse who was checking me would listen to the heartbeat of the baby, and finally she said the heartbeat was getting very, very faint and she was going to have to call the doctor. But you know, for twenty-eight hours the doctor didn't come to see me. So then the doctor came and checked me and then he informed me that, yes, they were going to have to use forceps to pull the baby out because they couldn't perform an operation because there was no anesthesiologist in camp. So that was the way they were going to do it.

They took me to the delivery room and gave me a local and I could see the knife to cut me. Then he used these huge forceps, and I kept watching that clock. He really had a hard time yanking her out, but I was conscious all the time. So it was really a horrible experience. And then I remember looking at the baby and saying, "Gee, I thought babies were bright red when they were born." This one was very pale and she gave one faint cry and they rushed her to the incubator and said she was very weak. Then I didn't get to see her for three days because they said she was too weak to be moved. When I did see her on the third day I noticed that she had scabs on her head where the forceps had been used. There's one spot where hair has never grown.

I'm convinced that she suffered permanent brain damage at birth, and I've read a lot of publications and medical books and they say that if you have hard labor and oxygen doesn't get to the fetus for one minute or something, it causes damage. There was another lady who had a baby about the same time and her baby started sitting up at six months or so. Well, my baby couldn't, and so I could see that her development was behind. Other children start walking, say at around a year, and Madeline couldn't walk. She couldn't walk until she was twenty-two months, so I know she was way behind in her development.

She was born in April. I wanted to join Fred, but the camp doctor said, "Oh, you can't travel with her, she's too weak. You'll have to wait until she's at least six months." So I waited until November and joined him in New York.

My father, who was at Gila, was a diabetic and so in our family we never had desserts because diabetics are not supposed to have a lot of starch or sweets. He always limited himself to one bowl of rice and he had whole wheat bread. He had always raised all kinds of vegetables in the backyard, fresh vegetables, because they were so essential to his diet. When we lived at camp, the diet at the beginning was really terrible—just starches, whatever they could ship in, and hardly any vegetables or fruits. One meal I think there were nothing but bread, potatoes, spaghetti, and macaroni. I looked at it, and I said, "My gosh, there's nothing but starch." I remember having breakfast, oatmeal, and it was full of those little black bugs, and I remember taking all those bugs out of that bowl and it made a black ring around the bowl.

The food, I'm sure was related to my father's death, but you see, they didn't diagnose it correctly. They put him in the hospital. I got a letter from my mother who said, "He's in the hospital, come quickly." I went back and she said, "They said it's not diabetes." And so I went to the hospital to see him and they said he's suffering from melancholia. And they said we have no way of treating him here, but we can arrange for him to go to the Phoenix Sanitarium, where he can get shock treatment, and maybe he'll come out of it. But they said, it will be at your own expense, because they didn't have any money to do that. We had some money from the sale of the grocery store, and so my mother said, "Well, let's go there."

The sanitarium was outside of Phoenix, and my father was there and was given shock treatments, but he was only there for about six weeks and then the doctor called the camp and said, "Come, your father is going to pass away." We went back and he passed away a short time after we arrived there. We got to see him before he died; and when I talked to the doctor the next day he said, "He didn't really have melancholia. It was brought on by his diabetes." The camp had only given him a urine test. They had not given him a blood analysis test, you see, and the urine test would come out okay. The diabetes wouldn't show up, but they had never given him a blood test and the doctor assumed that the camp had made the correct diagnosis, and he accepted it. So he went through all that for nothing. But his death certificate definitely says, "Died from diabetes," so he went into a diabetic coma, that's what it was, and then he died. If he didn't go to camp I'm sure he would have lived to a ripe old age because he was very careful watching his diet. The person himself has to do it, and he was always very careful.

I think the government was very wrong. This is why, although it is a very painful subject, I decided that I need to tell my story so that this kind of thing won't happen again. If people don't tell, no one will know the kinds of things that happened to loyal American citizens. I always considered myself loyal all through those years, and so it was a real shock that a loyal American citizen could be incarcerated like that and treated like a criminal. Maybe I should feel some anger or bitterness towards the government, because if the evacuation had not happened, then the tragedies in my life wouldn't have occurred. But, you know, you always have to roll with the punches, and I always look on the good side too.

MORGAN YAMANAKA

Tule Lake

The questionnaire came up while my brother was in Japan and very likely in the Japanese military, and my younger sister was God knows where in Japan. We were very close to my mother's family, and everybody there was in the military in Japan, we knew this. So the question here comes up, What do we do? We had this background. My older brother Al and I talked about it. The family wanted to go back to Japan sometime in the future, but then this questionnaire comes up.

We didn't know what the hell the questionnaire was. At that time it was interpreted for us as, Do you want to go out or don't you want to go out? If you want to leave the camp, you have to say yes-yes. But we weren't sure whether we wanted to leave the camp. The discussion went all over the camp that the Yamanaka family didn't want to leave the camp. One of the reasons is we were very provincial, we didn't know a damn thing outside of San Francisco. I think that was one of the variables.

The other thing was, as we discussed the questionnaire, the issue became clouded. It was no longer, leave the camp or stay in camp; it was loyalty. The wording of questions 27 and 28 became an issue —no longer an issue of leaving camp or not leaving camp, but a conceptual issue: loyalty to the United States versus loyalty to Japan. We felt we had done nothing, and we wanted to be good citizens. Then essentially we said, hell, we're not citizens anyway;

otherwise we wouldn't be here. The logical thing appears to be no-no. Once we said no-no, the next logical step was renunciation.

We did not want to leave camp; we thought about my brother and sister in Japan—do we fight them? Then there was the question of the word "loyalty"; loyalty means in wartime you fight. Up to the issue of loyalty, my plans, my ideas, were you must be a good citizen. But you see being a good citizen for me didn't involve fighting against Japan. You do whatever you can to be a good American citizen, but it never occurred to them you might have to fight your brother or uncles. When that came up, my father was not really a direct influencing factor. His influence was felt by Al and me, but he didn't say so in so many words. The major decision as I recall was between Al and me. We knew pretty well which way my father wanted us to go. But as I recall, he didn't really tell us what to do. So when I answered no-no on the questionnaire, the basic reason was that Al and I would not want to fight our brother.

At this point we were being transferred from Topaz to Tule Lake. It was just another transfer from one domicile to another, one camp to another camp; that in itself didn't faze me. My life at Tule during the earlier stages was really no different than at Topaz. It was when the rounding up of the people to put in the stockades started that I became conscious I was no longer in a place where I could be as free as I wanted to be.

There was some feeling of suppression, oppression, more so than at Topaz. Fences were there, guards were much more evident than in Topaz. But so what? We were in camp anyway. But what we were really made conscious of was more physical—the more apparent presence of the military. And you came up against them whenever something happened. At Topaz you seldom ran into a unit of them, except to see them in the towers, but at Tule there was much more awareness, and then our awareness was increased by Tulians who were there before we arrived, who said to us, "Hell, before you bastards came, we used to have Clam Castle Mountain and Abalone Mountain."

But once we got to Tule, the fences were closed, and none of us at Tule could leave the compounded area of the camp. The military presence was there. I happened to be a fireman, and I didn't have too much business outside of the campgrounds. No experience at all. But curiosity made us go to the fence every so often, especially toward the administration building once, and then you felt the physical presence of the MPs. I think those people who were able to go in and out of camp felt it more than I did. But they knew I felt it. More so than at Topaz. And I really felt it when my name appeared to be on the group that was to be placed in the stockade.

I still don't know why my name was on that list. I was not an agitator. I had never agitated at Santa Anita, nor at Topaz, nor at Tule. At Tule I was a fireman, captain of a fire department, and I allowed gambling in the fire department, but nobody knew we were gambling. It was a very good fire unit. Other than that I don't know. Now my dad was not the quietest person with his opinions, but he was not placed in the stockade, so we can't attribute my being on the list to my father's being a little bit outspoken, because he didn't go to the stockades. My brother and I both did. My brother was working in the kitchen crew and was not agitating. So I maintain there was no rhyme or reason as to who, other than the selected agitators, was placed in the stockade. Naturally there were several people who were identified as leaders of this or that group, but when it came to people like me and Al, I couldn't see any rhyme or reason.

The day we got in the stockade, it was a military area and I forgot what the situation was—whether they were searching for contraband or looking for people. In a camp of over twenty thousand the military went from one end of the camp in a straight row, and they covered the whole camp. As the military came closer, we were running away from them. It was a dragnet; they had my name on the list. That was when we were picked up. We were herded into army trucks, and we were shoved into a room in the military barracks and we waited interminably. We were just squatting on the floor, no furniture. We were jam-packed on the floor for hours on end, and every so often one of us would be called. And then I was finally called. We didn't know what the hell was happening. Then I was led, not blindfolded, by the military. "Okay," they said, "your turn next, Kunitake Yamanaka," and then I was led somewhere down the hall, placed in a dark room, shoved into a chair, and all of a sudden the light went on—classic third degree.

Then they started firing, and more questions started firing from the dark. Some of my friends told me they were beaten, the rubber hose type of beating. I was the youngest kid there in the whole damn stockade, and I don't remember how long that classic third degree quizzing went on. Then I was shoved in somewhere, taken away, and after that I don't remember. I just remember sitting on the floor, waiting in a very crowded place. One thing I do remember was when some of us had to go to the latrine. We called the MP and said we had to go, and his attitude was just, fuck you; don't pee on the floor. So the question became, what the hell do you do? We used to wear engineering boots, and somebody offered his boot. But we just held it, and that was the most uncomfortable, that's about the most stupid law, not knowing how long it is going to be and then one person being called out.

The stockade had three barracks; the third barrack was the washroom and the kitchen. There were, as I recall, something like 130 of us in the stockade, give or take a few. We were searched and then dumped there, and we slept on cots, with a couple of blankets—it was cold, wintertime—about 130 of us, dormitory-style. So from the quizzing to the time I ended up in the stockade, I don't recall specifics.

Every so often we would have raids. Now why in the hell did we have raids when we were already searched, but they would come in the middle of the night to do a raid. Having taught sociology and sociology of law, I don't think it was only harassment. I think it was fear that the prisoners might have something—just like San Quentin has its "rock downs," and they do find homemade knives. I think it was mainly harassment. There was this mentality of the people in the military police. Something might be going on so we better have a raid kind of thing.

I don't ever remember being scared for my life by a physical thing—I could get into a fight; my martial arts training put me in good standing. I'm seldom scared if ever, but one time I was scared. There was a midnight raid and a Thompson machine gun. A guy was holding it; he was shaking, this young kid, younger than I. I had practiced martial arts with .38s, .45s—you know, judo, where I knew something about firearms. And here this young kid was shaking in his boots, scared stiff I'm sure of these goddamned troublemakers in the stockade, and he has this damn submachine gun pointed straight at my belly, just shaking away. I think I was scared that he was scared that he would pull the trigger. I can't remember any other time that I was ever scared.

It was one of those midnight raids they used to do. I remember having that machine gun in back of a personnel carrier at the stockade aimed at our group. We were told to line up and I somehow ended up in the front row. I remember it was snowing, truly cold. We were told, "Get out, inspection," or whatever, and they surrounded us with soldiers in uniforms with heavy army coats, and they brought a half truck I remember, put it in reverse so the tailgate faced us, and they had a machine gun aimed at us, and we stood in the snow for three, four, five hours in our underwear and zoris. We stood in the snow. What the hell could we do? I don't know whether they would have shot us if we had gone back. We walked away, but here we were and there was that damn Army machine gun from a half personnel carrier aimed at us, and we stood there until something happened. After I don't know what—at that point I think—we decided to go on a hunger strike.

About the fifth day as I recall, some people became ill—frail types—and they were taken to the hospital. The Army medic would come and check our health. I don't remember what they did, but I do remember them coming in and checking us. The sixth day a couple more went, and the seventh day we decided to give it up. Nothing was accomplished.

The bullpen was part of the stockade. I did not experience it, but every so often people would be questioned, and they didn't come back after being questioned. There's only one entrance to the stockade, and the person being questioned would go through there and wouldn't come back. So the question was whether he was released or sent to the bullpen. Some people went to the bullpen and came back. I don't remember exactly; I think I'm talking about the bullpen, because I remember it, but for the life of me I can't describe it. I knew about the bullpen, and deep in my unconscious I must know more because we discussed it. I recall other parts of camp vividly, but the bullpen doesn't come back. So there was that kind of a fear; it was part of the stockade experience.

I stayed at Tule for quite a bit after the end of the war. I was released in 1946. I had to get a special paper from the Justice Department to say I could be released. I think, again, that was the stockade experience that made me a special person, and I needed the special release papers.

In 1946 I found myself in Chicago, at the bottom of the social heap. I was already twenty-three—twenty-three with no skills, nineteen bucks in my pocket, no knowledge whatsoever to do anything. This didn't jibe with the old Yamanaka image of who Yamanaka should be. But there I was. The reality was I was a dishwasher, and it was not in the best restaurant. But there I was. Hell, anybody can do that—the guy before me was a wino, and the only reason I became a dishwasher was because the wino never came back. He got his check and probably was on a wine trip, and there I was, no more, no less than a wino. And I think at that time I decided to earn money and then see something of New York, come back to San Francisco, and go to school.

When I left Chicago I do remember going to New York where my brother was and staying with him a couple of days. And then, on a lark I met a fellow from camp, and we said, "Hey, let's go to Washington, D.C." Now that was the most uncomfortable trip, goddamn; that's the first time I'm saying this. That was one lousy trip. Here this fucking country placed me in this camp, and here is the seat of the country where they made this decision essentially, and it was not a pleasant decision. Whether I'm still suppressing, I don't know. But all I can say is, in retrospect, that was not a comfortable trip. Hell, what was interesting is that Washington should have been more interesting; it wasn't. Nothing, this whole idea is suppressed. I never thought about it that way.

Because of my experience in the concentration camp I am more conscious of how individuals can become tools of large forces, and how those large forces have to be as controlled as much as possible by those individuals. If such a thing is going to take place it's going to be individuals that will have to stop it. In actual fact, it is good for me to think that way. I think I'm a damned sight better American than a lot of Americans because I think this way. How can a government put me in a concentration camp? That I think is the damnedest government in the world.

If we had resisted in 1942, I think we would have gotten our heads beaten. We would have gone anyway, by force. Force was there. The Army was there, and it would have been unpleasant force. As it was, the force was felt. And although at that time I believed the JACL was wrong, in retrospect I think they did the right thing. I think it would have been stupid to go against the military. All of us would have ended up with gunshot wounds. So, in retrospect, I think it was a right thing for that time. When I teach my course I say, "Imagine yourself in an airplane, it is hijacked, you going to go against the hijacker?" I say, "I'm not!"

And I don't think anybody would. I use that analogy—being hijacked—because we felt in World War II we were held in a hijacked airplane. And the airplane was going to the concentration camp. There was nothing we could do at that point.

JOHN KANDA

Tule Lake
442nd Regimental
Combat Team,
France, Italy

I was born in Seattle, Washington, in July 1925. We moved to an area between Auburn and Kent, twenty-five miles south of Seattle, called Thomas. Later we moved to Auburn until the evacuation.

It was just prior to our fourth year of harvesting when we were evacuated. At that time I was a junior in high school in Auburn, and I certainly didn't feel that my brother, my sisters, or I would be evacuated. We thought there was a possibility of our parents possibly being put into some detention camp; so all the plantings were put in, and we were working as if the harvest would be coming in. The evacuation took place about a week or ten days before the first harvesting of the lettuce crop. In March 1942, we were sent to Pinedale Assembly Camp, which is right outside of Fresno, California.

The day we left as we gathered at Auburn train depot, I was very sad. I thought it couldn't be happening; and believing what was in the textbooks and all on government and the Constitution, I just said, hey, this can't be happening to us; but it was.

Pinedale was a camp like all camps, surrounded by barbed wire, and inside there was a sentry line which you're not supposed to pass. There wasn't a blade of grass in that place or a tree. It was just sand and dust and the tar-paper barracks, and it was really hot. I can recall everything the neighbors said; they were talking on either side of you, and it was just like you were right next to them. There was no privacy. You could even hear people whisper; it was just dreadful.

We were sent to Tule Lake in September, and school started late, sometime after we arrived there. It was even a more desolate place than Fresno. The teachers that taught grade school or high school were just volunteer people who had some experience in the line of whatever course they were asked to teach. So I'd have to say they were far inferior to other teachers in the state. And there was absolutely no equipment—especially for laboratory courses—and there was really a shortage beyond comprehension of textbooks. There were no textbooks to take home or even to borrow to take home, and there weren't enough even to be distributed one to each pupil during the class hour. Whatever you had almost always had to be shared, and this was my senior year in a college preparatory course. I really feel that I was handicapped in many, many ways when I entered college after I came back from the service. I finished the chemistry course in high school at Tule, but when I went to college I knew zero. I never saw a Bunsen burner or a beaker or a flask until I got to college, and so I had to watch my fellow lab students and ask them what I was supposed to be getting. I have to feel that not only myself but almost every student in the camp school system suffered a great deal. I think they tried hard, but the equipment wasn't there, and the school was in a barracks. They had a blackboard and chalk and that was about it.

I finished high school in Tule Lake in 1943, and that's the only graduating class from this high school, which was named Tri-State, because students came from California, Oregon, and Washington.

I was at Tule Lake from September 1943, through just about the following September—about a year. Then I went to Minidoka. I was there only a short time. The draft was reinstated, and so I was eligible. I did get drafted eventually as a replacement for the 442nd Combat Team. At the time I got drafted, there were many of my real buddies, people I had grown up and went to school with who chose not to be drafted. Now there were some of them who because of family ties chose to stay with their parents in Tule Lake. For me, there was a real sad parting. I mean, I felt very sad about leaving those people; I could see their viewpoint. But many of the friends I made who chose not to register were eventually taken to

McNeil Island for the federal offense of draft evasion. I can see their position too, and I often think they may have been braver than I. I still have friends amongst these people.

When I got drafted, this was the government calling me to serve and maybe die for the country that put me behind barbed wire. Just about a year prior to this, there was a group of Army officers who came through the camps. I was still a senior in high school at Tule Lake at that time, and that's when they were looking for volunteers for the 442nd Combat Team. I knew what we were being asked to do, in spite of what was being done to us. Even to this day I really at times wonder if I had made the right choice. I don't mean to say I'm not patriotic. I feel I am patriotic, but I might have been more patriotic if I refused at that point. I'm just not sure.

It was 1944 before I was called to active duty. I went as a replacement for the 442nd and went overseas in 1944. But before we shipped overseas, my brother, who was also in the 442nd, and I had a very unpleasant experience. We received our furlough at the same time, so we were on the same train coming back to Minidoka to visit our parents. A group of schoolteachers got on the train, and they were just leaving a convention of schoolteachers. They were not going very far, but they were kind of tired-looking, so we gave up our seats and we sat on our duffle bags and were chatting, and as the conversation went along one of the school-teachers asked us, "You're Chinese, aren't you?" And we said, "We're Japanese Americans," and that just finished the conversation for the rest of their trip. I still don't understand. The way the conversation just ended right there really hurt us. Here we were in American uniforms and chatting with them about things, and then all of a sudden just because we're Japanese Americans the conversation ended right there. I still remember. My brother is more sensitive about all these things and the hurt feelings he had about the thing. It's one of those things, you know.

When we got to the Minidoka camp, the military police at the gate checked our papers before we went through even though we were in uniform. Our folks, knowing that the combat casualties of the 442nd were pretty high, were kind of mopey, even though the two of us were back together to visit them.

We shipped out for Europe on the *Queen Mary* in October 1944. I remember there were many Italian prisoners of war being returned to Europe, and they had the luxury cabins upstairs, and all of us 442nd guys were in the open troop berths below the water level. I still kind of smart at the idea of that.

When we got to Glasgow, Scotland, we were the first ones to disembark immediately after we dropped anchor. We ended up at Southampton in the morning and boarded another smaller passenger ship that took us to Le Havre. Then we were hauled immediately eastward and joined the 442nd Combat Team just after they had rescued the Lost Battalion. There were only two people left in our squad at the time four or five of us joined it as replacements, bringing the squad to about half-strength. In L Company, which I joined, the two men I met were both looking dazed and just worn out. The normal strength of a squad is twelve men, and there were just two people left before we came. Most of the companies had been completely wiped out in that campaign. As it turned out, the replacements were hit quite heavy too in the end.

During the lulls in combat, I used to write home, and they would write back and sometimes send little things, and my sister wrote quite often. My brother, who got married after he got out of Minidoka, was in E Company, and we visited whenever we could. We had a lot of time to think about what was going on back home. I felt no real bitterness then, and I can't say I'm bitter now. I just knew that it was an awful price to pay.

For my parents and my brother, who had put a lot of effort, sweat, and dollars into their farm, you know, and literally got wiped out especially as far the finances go, I just feel it's not right. It's more a matter of principle to me than anything else. It just is not right.

I think the whole experience has colored my life tremendously. Certainly I do not know where I would be if it were not for the war, but what happened with the evacuation and my wartime experience where I was in three campaigns has colored my outlook a whole lot.

VIOLET DE CRISTOFORO

Tule Lake

Before the war I lived in Fresno, California. When evacuation came I was married and had two children, seven and five years old. I was also pregnant three months. The day of the order was just about two weeks after my operation for a tumor. The doctor tried to have my internment delayed for a while and so asked the provost marshal, but it was not allowed. So I closed the bookshop, closed the home with my two children, carried whatever we were allowed to carry, and left for the camp, which was Fresno Assembly Center.

I couldn't believe that American citizens were being uprooted, especially since my children were so young. I was just unable to answer the question myself as to why such a thing was being done to us. This kept hounding us over and over. Why? What necessity? It just didn't make sense. But to tell the truth, we were brought up to be very law-abiding citizens. We felt that we were compelled to go, and it was not easy: not being able to convince myself, not being able to convince the children. My children and I decided that we would do whatever we had to do in order to survive. It was a matter of survival and nothing else that had made us go to camp and stay there for the next four years. Whether they call this injustice or inhumanity, I don't know, and history must decide. But for me it was an individual tragedy that should never have happened, and I don't think that it could ever be remedied by anyone, or any government.

Because in 1942 I believed in this country wholeheartedly, I wanted to offer something to the United States government at the time Japan bombed Pearl Harbor. But all I had was a Red Cross certificate, my only asset, and I went to Red Cross headquarters and said, "The only thing I have is an advanced certificate in Red Cross training. If at anytime you need my services I will gladly give them to you." And that was the fullest I was able to give, the fullest the United States government could receive from me. I believed in the U.S. government so, so much that I went to the Red Cross and volunteered myself.

In April 1942, my husband and I and our two children left for camp, and my mother-in-law and father-in-law came about a month later. I wasn't afraid, but I kept asking in my mind, how could they? This is impossible. Even today I still think it was a nightmarish thing. I cannot reconcile myself to the fact that I had to go, that I was interned, that I was segregated, that I was taken away, even though it goes back forty years.

But we went to the Fresno Assembly Center. And you know what the summer is like in Fresno—110 degrees—and we were living under a low, tar-paper roof. The floors were built right on top of the racetrack. And there was the manure, and there were cracks in the floor, so that every bit of summer heat, every minute of the day when you're in the barracks, pushed the smell up. It was unbearable, the heat and the smell, and being pregnant and very weak, I sheltered myself under the bed and put wet towels on myself as much as I could. Some days we would dig into the ground and get into the ground, but we couldn't do that very well. As the days went on, the alfalfa started growing from under the floor between the cracks. People pinched the alfalfa and started eating it, and I became violently ill because I'm very allergic to hay and to many grasses and seeds.

Then there was the food poisoning. I was the first to succumb. We usually had to wait something like an hour or an hour and a half to be served any food. The line was so long, and things were so disorganized that they didn't have a system that let a sick woman or an older person or pregnant woman go first. They never did that. So if you wanted to eat something, you stayed in line in that hot sun for an hour, sometimes two hours, and by the time you got your food and took it back to your barracks to eat, the food was spoiled. The first time I got food poisoning I thought I would lose the baby, and I was confined to the hospital, which had no roof, no windows, hardly anything. I was there for about a week and barely sustained the baby's life. When I was released to the barracks, I was under the doctor's care for about a month. But all during that pregnancy, I hemorrhaged, and so the doctor thought that if the baby was to be born, it might not be normal.

Towards the later part of my pregnancy I was in the hospital for about two months, and I had the baby. It wasn't quite a full pregnancy, and she was about five pounds, a very small child. During the stay in Fresno, my mother-in-law was quite ill too, and she wasn't given much medical attention. So with that, and with my two young children not having any schools to go to, not having anything to do, I had my hands full in trying to just look after myself plus my children and the rest of the family.

We stayed there until September. The day my second daughter was born was September 2, and September 18 we were herded off to Arkansas on a dilapidated train which had nothing for babies or sick women. It was a five-day, five-night trip—the most horrible, horrible conditions. The shades were drawn for security reasons, and there was no air. Whenever a troop train came by, we had to sidetrack and let it go first. Even on those little stops, we were not allowed to get off the train. And my two-week-old baby developed double pneumonia the third day out, and there was no formula, no sanitation.

By the time we got to Jerome, Arkansas, the ambulance was waiting for her and she was taken off to a hospital, which had no roof, no windows, no nothing. She stayed there for about two and a half months. After that, in Jerome, she was in the hospital most of the time. But let me tell you, they never let us off the train. There were three or four shipments of internees from the Fresno Center to Jerome. And I guess the husky men for building the camp at Jerome were the first ones to leave, and the sick and the old were the last to leave. And I was on the last trip. But we were not allowed to get off the train. And there was no way babies could sleep in a compartment or a sick woman could stretch out.

So I carried the baby for five days, and she lay on the seat for five days. And we were supposed to be on a medical train. There was only one doctor on the train, but he had his hands full, and his wife couldn't even get hot water for the baby's formula. But there were MPs all over, everywhere. And like I said, we were very, very naïve, very trustworthy, very law-abiding. Or maybe stupid, because if they said don't get up, don't do this, don't go to the next coach, we didn't. We absolutely did just as we were told to do. I know they told us not to draw the shade up. We just didn't.

Dr. Miyamoto, who was interned at Jerome with us, took care of my baby. There were many nights we were called, and he would say, tonight is the crisis, would you come and sit. I don't know how many nights we went from the barracks to the hospital, which was from one end of the camp to the other. The ambulance would come and get us, and we would stay there many, many nights. I took my children with me, and we would stay there. I couldn't leave the children in the barracks alone, so we sat there all night long, many, many nights in the two and a half months she was there. Then they said we could bring her home, but the weather was very bad in Arkansas. It was just that every little sore would infect, and there was ticks and all kinds of things. So most of the one year that we stayed in Jerome, our youngest daughter was confined in the hospital.

That is when I said that if this child should ever, ever live, she would be dedicated to God. She really owed it to the doctor, or willpower, or our intense prayer for her that she lived through this thing. And do you know, my feelings were, What have I done? That question, What have I done? went away recently. But it was there for the longest time. That was the thing that bothered me. I didn't try to blame it on the government; I didn't try to blame it on anybody—but the self-recrimination: What have I done to deserve this? Why? Why? I love my children dearly, I haven't done anything wrong, and why? That was the only thing that bothered me.

For the longest time, I was a sick woman. It's just in recent years that I have become healthy, and Cris, my husband, knows that. I was always a sickly woman, and because of that maybe I never spoke about all these things. I kept it to myself. Even my child, the other day when she first learned about it, asked, "Mama, why didn't you tell me these things?" Well, for some reason I just didn't speak, you know, and I told her that she had a very rough childhood.

After I went to live in Japan and sent my two older children back to the States, I told them that Kimi had gone through a very trying time, and the fact that she's living is because God has meant for her to live. And that I owed her more than I owed the other two kids, and that was the reason that if I cannot have the three of them to raise them properly, I felt the younger one, who was always more sickly, should be the one to stay with me. The others should go back to the States where they could be given proper education.

At Jerome, my in-laws were in a separate barracks, because we were from different parts of Fresno, and certain parts got evacuated at different times. But because my mother-in-law was very sick, I had to go to their place to take care of her, come back and take care of my kids, and then go to the hospital. When the loyalty questionnaire came up, my father-in-law looked at it this way: he was a Japanese; he had been in the Japan-Russia war, and he had quite a bit of property back in Japan. He figured that he was considered an enemy alien, all his assets were frozen, and he had nothing to go back to in California. He was at that time quite elderly too. His wife was very sickly, and he figured that there was no use in even trying to stay in the United States. And he decided to go back to Japan. And naturally, my former husband who was the only child decided that he would go back too. They didn't have anything left in Fresno, and they all decided that if they went to Japan they have so many rentals, they have so much land, they have so much money that they can live off the interest. So they chose to repatriate. I don't believe they answered the questionnaire yes or no; they just said "refuse to answer, seek repatriation." I didn't know what they were saying at the time, but I wrote the same thing. My husband had told me, "Don't answer this because this could be a very involving matter. Don't trust the government, don't trust anybody, just say you're seeking repatriation with my family." And that is the only thing that I wrote. I did not answer yes or no to the questionnaire. "Seek repatriation with the family" —that was the only thing I wrote.

That meant I was segregated to Tule Lake, but before that we were separated again. My father-in-law went first. Then because my mother-in-law was ill and I had a sick child, we were on the last train again. In going to Tule Lake, my mother-in-law became very ill in some little town in Kansas. She became violently ill, and the train's doctor . . . I don't know whether he was a Japanese doctor or whether he was a Caucasian doctor . . . anyway, he decided that the train should stop, that she should be hospitalized right away. They took her off the train, and she stayed behind for about two months in a hospital in Kansas. I had asked to remain with her, and they wouldn't allow it.

She did not speak any English at all. She was an elderly woman, and a very devout Buddhist, very, very devout. And so she was left behind, and when she came back to Tule Lake about two months or so later, oh, she was in a ghastly condition, just absolutely as if death had walked in. She was confined to the hospital right away. When I asked the doctor just what caused her illness, he said she had motion sickness, or wasn't able to withstand long trips like that. Various reasons other than medical reasons were given to me, but I believe at that time she already had cancer.

But our family were all reunited at Tule Lake, and my brother was in Tule Lake too. The camp had already been established two years or so, and a lot of original Tule Lake people were there. But with the segregation movement, those who had decided not to go back to Japan were sent to other camps. And those who were going to Japan remained there. So we were scattered to wherever there was an empty room. So my brother was way on one end, I was someplace else, my in-laws were someplace else, although we did request to have the family together as close as possible. But that wasn't done, and we stayed wherever they had assigned us.

As soon as we got there, we realized certain things were lacking. The mess hall was not quite adequate, we were not given the proportion of food that we were supposed to be given like sugar and milk and butter. We lacked lots of things. Those people who came from other centers decided they would form a Better Living Condition Association to negotiate with the authorities. By then a lot of boys suspected that something must have been going on for them to be getting away with less food for the evacuees, less medical facilities, and such decrepit facilities. That was organized and they started negotiating with the administration. The administration was not very cooperative, and a meeting didn't materialize. And my former husband and brother being young and being community leaders, were naturally in that group to negotiate.

Well, one thing led to another, and before you know, they were arrested. Those who were trying to investigate the shortage of food got beaten up and thrown into the stockade, and people like my former husband who were considered leaders—anybody like Buddhist priests, or schoolteachers, or newspaper correspondents— were rounded up and sent to Justice Department camps. That was soon after we went to Tule Lake. Within three months, they were rounded up and sent to different camps.

I was separated from my husband; he went to a Santa Fe, New Mexico, camp. All our letters were censored; all our letters were cut in parts and all that. So we were not too sure what messages was getting through and not getting through, but I do know that I informed him many times of his mother's condition. He should have been allowed to come back to see her, because I thought she wouldn't live too long, but they never did allow him to come back, even for her funeral. They did not allow that. I learned that a lot of the messages didn't get to him; they were crossed out. I now have those letters with me.

In 1944 I was left with his parents and our kids. But I had no time to think of what was going to happen because my child was always sick and I had been quite sick. I didn't realize it until I recently got my camp records from the archives telling that I was hospitalized many times in Tule Lake myself. My mother-in-law was quite sick, my youngest child was sick, and I'd been sick, and my other daughter was in and out of the hospital with nephritis and other things. So in fact, my son was the only one who was healthy. My husband was gone, my brother was by that time in the "bullpen," as some called the torture chamber of the Tule Lake stockade. And I had to care for my mother-in-law who eventually died.

My son knew what was going on, and he too had many times asked me why . . . you know, why? why? Of course, I had no explanation why this was happening to us. He said if other families decided to go out, they were able to go out. When I tried to seek permission to go out, I was denied.

I tried to remain in this country after my husband and father-in-law had gone back to Japan, but I was denied that. So naturally I had no recourse but to go back to Japan. At that time, the Justice Department which conducted the hearing did not give me the reason as to why my leave authorization was not granted. It was on account of that paper, the FBI report against my husband, saying that he was considered an undesirable enemy alien. So that prevented me, but I did everything possible to remain in this country.

Then after my mother-in-law's illness was diagnosed as cancer, there was no way to treat the cancer patient there. Of course, I understand now there were others who died of cancer while they were interned. But at that time I thought she was the only one. I asked the camp authorities, the doctors, and everybody, to send her to a hospital outside where there was a facility to treat cancer patients. And that was denied. I don't know how often I had gone to the hospital, to the administration building, asking for permission to have her sent. It took them so long to answer me, so much red tape and everything. But when she finally did go, it was with two MPs armed with rifles, who came and got her at the hospital. My mother-in-law got up and cried and hugged me and said, "They're going to kill me, they're going to kill me. I've been hospitalized so long since I came into the camp, I'm a nuisance, and they going to kill me. Kazue-san, I don't want to go, don't let them take me." And I said, "Well, I had asked for them to take you to a hospital where you can be treated. Isn't that better?"

She didn't want to go. She wanted to stay with us. And she cried. She cried and she hugged. Sometimes I wish I hadn't let her go. I wish I hadn't let her go. When she went and she came back three weeks later, she looked worse than before. She said the MPs guarded her, sat beside her on the train, and when she went to the bathroom, they went with her and stayed outside the door. Throughout the cancer treatment the MPs stayed outside the door. She said she didn't know what kind of treatment she received. She couldn't understand what the doctor had said to her. But she said to me, "I prayed and I prayed and I prayed," but she said, "Sometimes the *hotokesama* ("Buddha") didn't answer me." And she had been such a devout, devout Buddhist woman. For her to say that must have been very difficult—for her to doubt Buddha for even one minute.

She didn't complain. That's one thing you can ask Dr. Miyamura, who treated her till the last moment. She never complained. All she said when she was in such gross pain—absolutely gross pain— all she said was *namu-amida-butsu* ("oneness with Buddha"), that's all she said and nothing else. She never had any unkind word for the United States government or for anybody. She worried about my brother, she worried about her son, she worried about her husband, and she made me promise her over and over that I would look after her husband, that I would look after her son. She was not quite sixty. And they had guards on her all the time, all the time. At that time, of course, I had no inclination about how advanced she was or anything. They knew that all along.

When she died, my husband was at Santa Fe. My father-in-law was still with me, in a different barracks. My father-in-law lost his mind ever since she died. We had a funeral for her when he found out that his son was not allowed to come back, and my brother was not allowed to come back. He became a different man from that day on. Then he carried his wife's ashes in a little box, and he had me order some material from Montgomery Ward, a white material. I must have ordered five or ten yards for him. He had that box wrapped around, tied to him. When he went to mess hall, he took her with him; when he went to the bathroom, he took her with him; and the day that he left Tule Lake for Japan, he had that thing on him. And he said, "Kameo, we're going to say good-bye to Tule Lake, we're going to say good-bye to Kazue, we're going to say good-bye to Ken." And he got the box and told us to say good-bye to obachan, "Say good-bye to obachan."

And I remember all my children came and cried and cried and cried. They said, "Why do *ojichan* ("grandfather") and obachan have to go back like this to Japan?" And as I understand it, my father-in-law, when he got on the boat, he was like that all the way and went home like that all the way, and so, he was never the same man again.

When I went back to Japan this time, I found her grave, but there's no grave for my father-in-law. Nobody did anything for him. You know, he was a very influential Buddhist leader in Fresno, one of the highest contributors. Anytime there was a donation, he was the first one and the biggest contributor. And both of them were very active in the Buddhist church in Fresno. And they had quite a bit of assets in Japan. They had quite a bit of frozen accounts, and as yet, I don't know what became of it all. And to think that he died in poverty. I spoke to my father-in-law's relatives and to the neighbors and found out how he had died, what condition he had died in. I couldn't believe it. This is the only time I have felt any bitterness against the U.S. government; for the way my father-in-law died and the fact that he has no tombstone.

He stayed in the United States forty years. Both of them had

OUSTER OF ALL JAPS IN CALIFORNIA NEAR!
San Francisco Examiner
6 AM EXTRA
Thousands of Allies Face Japs in Java
OUSTER OF ALL JAPS IN CALIFORNIA NEAR!
EXTRA
Thousands of Allies Face Japs in Java

Donald Nakahata

Yoshiye Togasaki

Ben Takeshita

Mabel Ota

Mitsuye Endo

Wilson Makabe

Fred Fujikawa

Frank Chuman

Mary Tsukamoto, with her husband, Alfred Iwao, and daughter

Theresa Takayoshi

Haruko and Njio Niwa

Emi Somekawa

John Kanda

Minoru Yasui

Bill Hosokawa

Donald Sakamoto

Violet de Cristoforo

Miyo Senzaki

Helen Murao

Sam and Yuri Tateishi

Chiye Tomihiro

Iwato Itow

Paul Shinoda

Harry Ueno

Morgan Yamanaka

worked so hard. They gained three, four rentals in Japan, but when he went to Japan, his tenant farmers were Koreans and lived in the house. Under MacArthur's law, they had the squatter's rights. And they wouldn't vacate the house for my father-in-law or later for me. So my children and I had to go and live with his relatives who had ten children. His own home, too—MacArthur's land reform act said you could only keep what you could cultivate yourself. My father-in-law had lost his wife, was not able to farm, and his son was not a farmer type. I didn't know how to farm, and we couldn't keep the land and had to sell at whatever price Mac-Arthur had set.

So that forty years of his fruit, all the land, was sold in pieces like that. We thought we would be able to live with interest alone, but the yen was devalued to a point where there was nothing left. His United States account was frozen by the government, and I read that it's considered enemy assets. Once you repatriate to Japan, you lose it all—$27,000 in 1942 for him. Still, the only bitterness I have is to think how my father-in-law died in the condition that he did. And there is no tomb for him.

I don't know, this is still my country, I was born here, my children are here, I probably will die here, and this is the place I'd like to be buried in. It's a certain faith I have in this country. I feel that a government such as ours has its good points, its bad points too, and we probably were caught in that. But people shouldn't be too self-centered, too selfish and take advantage of another race or a situation such as ours and make profit out of it. But that's probably an individual act, not a government act.

My life will never be the same. I will take this with me till I die, and I'm sure my children would bear some of the burden too. Three generations of my family has disintegrated as a result of this. I don't know why I'm not bitter. But what good does it do. It would only make me sick. Remember when I told you how I kept on saying, why? why? why?—when I questioned so much—that was when I was getting so sick all the time. I was really sick. I was skin and bone. My husband, Cris, had to nurse me a long time. And when I got that feeling, I was converted to a Catholic after the war. I wasn't a fervent Buddhist but my family was; my in-laws were very, very fervent Buddhist people. I was brought up by an American family, and there was something about their religion even though I wasn't too serious about it. But all during the four years of camp when this was all happening, and having seen my mother-in-law die the way she did, and she being a very, very devout woman, when she said to me, "I must have done something in my other life for hotokesama to ignore me or not listen to me" . . .

I got to thinking when I went back to Japan. When I got to Japan we were thrown in the same place where the Japanese soldiers were being returned. We had soldiers from Manchuria, soldiers from China, and Japanese roughnecks all in the same place. There must have been only two hundred or so of us Tule Lake repatriates at that time, and we were thrown in with the soldiers. If you talk about fear, I was afraid that night. We slept there for about a week with the same clothes that we wore when we left Tule Lake. We wouldn't take them off. There was no place to take them off. We were given something like a millet, not even rice *okayu* ("recooked rice"), and some fish and some seaweed. And what I had with me was some crackers and other things that my brother, who was in the U.S. Army, gave me—a few things to take back to Japan, plus some warm clothes and that sort of thing. Having the Japanese soldiers, those who had just come back from the war zone, sleep with us and go to the same bathroom, that was the most horrible experience I ever had. Then we went on a train that was dilapidated—no windows, hardly any seats, no doors. We were shoved in from the window, a broken window; the MP broke the window and shoved us in.

I don't know how many days it took us to go to Hiroshima. When we got off, there was not even a Hiroshima station; it was just a cement block, and we were told to get off there. I knew where my mother's home was. I went there, but there was no bridge to cross to get to my mother's place, because it had been bombed—the atomic bomb. We didn't know how to go anywhere, so we stayed there that night. This was in March of 1946. We stayed there that night, huddled up against each other and found some newspaper or something for cover and cried, and just about froze to death that night.

The next day we went to a Japanese policeman, and I said that this is where my mother's home was, how do I get there? He said, "Nobody can go there, everybody's been evacuated, your mother's not there, nobody's living there. She's either dead or she's gone to wherever she can go." I said, "How do I find out?" The police said, "There's no way we can find out."

So then I decided the next best thing was to go to such and such a relative at another place. So I asked how to go there, and the policeman said I'd have to walk. I took my three children, what little luggage I had, and we walked. We walked for about two days and got to our relative's place. And you think they were glad to see us? They were not glad to see us at all. They had no news of my mother. Then I asked this person to take me to my father-in-law's place, which was way out in the country. And there was one train a day or something like that, and we went to my father-in-law's place. And like I said, he had no home to go to; he had been living with his relative who had ten children. Then with my children, we all lived there together for about two months or so.

At that time, my husband was in Nagasaki, and I guess he had already started a family or was living with somebody else. My brother was there too, because they thought that they might find some opportunity for repatriates. There were no jobs in Japan. People who had come back from war and the real Japanese had the priorities if there were any jobs at all. Repatriates had no place to go. Most everything had to be gotten on the barter system, and we had nothing to barter with.

So I stayed with my father-in-law as American forces came in. I pleaded with them to help me find my mother who had lived in such and such a place. After a while, with the help of Japanese police they found out my mother was at the place where she was born, which was two mountains away, but there was no transportation to get there. The Counter Intelligence Corps (CIC) officer said, "If you come and work for us, I will take you to the river, by the river where the bridges were blown up, and from there you'll have to walk on your own." I said okay, and I set a date for him when he was to take me to that river. Then he gave me some rations of his own.

Then I walked about a day or day and a half across two mountains and went to see my mother. I was told that was the house where she was. There were so many women like her. No hair— their hair was just about like a chick's, just a fizzle about half an inch or so—you know, just coming out. And naturally my mother was burnt on her right side where the ray had hit her, and she looked like a monster with her hair like that. I said, "That's not her, that's not her." Then I started explaining, my name is Kazue Yamane, Kazue. My mother lived at such and such a place; do any of you know where my mother is? And the lady said, "That's her, that's her." So I went up to her, and I said no, that couldn't be her. Then she looked at me and she tried to talk to me. And then, I have a little mole on my back and I showed that to her and then she remembered. She was in such a state of shock or something, she wasn't herself either. And then we got to talking and we got to crying; I think we did more crying than we did talking. Then I found out that she had lost all her hair.

Our house was a very nice house in the city of Hiroshima. But the impact of the bomb had flattened it, and there was only one thing remaining. Just before the war got very bad, my mother had dug a hole and buried those big *kame* ("stoneware vats"), and put the albums in. She had one for me, one for my brother, things we had left behind—whatever she had in those days—and that was the only thing she had. That's the reason that we don't have any pictures of our family or my father or anybody; everything just went with the A-bomb. Anyway, she said that she crawled and crawled and got on somebody else's little wagon and then came as far as where she was now. They hardly had anything to eat.

I stayed with my mother and then I learned how to get back, to go over the two mountains, and walk some more, and take the train, and finally get to my father-in-law's place. And that I did twice. Then I got a job in Kure, which was the headquarters for the British Commonwealth and the American forces. But when the Americans found out that I had renounced my citizenship, they couldn't hire me. But they asked the British forces to take care of me. I worked for my uncle's construction company which got contracts like Fukuoka maintenance, Air Force maintenance, Etajima troop housing, and so forth. In the afternoons I worked for British forces training clerks, interpreters, and translators for the gift shops and the mess halls. I interpreted and taught them how to go about doing things.

I was being paid in the wages of indigenous personnel, Japanese wages, because I did not have United States citizenship and could not be hired as an American citizen. They paid me in terms of indigenous wages, but from them I got American food. But that too had to be bartered because we needed other things. We subsisted on sweet potatoes for two or three weeks and then on leaves of sweet potatoes for two or three weeks. In other words, we had very little to eat for the first two, three, months we were in Japan. I should show you some of the pictures of how my children looked when they were going to Japanese school. In midwinter they were wearing straw sandals, because we had to barter shoes to get rice. My brother had bought them some overcoats, but we had to barter them to buy futon.

When I sent my son Ken back to the States, that was the hardest decision ever for me to make. The economy was so bad in Japan that I could not raise my children, and Japan was no place for them. I wanted them to be brought up as Americans. Why? Because they were born there, and I still thought they had many opportunities there. The war devastated Japan, and we were not accepted in Japan either, first of all because we were different. But I had no one to send him to other than the family that brought me up, Mr. and Mrs. Stewart, who were attorneys. When I wrote to them, I told them all about my condition and that my children had to get back to the States where they must be brought up. Twelve years old was getting too old for Ken to start all over again, so I must send him. I asked Mrs. Stewart—I pleaded with her—if she could find some of her friends who would be willing to take our son. And she inquired many places and finally said there was a family in Marysville who would be glad to have Ken, and he could go to school there.

So I sent Ken over, all by himself, and I had to borrow money to send him back. I borrowed from the CIC officers with the understanding that in five years' time I would pay them back so much a month. And, so, when he was sent back, he stayed with this family in Marysville. Within six months I got a letter saying they did not want him anymore because he had taken some whiskey and things out of their home to the school. What happened was, first he was put in the first grade, then within two months he went up to the third grade and then fourth grade. Well, he wanted to play with the older children, and there was no way he could get in to play with them. He wanted to play football and basketball with them. They wouldn't let him. So he took whiskey out and gave it to the coach so that he would be allowed to play. Well, I didn't know that part of it. All I knew was that he had stolen some things and went to school, and school found out, and the school didn't want him. This family didn't want him either.

They told me to come and get him. Well, I went to the American Consulate with the letter, and they said, no, there's no way you can go to the United States because you haven't got U.S. citizenship. We only serve people who have American citizenship. So then I went to a Catholic priest, and I asked him, what do I do now? He said he would plead with the American Consulate. There was no way. I went to CIC and showed them the letter. There was no way.

Then I got another letter. They no longer could care for him and they were going to dump him, because they had found out that I had a distant relative in Los Angeles somewhere, and they were going to dump him there. So with that, I went to the American Consulate again and they said there was no way I could be allowed to go back. Then I heard nothing. I had no way of knowing where he was until one day I got a letter from him about six months later or so, saying that he was with a distant relative of ours, but they were so mean to him. They said that he was a thief, that the people who brought him down said that he was a thief. My distant relatives then said they didn't want a thief around the house and to get out.

He had no place to go. And he said he was going to school, and he went to see the counselor, and the counselor said, well, maybe we'll have one of the coaches take you in because he has a mother who is sick, and maybe you can stay there. In the meantime the Catholic priest and I were trying everything possible to see if we could locate him again and put him in someplace.

Well, since Ken didn't write to us, there was no way that we could get in touch with him. Then, the Catholic priest wrote to many Catholic churches around southern California and northern California. And I tried to find him through *Rafu Shimpo*. I put an ad in the newspaper, and I found him that way.

Finally a family came forth and said, they will take care of him until I was able to come back to the United States. And that was Mrs. Hendry who took care of Ken, and Ken from there went to Santa Clara and to San Jose and got a football scholarship. He then got his M.A., and he taught at Foothill College. Then the Hendrys, being alumni of the University of Southern California, obtained a job for him, and he's been there all these years. He's a very good coach, but as far as Ken is concerned, he has no mother—she died in Japan. He doesn't know anything about the life in Japan; he has nothing to do with that. Ken will not forgive me. I was not given a chance to explain the decision I made to send him back, but I'm glad I did because he is what he is today because I did. Whether he realizes it or not, I don't know, but I don't think I made a mistake. . . . He's doing all right.

I sent my second daughter back two years later, back to the United States for the same reason. I borrowed money again. It took me a long time to pay these debts—and to think my father-in-law had left enough money for them to be educated and all that. We haven't got a cent from that. My daughter Reiko went to Fresno because that's where we lived, and Mrs. Stewart had many lawyers and judges for friends. She said Judge Hoffman would be very glad to take her, somebody whom I had known from the days I was in Fresno too. Judge Hoffman took Reiko in. She, too, I guess tried very hard to be accepted and wanted, but within two or three years, she was let go for the simple reason that while she was bathing a child, she left the child and went to the telephone and the baby almost drowned. And this happened twice.

And then she was taken from home to home, and every time it happened I went to the American Consulate, I went to the Catholic priest, I went to the CIC, the American forces, and everywhere, but I was not able to come back. The Japanese homes in Fresno soon after the war barely had enough to subsist on, let alone take a stranger's child. So they only took her for one month here, two months there, because they knew my former husband and me. So they would write and write and write and say come and get her, we can't take care of her, she's done this, she's got boy-friends . . . and that tormented me no end. But like I said, I had no way of coming back to the States, so Ken and Reiko had to shift for themselves.

And, because of this trying period they decided that I had let them go because I didn't want them. But Reiko is a registered nurse now, and her daughter is becoming a registered nurse. I met her in Japan this time when I visited. A strange coincidence. I went over to my aunt's house, and who do I see but my daughter? All these years. We didn't have much to say. My aunt had tried awfully hard to establish contact there, but there were very few words spoken between us, and she took off.

You can cry about it, but what good does it do me? None. I like to help people. I like to live comfortably. I'd like to live in peace. I know in my own mind now from my last trip to Japan, that what I did for the children, for myself, for others, was the best course that I was able to take. I have no regrets whatsoever. I guess I came through, I had to live, I had to work.

In the days when this was all happening to me I had to take it day by day. But in the last six months since I started reliving this thing it was very hard. I have more peace of mind now. And seeing the children, even though they don't know that I'm up on their activities, that's a big consolation. They've done well. I think only America could have given them that opportunity.

IWATO ITOW

Bismarck, North Dakota

I was born in Cupertino, California, in December 1918. My family mostly raised strawberries and did sharecropping. We were poor farmers, and I started to work when I was about five years old. In strawberry farming we had to keep moving every so often, for new land, so we kept moving, like to San Martin and Watsonville. We moved to three or four places, even in Watsonville.

My schooling started in Redwood City; they called it Washington Elementary School, and that's where I started. Then I moved to San Martin. I went to elementary school there, and from there I went to Watsonville schools. When I graduated high school from Watsonville, I helped out with my father on a farm. My father wanted to go see his mother. He wanted to see her pretty badly, so he left in September 1941 for Japan. The day before he reached Japan they had a party on the boat, and he caught this ptomaine poisoning. He almost died. The Japanese papers here said one of the Itows from Salinas died. Salinas is about twenty miles away from Watsonville, so my mother wanted me to check and see if there's a person by the name of Itow who left Salinas for Japan. I went over to Salinas to check around, and they said nobody, so my mother said it must be your father. My mother and my sister left on the next boat, right away, to Japan to see what happened to my father. We had no news or anything like that. My mother and sister left America November 3; that was the last boat that left this country. After they left, I was the only one left here, and I had no contact with them.

In November 1941 I entered the Curtis Wright Technical Institute to learn to become a master aviation mechanic, and right after the war started they rejected all the Niseis. Then they let us go back with a permit for about a month or a month and a half, and after that we had to get out on account of our Japanese ancestry. There were fourteen of us and more than half were graduate aeronautical engineers, and they were taking a quick brushup course. But I was taking a master aviation mechanics course.

When they kicked us out, I mean the whole thing went black, and it just wiped me out. There was nothing I could do; I was just bitter. I'm still bitter about that, you know, my whole life is just ruined. It just went out the window and I can't understand why they did such a thing, and then they called this country a free country and justice and all this thing. I thought, well, I don't know, I just can't believe it. That was my dream school, you know. To become a master aviation mechanic. My father always said, to be an aviation mechanic, you have to have a steady hand and you have to be honest. You had to prepare for the school—like no smoking, no strong tea or coffee or things like that. See, you have to have a steady hand to work on instruments, and nearly all the measurements you make with a micrometer. You have to read small print and things like that. Actually it was my dream school, so when they kicked me out of the school I was bitter, I'm telling you. I was so bitter and still can't do anything about it.

Then I returned to Watsonville, and I stayed with my friends there. At that time we were frozen there; we couldn't move anymore. So with my friend, Mr. Fukuba, we voluntarily evacuated to Reedly, California. They said if we lived east of Highway 99, they wouldn't evacuate us or wouldn't put us in a camp. Mr. Fubuka bought property in Reedly, and we moved there in April, and then they said we had to evacuate. The funny thing is, they evacuated us and put us in camp just a week before he started to harvest the Thompson grapes. Everybody was ready to harvest the grapes at that time you know, and it seemed like everytime someone was ready to harvest something, they evacuated them just before they started harvesting. It seemed that way because I checked in Watsonville, I checked with a friend. They had strawberries, and they had everything all ready to harvest, and then suddenly they went to camp in Salinas. And they went to Poston too.

We didn't go to an assembly center. We got on a train, destination unknown. Everybody took it as it came. Reedly is a hot place around August, but when we got to Poston, it was real hot; it was about 125 degrees and I was sick. For about a week after we went to camp I could hardly eat or get a good night's sleep because it was so hot, and you have to live in a place like that for a while before you get used to it. And when it's 125 degrees, it's terrible, and lots of the people from places like Salinas passed out on account of the heat.

With all that kind of dirty treatment, we have to take all that, and they don't think nothing of it. Boy, talk about cruel! I mean, that's like taking a two- or three-year-old kid out in the desert and then tromping on and kicking him. That's pretty dirty, you know, and then on top of that they came around with a loyalty questionnaire. So I said yes, if drafted I'm willing to serve in the Army. And that caused a lot of trouble in camp too.

In Poston, I washed dishes for four months, and the other six months I drove a press car for the Poston *Chronicle News*, and I used to go from camps I, II, III, back and forth. But you know, I never tried to get away even though I had the car. Oh, not me. I know what some of those guards would probably do. They had a guard at the entrance, and then another thing, you couldn't go too far without suffering from heat and lack of water. Nobody ever attempted to do anything, even though, if you look across the Colorado River, there's California, but nobody would dare try to go through. Oh yeah, you couldn't get away from there. Not a chance.

In a camp, I'm a nervous guy and we're not doing nothing, just sitting around, wasting our life away. I said through all that it wasn't right for the government to do this, to a citizen. Anyway if I had to do my life over again I never want to stay here.

I was in Poston ten months. Then I got a permit to leave camp, so I went to Cleveland, Ohio. I got a job in Cleveland at the Lake City Malibu Company that made cast-iron parts for military equipment and things like that. But the main thing was to get an education, or become a master aviation mechanic. I was going to do it somehow, and I didn't give a darn what happened, I was going to complete the school. So I got the job, and I said to myself I was going to get the job and get out of there. Some way I could probably work my way into a school or even join the military air force. The FBI called all the ones that came out from the camp, and we had to get fingerprinted. I worked for about two to three months, and then I started looking around for another job myself. I was going to get some job, and in between try to get into an aeronautical school there. I went over and tried to get in some way, but I couldn't even get near the school, so I thought, oh well, I don't think I'll ever get a job.

It was about five and a half months later when the WRA officer called me into the office, and he got mad about me changing jobs and doing stuff like that on my own. They weren't about to help us out anyway, so I went over there and they kicked me out of the office. There was another guy in the next office, and he called me in there and he asked me what I'm going to do. I said, "I'm going to go to Tule Lake and probably from there on to Japan." And he said, "How about joining the 442nd?" I said, "Nothing doing." I said, "I'll volunteer for the U.S. Army Air Force ground crew, yes, any day." So I would've volunteered for Army Air Force ground crew, but he said, "Sorry, that's one place you can't go in."

So around November 10 I went to Tule Lake and was working on a hog farm with my friends and then I also joined a pro-Japan group that did morning exercises. I decided, I'm not about to rot in the camp, I mean, I'm going to join them and get up early in the morning and keep my health. We got up early in the morning and exercised and made noise you know. Everybody got mad at us, people got mad and they segregated us from the other people. I guess I was considered a troublemaker in camp, but we didn't make any trouble. What I did was get up early in the morning and made those noises, exercise you know. So they got tired of that and sent us to Bismarck, North Dakota. guess I was identified as pro Japan and a militant. I guess that's what they were saying, I don't know.

Fort Lincoln was at Bismarck, and it had a big building, an all-brick type of building, and it had a good-size room too, and it was sort of a military camp I guess. And nobody made any trouble there, and everybody was quiet. It was all fenced in and we could move around, but our letters were censored. Some of my friends wrote me a letter; it was all cut out.

All we did was go to the dining room about a half a block away and come back. And around May or June it started getting warm, and then they used to let us go out and do some sunbathing, and that's about it. I went through interrogation one time. The main thing they wanted to find out was whether we were pro Japan or something like that, I guess. At the end of November, somewhere around Thanksgiving, we got on a train. That was at the end of the war. Then I went to Japan from there.

I am bitter. There's a constant reminder of what I missed or lost out on because of the war, and then how they treated us. I am still bitter about that, and I don't think I'll ever forget, because every day there's a plane flying overhead, and when I'm working hard on a hot summer day and when I get pretty tired, I think about if I was working as a master aviation mechanic I wouldn't be sweating like that, you know, wouldn't have to work as hard, and I think of it every day.

My occupation now is gardener, and working the soil is one thing I wanted to get away from. It's real hard money, hard to do. That's why I went to Curtis Wright Technical Institute, but instead of that I'm right back again. I don't know.

EMI SOMEKAWA
Tule Lake

At the time of evacuation, I was married and had one child and was pregnant with another. I was born in Portland, Oregon. My family moved to Salem, Oregon, and was in farming. I graduated from high school in Salem and then went to train as a nurse in Portland, where I met my husband. And we lived there for two years, until the outbreak of the war when we were evacuated to the Portland Assembly Center. I graduated from nursing school in 1939. My husband was in business with his father, The Nichi Bey Fish Company, right in the heart of Japanese Town.

There were three of us Nisei nurses then at Emmanuel Hospital. We were received very well. At the time of Pearl Harbor, I was supervising at Emmanuel in the labor rooms. I had my training there, and when evacuation came, the administrator told me that any time I came back to Portland, that job would be there for me. But I wasn't too sure whether I was ever going to come back to Portland.

On December 7 we had just come home from church, and we heard it over the radio. Of course, everything goes through your mind. Now what? We're Japanese; I wonder how the neighbors feel toward us. But the neighbors were all very friendly; we had a German family living right next door. The family that we went to church with was a Caucasian family that lived right across the street. We felt like we were getting along fine in that neighborhood. For a few days we tried to stay close to home. We didn't go out shopping, but my husband did go to work. I think the thing that we felt the most was that the people who stopped in at our store thought maybe we should close it up. For our safety. But my husband said, "No, there's no need to do that. We're American citizens." But as things came out in the newspaper and on the radio as days went by, it really got worse. So then I felt, too, that we had to stay inside, and then we had a curfew. We had to have our lights out at eight. I had this small baby that was born August 31. So we just felt that we had to abide by all the rules and regulations that the government made. When April came along, we knew that we had to go. So my husband started selling things in the store.

When we first realized that an evacuation would take place, it was a depressing feeling that's hard to explain to you. My husband's father was an invalid by that time—I think he'd had his third stroke—and so he wasn't able to walk in May. I thought, well, the only thing that I can do is to take care of my small son and my husband's father. As long as we take care of these two people, I felt that that was the best thing that we could do. I didn't know whether we'd ever come back to our home again, but it was a feeling that all these years we'd worked for nothing. That kind of a feeling, you know, that you're just losing everything.

One thing that upset me, that was hard to take, was that we had this German family right next door, and they were as German as German could be, and they were free, they could do anything they wanted and nothing was bothering them. Why us? I felt like we were just being punished for nothing. It's something very, very difficult to explain. I don't really know how to put it in words, but the day we left the house, this German lady came with a cake, and she said that if there was anything that they could do for us, to call. So twice they came out to the assembly center. I think they felt like they were a little bit displaced too. I don't think they could help but feel that way.

The Portland Assembly Center was terrible. It's just amazing how people can think of putting another group of human beings into a place like that. There was so much horse and cow manure around. We were put into a cubicle that just had plywood walls and it was a horse stall with planks on the floor with about an inch of space between them. You'd find grass growing through the planks already, and it was just terrible. In the corner we saw this folding bed, army camp cot, with mattress ticking, and we were supposed to go out there and fill it with straw so that we would have a mattress. It's a depressing thing to think that we had to go into a place like that, but we were all there.

This was May of 1942. We were there until September of 1942. We lived in a horse stall from May to September, and my son was born in a horse stall. It was terrible, and that stench that came up from the ground, you know, was just terrible. So of course we didn't want to stay in it any longer than we had to; we'd just go over there and sleep at night. So most of the time people would spend the time right outside the door. Of course, there was a barbed-wire fence, only about five feet from the outside. That was more comfortable than being in our cubicle.

In September we went to Tule Lake. Now the reason we went there was that they needed nurses in the hospital. They did have a few RNs, but they needed more. When we arrived there, they had a message for me saying that they needed me at the hospital right away. They had about three Caucasian nurses. Of course, they took all the top priority jobs, and they didn't do any work. They just kind of watched over us and ran around the halls.

While we were at Tule my father-in-law, who was in Minidoka, became very ill, and we were given permission to go see him. That was a miserable, miserable trip. We were again put on a bus. My two children were still very small. This was in the spring of 1943. They both needed bottles and baby food, and we didn't have too much priority for seats on the bus. So my husband carried the older one, and I carried the little one, and we traveled that way.

We got to Burns, Oregon, and ran out of milk. Oh, gosh, that was terrible. They knew at the camp that you needed those red tokens to buy anything—canned foods or meat products. Everything was rationed. And of course, we didn't have anything like that when we were in camp. So I thought, well, there's not a thing I can do; I don't have any more. While we were in camp, we were allotted so much canned milk. So, I thought, I'll just have to go to the Safeway store and buy a can anyway, regardless of how much I'm going to have to pay for it. So I got my can of milk, and my son was allergic to just any kind of milk, so I had to get this special morning milk for him. I went up to the cashier and I said, "You know, I don't have a red token to buy this, but I need it for my baby because I'm traveling from Tule Lake, California, to another camp. I have no other way of providing him milk." Right then there was this lady right behind me, and she gave me the red token to pay for that milk. You know, right there in Burns, which is a real bad area, I think. There was a lot of discrimination and prejudice. But anyway, I was thrilled to death, because I didn't know how else I was going to ever buy it. I thanked her and bought the milk. It was one of the things that you just can't forget.

There was a case at Tule Lake of a lady who was pregnant, and she had a very serious cardiac condition. All through her pregnancy she spent most of her time in bed, under medication. She didn't quite reach full term, but she went into labor. The baby was in the neighborhood of about five and a half pounds when it was born, and the mother seemed to be in a coma at the time she delivered. I was there at the time of her delivery. I was on from three to eleven, supervising deliveries during those hours. The doctor who was attending her said that they didn't think that she would ever come out of it. The baby was good and healthy and a beautiful baby. She wasn't able to nurse the baby or do anything for the baby, because she was constantly under an oxygen tent. This went on for about ten days and she never improved. I felt, at that time, that there was really no other choice but to just keep her under oxygen, hoping that maybe there would be some miracle and she would improve.

One day her husband came and said that he just couldn't stand watching breathing, a very labored type of breathing, day after day. Would we please take her out of her misery. I was kind of shocked to hear him say that, but I said, "Well, I will talk to the doctor and see what he says." The doctor said we had nothing here to offer her, and if that's the wishes of the family, then he'll go along with it. And so then we talked about it and I think it was the next day the husband came back again with his family. This was her fifth pregnancy. He had four children, and they were all still little. The first one might have been in grammar school, but not much older. They all came. He had made his decision; this was what he was going to do.

So he talked to the doctor again, who told me to fix up a fourth of morphine. So I was there. There was a teaspoon there with some water in it, and the father told each child to give the mother a sip of water, and after the last child gave the sip of water, the father did the same thing, and then he was ready for the morphine.

That was it. That was it. Right away the oxygen tent was removed and she just went to sleep. You know, I feel this might have been a legitimate thing to do for a woman in that condition. But I still feel that if we were not in camp, that there might have been some other treatment.

The hospital facilities, of course, were very minimal, to say the least. The camp-based hospitals were not furnished with a sufficient number of bedpans, urinals, or washbasins. We never had enough linens, and we'd run around looking for blankets and pillows. The facilities were not there to take care of a hospital full of patients, and I think our base hospital in Tule Lake always had about eighty or ninety patients.

We had . . . oh . . . sad cases. We had one boy there, who was in his teens, and he was epileptic. We used all kinds of girls and anybody who wanted to help in the hospital. We had routine times when we'd take the temperature of all the patients. The girls would put thermometers in everybody's mouth; maybe we'd have half a dozen thermometers. Well, one time, one of the girls didn't know that the boy was epileptic. Anyway, he bit the thermometer, and he got all of that mercury in him. Well, you know, the hospital records didn't say anything like that. Just that he just died of natural causes. It's just one of these things that if you know the patient is epileptic, you use a rectal thermometer.
more." So he said, "Why don't you get organized the Japanese
These were just some of the things that happened. There were a lot of unnecessary deaths in camp. You wouldn't believe it. It's just that there were not enough people to watch the patients, not enough professionals. It's just that kind of thing.

We had another case where I remember a pregnant woman came in with just terrible pain, and she was having what we call an abruptio placentae, where there's bleeding in the uterus and it's absolutely necessary to operate right away and do a cesarean section. But there was no doctor to do the surgery. The woman died of a hemorrhage without delivering her baby.

I feel very bitter towards the whole thing. Now, this is just my feeling. I can't help but think that if it wasn't for evacuation, maybe I would have had a little different kind of a life. For one thing, when we got married in 1940, my husband didn't have any college education. We were thinking at the time that he would be going on to college while I worked. I felt it was time my husband got some education too. When he didn't have a chance to get that education, I think this was the thing that bothered me most, and that was what I was thinking about when we were put into camp.

Not only was it a most traumatic time in my life, but it was also the most frustrating period, because I felt that all of our accomplishments up to that time were gone. Yet, if it had to be this way with President Roosevelt's orders, we just had to make the best of it. I've often felt that we'd lost several years of my younger life because of being in camp. I'm bitter towards it. I have tried to cope with it the best I can by educating my children, and I've tried to serve the community the best I know how. I hope that something like this will never happen to another group of people or to us ever again. But sometimes I wonder.

RAYMOND KATAGI

Heart Mountain

I was born in Osaka, Japan, in January 1903. I have education in Japan, and I was working for the government for about three years, the Department of Finance. Meantime I was going to night school. My father was in the United States. I came here at twenty-one. That was 1924, before the new immigration law. If I miss that chance, then I won't never to come here. I came to Seattle where my father was. I went one year for the high school, and then I went into University of Washington for about a couple of years. I was studying journalism. I was in Seattle about four years, and then I came here to Los Angeles.

There was quite a few discrimination for some people; but in Seattle, their leaders among Japanese were very much Americanized mind, so in Seattle they didn't have too much of a discrimination compared with those people in California. Those people in Los Angeles who were educated here, they graduate from USC or UCLA but they cannot be able to get the job among the Caucasians. They all graduate from college, but they were working for the produce market.

The whole thing was more or less that those people are living in the country and they're doing the farming, and they always work hard, but they compete with Italians and Greeks. Between those people and Japanese was kind of competing each other, and Japanese was always came from behind, but they always get ahead of them. But in the business world, Japanese was way behind, so there's no competition, because they are all big, you know, big fellows in business. At that time, already in California, they have all kind of law that prohibit Japanese to own the land, and they separate Japanese school kids from Caucasians, and those sentiments just run all over.

I had the fruit market, three of them, but those people come around to me and then they say since Japan and America is close to the war and they ask labor union not to deal with Japan. But instead, you know, those people they took it, don't associate with Japanese, so I got so many customers stopped coming.

By December 7, I start working for the fellow by the name of Vincent Hallinan. I was working for the Vince. That was a Sunday, so we were eating together, lunch. Then that time, the news came. So all of a sudden, you know, Vince he was so surprised and I was surprised too. Then Vince said, "You know, maybe this sentiment, how it is now, you may not be able to stay here anymore." So he said, "Why don't you get organized the Japanese farmers and go to some other place, I mean beyond this restriction, and start a new farming, you know, some other place. Then I will furnish you money." But things gets worse and worse. Vince Hallinan told me if I could organize those farmers to go some other place, such as Colorado, or Arizona, but there was no time.

We had resentment, not about evacuation, but since I'm a enemy alien. I'm not the American born. My kids are. I only have one boy that time—he was only about four—so I didn't have anything, but so many people were arrested. So when evacuation came, I went to Santa Anita first.

But I never felt resentment for that, you know, because since war start already and we didn't start the war, we are all still enemy aliens. Whoever born in this country, you know, they have all kind of resentment. I didn't try to resist those things. I think end of August, we move into Heart Mountain.

At Heart Mountain, we were this council. We meet every morning, block managers mostly. These group is mostly Isseis, and we had argument among the councilmen's meeting that we should help the American side, to okay draft in Heart Mountain. There's so many people, they have their sons already grown—about seventeen, eighteen—and they were the one, to really start to talking about those thing. And their idea was they want their sons to be American citizens, full-fledged American citizens. So they should take the draft, and if they have to go to war, let them go. Most of the fathers said that way. Their sons went the same way, most of them. But I, at that time, I told them we shouldn't influence the Niseis. Let them decide themselves, see. As a council, we trying to promote those things, I don't like that idea. Let the young people decide themselves whether they want to okay draft or not. That's up to them. So, anyway, the decision in our council was yes on the draft.

But for their sons, they're born in this country, and they want them to get to be real American citizen, so they want them to fight for America. Mostly the Heart Mountain people are more or less well-educated people, among Japanese, and they were the community leaders before they go into the camps. They are rather to be Americans. When they came to America, at first, they were trying to make money. But as they live long in this country, they found out that this is a really good place to live, and their descendants have so much opportunity in this country, so they want their descendants to want to stay in this country, and they have same idea as those pilgrim fathers. So they wanted their sons to have chance to go in the Army. America is a land of opportunity, as long as you have a liberty. So they love the life to stay in this country and make their children to be staying here and contribute something to America. That was the Issei's idea, that we should let the Nisei go in the Army. That's the only way to get the full-fledged American citizenship. American citizenship is just a paper. You have to have some kind of contribution, so you could say in the community, Japanese did this and that.

There's so many capable people among Japanese farmers, they specialized in the chicken farm and hog farm and just regular garden, vegetables such as turnip, carrots, peas, and tomatoes. Things like that you know. They trying to start that themselves instead of just working for the camp. They just made up their mind and soul, they could able to do so. So they like to do it, since this Heart Mountain desert make one of the outstanding rich place in Wyoming. So they start and they made so many things, just like they raised the hog, they raised the chicken, and the eggs and things like

that just come from their own ground. They start having confidence, you know, desert like this could be a rich land. They raised
the vegetables and all kind of roots things. Finally they had so
many things abundant, so they send them out—potatoes, ruta-
bagas, carrots, and things like that; they send them out to the other
camps trying to help a little bit.

They saw foresight, you know. Clear, after the war. During the
war they trying to help the war effort. They see things because the
wars only last so many years. But after the war, Japanese could able
to do something for the benefit of this country. The same attitude
lead the Issei to say, let our sons go in the Army. They start thinking about whatever we do here now will contribute to the Japanese
in later life.

Those sixty-three people that resisted the draft, they have their
rights to do so, and they have so many resentments, you know, but
in any kind of movement like that, there is a people behind of
them. Many young people are just very pure of heart, but some
people just trying to make, well, hero out of themselves.

I came back to Los Angeles, but that was 1944. See, again, I
thought, you know, there's so many Japanese in camp. There's so
many people they have not the money. They have so many kids
and they can't start. They don't know how to start. So this Seabrook Farm, they offer us the job. I became the relocation coor-
dinator, so I studied about those things and finally came to see the
point that those people who has not anything, they should go out
and prepare for the end of the war. So I told those people, why
don't we start to prepare for after the war? About one hundred
people went with me to Seabrook. But, I told them, some people
who's got enough land in California or elsewhere, they shouldn't
go to any other place. They should go back to California. So I just
decide to get those people who have not money to go with me and
trying to find out something new. Even this you know, things not
come out so good, but still, they have that much experience.

I am an American citizen now. I got the citizenship in 1959. This
is my country. I went through all kind of troubles, but even so, I
know Japan, and then I know this country. I start knowing this
country, and there's so many resentment towards the Japanese,
but that all could eliminate, see; that's up to us.

When come to the war, this country is the almighty, and each individual can't say too much about it. We resent it, all right, but you can do nothing about it. The order come, you have to sell out the house and move into some other place. But I do not resent it. The only thing is, see, what do you get out of it? My way is, whatever comes ill-fortune to us, that isn't real. Ill-fortune inside of us, see. Not come from outside. The fighting spirit is also inside. That's my idea, see.

SHIG DOI

Tule Lake 442nd Regimental Combat Team, France, Italy

I was born in Auburn, a little town about thirty miles northeast of Sacramento, on March 30, 1920.

The whole family worked on an eighty-five-acre orchard, with grapes, peaches, and pears. We bought it a couple of years before the war broke out. My folks were aliens. They weren't allowed to become citizens, and aliens in California couldn't own land. This is what most of the Issei did: when my oldest brother got to be twenty-one, they used his name to purchase the land. It was a good opportunity, eighty-five acres. We were all just coming out of the Depression, but the land that we wanted was just perfect for us, and it came with the horses and a tractor and some other things. It was really a good deal.

So in 1939 and 1940, we worked it within our family. I guess all the Nihonjin, that's how they did it—a family deal, so a lot of the money didn't go out of the family. Even if the fruit didn't sell for a good price, we were able to pay the taxes and keep going.

In the meantime, around 1940 or so, we had this Sino-Japanese war going on in Manchuria, and things were getting rough. But we still decided to keep on adding farming equipment; we bought a tractor, a disc, and a truck—all the things that you want to farm. So we were getting self-sufficient with all the money we were making.

But, at the time, Placer County, where we lived, was a hotbed of prejudice and discrimination. It was really a hotbed. Many rednecks, I guess they call them. Even when we were in elementary school we would always have fights. If somebody said, "Why, you dirty Jap . . ." those were fighting words. We used to get even with the whites when it snowed. Once in awhile, it snows up there. Then we had these snowball fights, and we would really give it to them. We'd soak up the snowball with cold water and really make it hard.

But during the high school, we didn't have that kind of fight except during the forty-niners celebration. I remember one time this kid had come from Japan. And this Hakujin kid didn't know he was a good judo man. So the Hakujins decided that anybody who wasn't dressed in a forty-niners costume, they were going to throw in the fishpond in front of the high school. They found out different after they picked on him. He took on about seven of them—bang, bang, bang. So after that, they left him alone.

But the hostility and prejudice . . . even the teachers were that way in the high school. There was a certain feeling—the white kids used to kind of keep to themselves, and we used to keep to ourselves. At certain times, some of us would mix with the whites, but as a whole, we kept to ourself. Our friends were always Nihonjin.

It's always been a prejudice country. You could feel it. You could feel it even more so during the war. And my folks felt the brunt of it when they came back from camp after the war. You see, some of the white kids that went to the school never made it back, because they went to the Pacific and they died there. So that explains the hostility. So during and after the war, in 1944 when my folks came back, they hit a brick wall.

They were the first ones released from the camp. They were in Amache, and they decided since we had the land they wanted to come home. They wanted to run the orchard and to come home. Since our land was debt free, not like others who had mortgages foreclosed, my dad had leased it out before we left for camp.

All this happened when I was overseas. I didn't know about it until I got back home. First, they were going to dynamite our packing shed, but somehow the fuse didn't go off. So second, they were going to burn it down. Well, there's always good in some people, and one of the fruit managers told my brother, "Watch out, they're going to burn your shed down tonight." So my brother had the firehose ready, and the minute he saw some flame he was able to put it out. Then the following night they fired a shotgun through our house. When I got home, my mother showed me where all these pellet marks were.

This was around November of 1944. That's just when we rescued the Lost Battalion and we were cut down to nothing. In fact, out of my company of 230 men, I was one of the 23 men to walk out, and I only had 6 riflemen left. See, I was getting shot at from the enemy, and then at home in my own country, people were shooting at my dad. I was risking my life for this country, and my government was not protecting my folks. And they came home from camp with nothing.

When my company got to southern France we were at a point where we just had to wait for the replacements. We just didn't have any fighting strength. This was a quiet front between France and Italy. So I had my platoon up the hills, and we used to go patrol every day. Some guys would talk about how people were shooting at my family, and then one would say, "Hey, why are you here risking your life? Why don't you go over the hill to Nice and enjoy yourself?" Well, God, you can't just take off. After all, you've got your whole platoon up there with you, and you can't say, "I'm gonna quit and take off." They would have probably court-martialed me anyway. So that's how the thing was.

All three of us boys were in the service. My youngest brother went in the service to Japan. He went late, which made things hard for my family. This shows you how harsh those Placer County guys were—the white guys up there on the draft board. And they drafted my oldest brother after the war was over. They didn't need to draft him when two of us were already in the service. One of us was deferred, and that's how we used to eat. So they made it hard for my dad who couldn't drive and my mom couldn't drive. In Placer County the lawyers' sons got deferred, but us peons got sent.

All the way through, they wouldn't even sell my parents anything. They wouldn't sell these boxes to pack fruit. So my oldest brother had to go all the way to Sacramento to buy boxes. Then they wouldn't handle my family's fruit, so the family had to take it up to Sacramento to ship it out. By then, the three of us were in the service.

In 1942, I went to the Monterey induction center and was sent to Camp Grant in Illinois as a basic trainee. After basic, I worked in the dental lab through part of 1944, and then all the Nisei got shipped out to Camp Blanding in Florida. Almost a thousand went down there. Later on we found out why we were there. The 442nd and the 100th were fighting in Italy. They needed replacements, so they scrounged the whole United States Army, and whoever had a Japanese surname ended up in Alabama or in Camp Blanding for combat training.

While we were at Blanding, we were due for furloughs, and they threw the loyalty questionnaire at us. We were supposed to answer those questions, Will you serve your country? and If you were asked to go overseas, will you go? So naturally, I said, if necessary, I'll go overseas. They gave me a twenty-one-day furlough to go home, but I couldn't come home to the West Coast. And by then, my folks had transferred from Tule Lake to Amache in Colorado.

But before that, when I was in Camp Grant, my first sergeant asked me once why I never went home on furlough. I said to him, "Where would I go? I have no home." He didn't believe me and said that everybody had a home, a family to go home to. So I told him, "Okay, if you don't believe me go ahead and look it up in my files. You'll find out I can't go back to the West Coast." So a couple of days later he calls me and says, "Yeah, goddammit, Shig, you're right, you can't go home."

So when I took that twenty-one-day furlough from Blanding, I didn't go home to the West Coast but went to see my folks at the Amache Relocation Center. I think I only spent two or three days at Amache because it was so depressing that I couldn't stay anymore. I told my mom that I was going back to the army camp, but I stopped in Omaha on the way to visit an army buddy. That was a lot better, you see, because my mom was trying to do her best to keep me happy. The day that I was supposed to leave she wanted to make me something, but she couldn't fix anything for me. There wasn't anything. She felt really bad about not having anything for me. So I took the bus from there to Omaha, and when I got on the train one Caucasian guy asked me, "What kind of camp is that? What kind of army camp is that?" And Jesus, I just couldn't tell him what the hell it was. So I kept my mouth shut.

At the end of my furlough, I had to report to Camp Shelby. It was at Shelby that the headquarters of the 442nd had some kind of idea that some of the Blanding group were no-noes and weren't willing to go overseas. So every night we had a bloody fight. They would come down from headquarters but they didn't know who to pick on, they didn't know who the no-noes were. But after we shipped out to Fort Meade, I found out who the guys were that refused to go, who became no-noes. Some of those guys were back here enjoying life. That's what hurts me, you know, because some of us went into the service together.

The guys in Shelby—some died, some got crippled. This redress thing should be for the people like that. But surely the people who deserve it are not going to benefit. Like my dad. They're gone. Like my wife's father. He was interned as an enemy alien for four years and separated from his own children. They're all gone. That's why I say it hurts, it hurts me a lot. Because we fought like this for the benefit of . . . Those who deserve it are not going to get it.

One of my friends and I were the only ones in ROTC in school. The other guys ridiculed us before the war. But it was really hard on my friend. When he volunteered from Tule Lake in 1942, they said you know, the Japanese line, *"Inu ga koko de taberu"* ("Dogs eat here"). They put a bone on a separate table. The people who gave everybody a hard time at Tule Lake today act as though nothing happened.

I have no regrets about what I did. I can look at everybody in the eye and I have no shame. I'm glad I served. I did what I had to do. And I have no regrets. I don't mind people calling me names as long as they don't do me body harm. That's their prerogative. And they said no-no. Well, how many who went back to Japan came back here? All of them. The 442nd wrote the history for the Japanese. It was a good stepping-stone for the Buddha-heads, and we paid dearly for it. It's something we left that the future generations can be proud of.

But I don't think that settles everything. Just think of all those people—of the 990 that went over, not more than 200 of them came back without getting hit. If you look at the 442nd boys, don't look at their faces, look at their bodies. Then you'll find out how much they've suffered. They got hit hard, some lost their limbs.

I could tell you all this, but actually, to feel it, you had to be there. You would know the agony, the frustration, everything, while you were there. All this, and then, you'll wonder why you get kicked around.

I had the 36th Division general hit me on the head. Twice in a row he wanted me to push on. He wasn't worried about the 442nd and us guys; he was worried about his own men, the 36th Lost

Battalion. So he committed all three of our battalions. I remember the first day he came up. He hits me on the head and says, "Soldier, you can't do anything here." Well, if you ever see the forest in the Vosges Mountains—my God, your enemy is ten or twenty feet away from you. The only reason I could fire at them is because the German has a white face, compared to the Nihonjin. So when he peeks out at us between the bushes and the tree, I fired. You hop from one tree to the next tree. We had them scattered so much, they might be in the back of us. The 36th Division took off and left a lot of their machine guns behind. So the Germans were firing our machine guns, and you couldn't tell the difference. It was really a mixed-up deal. I don't know why we went. I guess it's just something we had to do.

There's a guy in Oakland, Akiyama, who I met years after the war. I was working for the county, and he was working over here in a factory. I was looking at his head, and he had a scar right up here. "Jesus," I said, "Goddammit, I know where you got hit. You got hit in that Banzai hill going after that Lost Battalion." He said, "How'd you know?" I said, "You went after that guy with a tommy gun and the other guy was already shot and you got shot by that sniper. I went after you, and I don't know why to this day that sniper didn't shoot me."

You see, the sniper took two guys right off. The first guy was dead. He got shot going after the guy with the tommy gun. We were using a lot of tommy guns then, because in a close-quarters fight, tommy guns are better—a tank can't move. But the only time you get .45 ammo is from the guys in the tank: You knock on them and say, "Hey, we need more ammo," and they'll just put their hand down and drop it out for you. And then they'll say, "Can't you see that machine gun right in front of you?" Well, they got a periscope, they could see really good. They could take their time and see, while us guys, we got to scan, you know, from here, and next, and next to see if the Germans are there. So if they're camouflaged really good, you're going to miss them. Well, tank guys say, "Right in front of you." This is how we fought in Vosges. That's why we lost so many men.

I also climbed that cliff at the Gothic Line. I was mad because we had a 10th Mountain Division out there trained for mountain fighting. And we were climbing just like goats. If you fall, you'll roll down, way down. We were lucky that day. Our company was the assaulting company. I was in the 3rd Battalion, so we got companies L, K, I, and M. The four companies are the rifle companies.

We assaulted that hill. We went into this little village there. We got there about two or three in the morning. They had a cobblestone street. And why the Germans never knew we were coming, I don't know, because when our guys said, ten minute break, everybody took his helmet off, and clonk, clonk, clonk, clonk. It hit the cobblestone and God, you could hear the thing go way down the valley.

Our guys said, "All right, nobody goes out in the daytime." I wasn't going to just sit. The whole company was in one small room. And everybody was saying, "God, I can't sleep." So I got my platoon and said, "Hey, I found a good place." I didn't know in the south part of Italy they sleep upstairs; and downstairs in a barn I found some nice corn stacked up, and it was really like a mattress. Hey, this is going to be a good idea. I got all my men down there. And Jesus, during the night something started crawling, and everybody said, "Hey did you guys feel any crawling last night?" and God, next morning, you're full of fleas. Man, I have everybody outside slapping themselves, and we're not supposed to get out there in the daytime, because the Germans were way up there and they could see us. The hell with the Germans, I said.

So I had fleas, and by the end of the campaign they were nice and fat. They chewed on me all the way through. We ordered a DDT powder and finally got rid of them. But we assaulted that night. L Company led. I Company followed. And we got on top of the ledge way up there and we caught them napping. And it's a good thing because they would have mowed us down like nothing. Because, yeah, the hill that we went up, a machine gun had the whole side covered. We caught that guy napping.

There was a guy who took basic with me named Hanamura in L Company, and he lives in Alameda. When we got up there, he was laying on a stretcher and I said, "Hey, what happened to you?" "Well, they shot me right through the . . ." They couldn't carry him down, it was so steep, so they left him there overnight.

The 92nd Division was sitting for a whole winter on the Gothic Line until we came in. It was the same with the 36th Division. They were sitting there until we made a breakthrough. Then they took off and went too fast and got trapped. That's why we were always, I think, expendable to our army. I don't know, all those stories—What the hell, they said, they're just Japs anyway.

That's the way I felt in the service. Because we always seemed to get the hard part of it. We'd get pushed out of towns we would take. We couldn't be there to enjoy it; we were always in the outskirts. We're always doing the flanking protection for somebody's division. The rear echelon guys always enjoyed the benefit of the whole thing. So you can't help but wonder, because we always seem to get the hard part. Okay, you take the Lost Battalion. You attack with two battalions. You never commit three. Why couldn't the 36th Division do their own rescue?

Why was the 442nd so good? It's not that we had to prove anything. We were reckless because we were young, you know. I will never do the things now that I did at that time. I would think twice. But if I had to do this thing over again and if I were to hit a front line, I'd rather be with the 442nd. I guess, it's upbringing, the family, the closeness of the family ties. When you're like that, you and your buddy are close. You have to figure also that the life of infantry is minutes. You count it in the minutes and seconds. If you're unlucky, boom, the first bullet has got you. So if you're a replacement, the saddest part is that you say, "What happened to that guy?" They say, "Oh, he *ma-ke up*," Hawaiian pidgin for "he got killed." They say nobody knows his name.

Like I was telling my wife, the last patrol I went on, I had a sergeant in communications who was a really good friend of mine. And he said, "Look, Shig, don't do anything reckless, I think the war's going to end." He kept telling me that. He said, "A and B tried to take that town. You're only taking one platoon, you're not going to do it." Then he said, "It took C Company to bring 'em out." So, I didn't get halfway in before I had a new communications sergeant. We had mail call and I said, "Go ahead and read your mail." We got mail a few more times, yet. He said, "Nah, I'll come back and read it." It was from his wife, I think; he was married. He didn't get back, he got killed. And to this day, I don't know where he got killed. So that's the sad part, one part of the life in the infantry. To this day, I don't know how I got through all those campaigns.

I was fighting almost by myself, and I was the twelfth man to hit the Lost Battalion. We were talking about Tak Senzaki, a real hotshot guy from Seattle. He never would stay quiet; he wanted to fight all the time. Golly, we got lost because we had a lieutenant who couldn't read a map worth a damn. He took us down the wrong hill, and we ended up in no-man's-land. I only had an M1 and eight cartridges, just eight rounds. The rest of them had the same rounds. So God, you looked down and somebody says, "Those guys are Germans." Holy cow!

Then we saw this yellow communication line going up to them and this guy said, "Shall we cut?" "Hell no, don't cut it, they're going to come looking for it." So we go up there and pretty quick we see a guy digging. We could hear the shovel. Than you peek over there, and those guys are setting up a machine gun. So then they heard us and they started chasing us, and that's where I got my ear blasted. Because, God, they had a flanking movement to catch us. We had about ten guys. We had a rookie and this guy from Seattle had a tommy gun, so he says, "Hey, let 'em come close, let 'em come close." We were waiting for them, letting them come close, but the rookie guy gets all scared, so he gets up and bam. . . . They missed him the first time but got him the second time. Then all hell broke loose. The big guy lobbed a hand grenade at us. Then they took off and we took off.

So we were going around this corner, around a bend, and God, here we meet again, ran right into each other. God, they started running, and everywhere, bang, bang. You know, it's hard to hit a running guy. I never have. We were lost the whole day. I had a hole right through my . . . somebody took a potshot out of my hide. Somebody said, "Shig's got a hole in his pants." I looked, and that's the closest one ever got to me. I came through all that.

The Lost Battalion was the worst because I had never seen men get cut down so fast, so furiously, caught in machine-gun crossfire. They were crafty fighters, too, you know. That's the reason, I think, they wanted people who were young—eighteen, nineteen, twenty—and reckless. In the infantry if you're married and you play it too cautiously, it seems like you get hit. They're too cautious on the line. I'd think they'd be worrying about lots of things, you know. But I was on top of Banzai Hill and somebody hollered, "Tank," and boy, I ran the other way because I wasn't going to tackle a tank by myself.

But this is the whole Lost Battalion thing. If we advanced a hundred yards, that was a good day's job. We'd dig in again, move up another hundred yards, and dig in. That's how we went. It took us a whole week to get to the Lost Battalion. It was just a tree-to-tree fight, and a tank couldn't go there.

I could never figure out why the Germans never attacked us right after we got to the Lost Battalion. They could have run us right off, but they must have been hurt just as bad as we were. We were so tired. The next morning we would have been all dead. But I found out everybody bleeds red, and it doesn't make a difference if he's white or black. And everybody hollers when he's hit. But it's hard to think that young men like that die by the hundreds, you know. You see a corpse lying there and turning wax blue. I guess ours wasn't too bad because at least the stink wasn't there. It was cold so the body didn't decay as much as during the summer.

I don't know, it's just that a lot of funny things go on. The people who's unlucky is just unlucky. You get it, that's all. You could hide underneath the biggest rock and still get it. There's a guy from Chicago; he used to always want to dig a foxhole with me. So he was digging under the great big rock on the other side of the Lost Battalion. All of a sudden he hit something and he said, "I can't dig anymore. Can I get in your foxhole?" "Yeah," I said, "you could stay with me tonight." The next morning the railroad gun hit that thing and knocked the rock to smithers. Wham . . . it hit underneath the rock. If he was underneath it, he would have been buried. And my bazooka man, we took him along on a last patrol. Good thing he was out of his foxhole. He came back and he saw a mortar shell right inside his foxhole.

Then I had another guy who would never fire at a German. He could spot them though; I couldn't spot them. He could tell me, "Hey, he's right over there, he's right over there." I would say, "Why don't you shoot 'em?" He couldn't shoot them. He would never shoot them. I think he got hit, and I never did see him after that. Funny, I don't know why he was there; he could have been a conscientious objector. He would have been better off instead of being out there. But he sure could spot them!

When it was all over for us, the guys who went through all the combat didn't get the glory. We were coming home on points, so we came back earlier to our homes. We didn't take the glory. The guys that came after, the ones that volunteered after awhile got to march down Pennsylvania Avenue.

After everything we went through—the evacuation, the war—

sure you're bitter. Somewhere in this corner I have a scar that will never be gone. If you hurt a person, you say something and you apologize, but that isn't going to bring anything back. You've been hurt and the scar is there and it'll stay till the dying day.

But mostly, it's just the people that gave my folks a bad time, that's what hurts me most. I don't know, I guess it's because they were back here enjoying the benefit of my protection, and my dad, my dad must have died with a broken heart. He died young. My mom died young, too.

I did what I had to do, and I have no regrets. But people made it rough for my family. And that's what hurts me most.

JACK
TONO

Heart Mountain

I was born in 1920 and grew up south of San Jose. My father was a strawberry farmer. Pearl Harbor day was in December, and in the wintertime there's not too much to do, so we were down in Edenville about eight miles south of San Jose. I was working in a packinghouse for Durio Brothers—broccoli, celery, all that stuff. There was about one-third Nihonjin and the rest of them Hakujin.

Well, we heard it over the radio and we figured it was one of those things. It didn't hit us that bad, you know; we all got along good with everybody. So the first impression was, it didn't affect me one way or the other. And the only country we knew was the U.S. All being citizens, a bunch of us were talking that we eventually would have to go. Go to the Army and defend the country, that was about the main thing. Other than that, there wasn't a hell of a lot else. At least I never ran into anything that was bias, nothing like that.

But when I heard we were going to be evacuated, I was really disappointed then. I said, what the heck, we didn't even commit a thing, and we have to be evacuated. I just couldn't understand the whole atmosphere of the whole thing, being a citizen. I could see it if I was an alien. You have no choice but to face things like that. But at the JACL meeting when they came out and nobody resisted—they're all for it in such a way to help the government out with this evacuation business—it was more shocking than the goddarn Pearl Harbor attack. It really frosted me. These people up front conducting that meeting—they're all professional people with college backgrounds, and none of them resisted. They just went along with voluntary evacuation because they said they had to. I think it was about two meetings that I went to in late January, 1942. This was prior to the order.

So that was a disappointing thing. Right then and there I thought there's something wrong because there was no ethnic group as straitlaced as the Japanese because of their historical background. Like my father, born in the Meiji era, those guys were pretty macho guys, you know. So we're all brought up with honor, shame, dignity; the moral code of standards is nothing but the best. When you talk about delinquency and other crime, for us there was nothing but traffic tickets. And yet they would commit us to a prison, in a camp, without a trial or nothing. That really got to me. To this day I'll never forget it. Really something.

I think we were the first batch to leave San Jose. We went to Santa Anita and stayed for three months, and then we went to Heart Mountain. How did I react to Heart Mountain? I didn't react. It didn't faze me one bit. After everything else, I don't think I gave a damn. After the treatment we got as citizens, I just, I just didn't care. So when you looked at it that way, it didn't faze you. I didn't care what was going to happen to me because we were put into camp without being tried or anything. You were committed without even being guilty. We learned nothing like that in school, you see. So that's where a lot of people just turned around and lost hope for the country, I think.

But before evacuation I was ready to join the Army, because this is the only country that I knew. I never traveled, nothing. Born and raised in this country, educated here. So I was all ready to go. When this evacuation started, that just broke the back of a lot of the guys. I'm not trying to be antagonistic, but from then on it made me fight for my rights and principles more and more, you know. From then, I said to myself, well doggone it. We were brought up with the very highest moral standards, and why should I take a backseat to anybody. From then on, I didn't take a backseat to nobody.

I was only a twenty-year-old kid then, and what we saw wasn't right, but we couldn't do much. We were up against the government to start with, and nobody was resisting, so I thought, what's the use? Everybody's for it, so you went along with the program.

As I got older and I went to different places, I got educated real fast. But at Heart Mountain I said to myself, here's a President saying that we have to go out and preserve democracy. You start thinking, where the hell is the democracy we learned in school? Hey, wait a minute now. When I have to give my life up for democracy, I want to see the goddamn thing first. That's the reason when I testified later at the trial I said all we wanted was our prior livelihoods, as in the prewar days. All the families living as they were. Then we said, we'd go. We weren't completely against defending the country, but we wanted what we had before first, and then we'd go and fight.

There was this Fair Play Committee. They were also the guys preaching democracy, what it should be. But what we were then going through had nothing to do with democracy. These other guys were trying to educate us and told us to go out and fight. But what kind of democracy is it when your parents, your brothers, and sisters are in camp and you have to die for the country? There's no such thing as that kind of democracy. At one meeting we had about two hundred or three hundred guys before the FBI come and picked us up. And they wanted a show of hands to see how many guys weren't going. Well, naturally, you know how they are. Everybody raised their hands. I thought to myself, holy Christ, this is great. Where the hell you going to put all our two or three hundred guys. So I'm really happy. At least this way we got the mass to fight for what's right. So come April 3, 4, what do you know, the FBI rounded us up. In two days there were sixty-three of us out of the whole mass left.

They knew who we were because we were the guys that didn't report for physicals when we were supposed to. Well, a week or two later, I think they came around. I happened to be at home and the FBI said, "You Jack Tono?" I said, "Yeah." "FBI." I said, "Okay." I had my stuff ready and went with the rest of the guys. Then we went to Cody, Wyoming, where we were interviewed and fingerprinted. And from there, I was sent to Casper, Wyoming, and then we had guys at Laramie, and Cheyenne, Wyoming. So we were put in three county jails: Casper, Laramie, and Cheyenne. This is April, and the trial wasn't until June, the third week in June, I believe. So we spent all that time in a county jail. In the meantime, the families got in touch with the American Civil Liberties Union, and they took the case.

Failure to report for physical, that's the only thing they could get us for. All the same convictions, so we had a mass trial for all sixty-three. That's why when our case went up to the Supreme Court, Fujii was aphabetically first on the list, so it's *Fujii v. the United States*.

The attorney told us that not reporting for the preinduction physicals is a federal offense. We knew that already. Then he said, "Well, you could have taken your physicals, but you're not in the Army until you take an oath." I didn't want to have nothing to do with that way of looking at things. When the trial started, the prosecuting attorney said that this group of boys, men, didn't report for their preinduction physical, which is a federal violation. So we knew right then that that was that. We told our attorney the reason why we didn't report was because we were put behind barbed-wire fences, the evacuation, and so forth. We were put into camp without even a trial. What crime did we commit? All that we brought to the trial.

By the time the judge sentenced us, it was about the 25th of July. In the meantime we were all in the county jail; sixty-three of us were put into a place that only holds twenty-four guys. They had bunks, but we had to sleep on the floor. We knew we were going to get it because at the end of the first day, the judge said, "You Jap boys," and then he corrected himself, see. So when we went back to the county jail I told the guys, I said, "This son of a bitch, he's got it in for us. Don't have high hopes. This guy, he's going to give it to us." And sure enough, he did.

We were sentenced to three years in the federal penitentiary, which didn't faze me one bit at that time. Of course, I was single. And we had older guys, married, with families. I don't know about those guys. It must have hurt them being the head of the family and going to the penitentiary. Yet, I give them a lot of credit because they stuck it out. Even putting the family through all the hardship. Us single guys, we didn't give a damn, you know. We weren't tied down to nothing. So when they separated us, those aged twenty-five and under went to McNeil Island outside of Tacoma, Washington. Thirty-three of us went there. They said, it's a much cleaner place and it's a much better place, and so they sent the young guys there. Then the married guys and their relatives all went to Leavenworth, Kansas. Thirty went there. They had it tough.

So at McNeil, for the quarantine period of one month, we had to stay in the big house. Naturally we got interviewed by all the psychiatrists and the doctors, and reverends come over. They tried to talk you out of it. We all had our minds set and that was it. There was nobody who could talk us out of nothing. I told the reverend, "Look, Reverend, suppose you were in my shoes? What would you do?" He said, "Personally I believe in what you guys are doing." That's what he said. I said, "I know that."

So after the quarantine period in the big house, we were all sent to the farm, which had a capacity for three hundred guys, and one hundred were Jehovah's Witnesses who were religious objectors, you know, who couldn't get ministerial deferments. And there were a lot of black-market violaters.

Oh, Christ, man, and those lifers were with us. Toughest criminals, but they're all human beings. They're no different. And life was no different at McNeil Island than at Heart Mountain. The only thing we didn't have was the family or the women. That's the only difference. They got the best of you, you know. Like the government says, we'll teach you. That's the attitude they had. So they put me with the worst goddarn guard over there. We used to call him Scrooge. He was a damn ignorant Oakie, and one time I told him, "You're so damn ignorant you couldn't hold a job on the outside. That's why you're working here." But, they can't do nothing to you in there.

So, here's a Jew and an Irishman and myself. The rest were about twenty Jehovah's Witnesses, and we went out to this tomato field and had to pull weeds. So I told Rosenthal and Hardy, I said, "The hell with this son of a bitch. Let's pull one little weed at a time. That's all we pulled, you know, one at a time. My God, the line was about a quarter mile long and we only got about two plants done. The guard was hotter than hell. So we got a pink slip, and you have to go to court.

Every Tuesday afternoon we had court. The superintendent was a judge, and then you had to look at a psychiatrist, a parole officer, and a doctor. They were the jury. They read out the offense. They said I wasn't putting out enough work. So I told them, "I'm doing my best out there. I can't do no better than that." "Oh yes, you can," they said. I said, "The hell with you. I can do only what I'm doing now." I lost some privileges but I didn't care.

So, you know, more and more you think about democracy, like a rubberband, you know, they stretch the law many different ways. One side they apply it this way; next one, they get it right up your neck and you're just about hung. I just thought that they were a bunch of idiots. First of all, I was 1A before I went into camp. Then I went into 4C classification. Now 4C is just for enemy aliens only, right? I said to myself, what's going on here? Then afterwards, I got a 1A classification right after that again, before I went for the physical. So I said, we're dealing with people that gave us all this classification without a hearing or interview of any kind. Why did we get the 4C? Why did we get the 4F or 1A? Every time we get some card from the draft board, it would change the classification. So more and more you start thinking, we're citizens and we're treated like enemy aliens. Then when they want you in the service, you're citizens again. Yet, you're in camp, you know, it's really confusing.

But then in the camp the JACL was going around telling the people that we have to go prove our loyalty. And then I said to myself, for Christ sake, what the hell do we have to prove it for? We haven't done nothing. That was a farce. I couldn't believe this kind of thing was going on. We have to prove our loyalty. I said, good God, and I told them where the hell to go. And then one of them got the goddamn gall to call us fascists and everything in the Wyoming paper. And I thought to myself, I could have shot him. But these were the kind of things they tried to pull on us guys—that we're doing an injustice to the men in uniform, that in time of war we have to go along with the government and work with the government—all this kind of stuff. Patriotic stuff. I said, like we stated in our trial, that we're more than willing to defend our country. Give us our priorities. What we had in the prewar days, that's all we want. We're not asking for the arm or the leg of the government. For crying out loud, give us what we had. That's all. Then we'll go.

Our parents were all aliens. They couldn't get their citizenship until 1952. When anything went against them, they had this last word, which they said all the time, *Shikataganai* ("Can't be helped"). So you hear this all the time as you're growing up, you know. They get discriminated against, and you hear this constantly, and it kind of gets bred into you. And I think that's the main drawback that's embedded into them, because even now when I talk to those guys they come out with that feeling, so why go into it?

Among my guys that resisted the draft, there was this reunion, and I was really disappointed. I said, "Gee whiz, a lot of you guys were leaders at that time." And I said, "We got pardoned by Truman. The only time you get pardoned is if you win the case." I said, "They wouldn't give it to you any other way. So, *we won*." I said, "We fought the goddarn thing during the war. It's twice as bad because we're Nihonjin, and the United States was fighting against Nihon. And I said, "The JACL bucked us in every way, even at parole time."

We had a guy in the parole office. He saw a letter, and he told us that there was a letter in the office saying this organization was against our parole. They advised the parole board to deny our parole. The guard, the inmates, used to tell us, "Oh, hell, you guys are clean as a whistle, no record. If you guys don't get paroled, there's something wrong." I said, "Yeah, there's something wrong. We didn't get it." Then they told us if we got parole, we were going into the service. This must have been about July of 1945 we went up for parole. So we said, sure, we'd go serve for our country. And then, well, geez, moments after that, we got a letter saying that parole was denied. So what. So we do another year.

The thing is, after I was put in Heart Mountain, put in McNeil Island, I was still willing to serve in the military. Why? Because we wanted the rights we had prior to the war, and our families' livelihoods. My whole family was out of camp now. Basically that was the main thing. Lots of those guys went over to Europe when their brothers and sisters, mother and father were still in camp. They died over there, not knowing what happened to their family. We didn't want that. If we went, we wanted to have security and everything for the family. Once they had it, I told them we would go; but we were denied parole.

I think our group respected citizenship more than anybody in this country, because we were actively trying to preserve our citizenship rights, instead of just *saying* that we're citizens of this country. If you're treated the way we were, there's no such thing as real citizenship. You have to fight and pay your dues. But I don't begrudge those who did volunteer. Most are still alive. My life was at stake. I treasure my life. If the others wanted to do it that way, that's their business. But the soldiers who died didn't know what happened to their families in camp. That's the sorry thing about it.

Meanwhile, I don't have one regret. If I had to do it over, I'd do the same thing. That's what I keep telling my family. I had nothing to hide. There's nothing shameful about how we lived, and we got treated like criminals without committing any kind of crime. I would still fight to the end. But I'm not bitter, only disappointed sometimes. It was good what I did; I did it with a clear conscience. Because what we fought for was a righteous cause, and we weren't going to back off for nothing.

So many people don't know about the evacuation that the Japanese Americans went through. I'm not ashamed of it. Some Nihonjin are ashamed to talk about it. They're ashamed to tell their kids. My God, what's wrong? There's something wrong with that. I told them, "You talk as if you committed a crime," I said. "We didn't commit anything. The only thing—the crime—was our face, the way we look, and goddamn it, that'll never change. You ought to be proud of being Japanese in this country and having those values that were instilled in us by our parents."

TOM KAWAGUCHI

Topaz
442nd Regimental
Combat Team,
France, Italy

My parents are from Kōchi, Japan. My father came to Seattle in 1898 and worked on the railroads. Then he got to Chicago where he attended watchmakers school, the Elgin School I believe it was, and learned to become a watchmaker. He also learned photography. So he opened up a watchmaking and photography shop in Seattle. My mother came over as a picture bride shortly thereafter from Kōchi and joined my father. I was the sixth child of seven children and was born in Tacoma. When I was three, my dad decided to open up a shop in San Francisco and for a while traveled back and forth between there and Tacoma. He then brought the family down and we settled here in San Francisco. I was raised in a Jewish neighborhood.

Most of my friends were Jewish kids. There were Russian Jews and German Jews on McAllister and Webster Street; as a matter of fact, I learned how to swear in Yiddish before I even knew how to swear in Japanese. I hadn't realized that there were that many Japanese until I went to John Muir Grammar School where I met Frank Hara for the first time and his sister, Misa, and others. It was a revelation to me that there was a Japantown and all these Japanese.

Then my dad had a stroke and his business folded with the Depression. When he got a chance to manage an apartment house in Japantown, the whole family moved there. We lived on Buchanan and Bush until the war broke out in 1941. Because my dad was an invalid, my brother and I had to go to work at a ripe young age. I was delivering papers and my brother was working in a grocery store.

I went to San Francisco Junior College for a couple of years, but because finances got real tight, I decided to work full-time. A lot of us didn't have much money, and jobs were very, very difficult for the Niseis and the Isseis to get. Most of the Isseis were either doing domestic work or they had small businesses of their own, and that was it. I was born in 1921 and was twenty when the war broke out, and turned twenty-one when I went to camp. But earlier I guess the stars were looking after me because Mitsubishi had an opening. I applied for the job and so did many others, but I was fortunate enough to be selected.

So I was working for Mitsubishi until the war broke out, and I learned an awful lot about the import-export business. At the same time I learned a lot about Japanese nationals and how they conducted business. To me the Niseis were being discriminated against. They expected a lot of work out of them and gave them minimum pay. That was a philosophy then. We used to work hard, we'd go to work early, we'd go home late, but our pay didn't change. They expected this from us, and in Japan I assume this was the way of life because jobs were scarce there, and, of course, in those days jobs were scarce here too.

On December 8, 1941, I was told to go to the FBI office where they interviewed me. I said that I was just a general clerk, that I was a flunky. But they were very much aware of my movements because I used to meet Japanese ships coming and going, to take down the bills of lading and trade acceptances and that sort of thing and turn them over to the purser. That's what I told the FBI. I was doing general work in accounting.

But on December 7? Let's see, I was at the public library. I was in there, and when I came out, the boys were screaming "Extra, Extra, Japs Bombed Pearl Harbor!" I wondered where in the world was Pearl Harbor? I didn't know it was in Hawaii until I started reading the paper and then . . .

I kind of got a funny feeling going home. I thought everybody and his uncle was staring at me, ready to pounce on me or something. I came back to Japantown and the place was just stone quiet. You didn't see anyone around. You felt very apprehensive and thought that something big was going to happen. You began to notice extra police cars and extra patrols coming into the area, and then plainclothesmen. I guess they were there to provide some security against reprisals. There were some Filipinos who lived in the area who would want to start a fight with you. We avoided being out in the street. And like everybody else, we listened to what was happening on the radio. We just didn't go out, period.

I wasn't frightened, just apprehensive. I'd go out and do whatever had to be done. If my sister went out, I went along with her to shop or whatever, just to ensure that nothing would happen. We didn't take any unnecessary chances.

Then, all of a sudden we lost our jobs. I was called down to the office, and the FBI was there. I opened the desk drawer and showed what I had and so forth. After that Mr. Babba, who was my boss, told me, "We'll call you if we need you," and that was the end of it. I never went back to the office again until I got my severance pay months later.

Since I was out of work, I put in for unemployment insurance. We all used to march down to Mission Street and get our unemployment checks. Morale was low. We knew we couldn't find jobs elsewhere, we could only get jobs inside Japantown. We were trying to help each other get through the upheaval. What was already happening was many of the community leaders were being picked up. And the mothers and the wives just didn't know what to do. People went over to console them and so forth. They got the word that they needed their toothbrush, shaving equipment, and change of clothes. They took the items to Solrab, which was the immigration center. And that was it. They wouldn't hear anything more.

Meantime, all kinds of rumors were flying around that we would all be placed in prison and so forth. I volunteered my services to the JACL because I didn't have a job. And that was my first real exposure to it. That's where I first met Mike Masaoka. Henry Tani was president of the San Francisco JACL and then there was Tomi Takagi, Terry Ishida and Saburo Kido. These people were all very, very much in the forefront and I just used to do a lot of message running.

Then the evacuation notices started being posted. I was very angry because the thing is, I am an American citizen. I said, "What am I being accused of?" And for the first time the full impact started to hit home. The newspapers, of course, were playing up the war like crazy, and the propaganda was unbelievable; that Japanese planes were coming into the Bay Area and so forth. We had blackouts and there was a local hysteria, but somehow in the Japantown area where we lived, things were very quiet. It was very subdued. You would expect people out there yelling and screaming, but instead, everybody kept a very low profile while activities were going on with the JACL around the clock. Mike wouldn't even be eating some times. One time he had to climb over the fence because there was a curfew. I really take my hat off to Mike, a young guy like that taking on a major problem.

A lot of people are now Monday-morning quarterbacking as to what he should have done, but the thing is, at the time what he did seemed right. I was twenty-one and, hell, I didn't know what to do. I didn't have the faintest idea. My life was very, very limited; all I knew was what I saw in front of me, literally. And I think most of the Niseis at that time were very small in their thinking because we never saw the real world. The real world was a revelation to me. When I joined the Army, that was the first time that I saw what the real world was like. I made up my mind, I said if this was the real world, I want my share, and I said I'm not going to go back to the shallow existence that I had.

Anyway, we were in Tanforan on May 1, 1942, and then in September of 1942 we went to Topaz. I was furious. No one really knew what was happening. For example, my Hakujin friends came under the scrutiny of the FBI. They were told not to become too close to Japanese families. There was a very good friend of ours, Sam Frusco, who was with the Boy Scouts—the FBI had him run out of town. He ended up in Utah. Sam was too close to the Japanese, fighting for their cause. The things that happened to him, it was pathetic. He just about lost his business and everything else. It's because he went to Seiko-kai ("Japanese Episcopalian Church") and was legal director for our Boy Scouts. He was a violinist and a good friend of Reverend Tsukamoto. He had sympathy for the Japanese and he finally ended up in Utah. But he went to school and got a law degree and came back.

It was just the frustration at Tanforan, that I couldn't do anything about it. Total frustration that something was happening to us and there was no way we could fight back because actually none of us had ever really been exposed to the majority culture. All of our lives we had been living in *Nihon-machi* ("Japantown"); our thinking was Nihon-machi, and we really didn't know what the real world was. We did go to school where we saw our Caucasian friends, but when we came home, it was back to our Issei parents again.

When we got to Topaz and saw the MP guards and the whole bit, we thought we were at the end of the world, a complete sense of loss. My stomach really just sank, and I thought, oh my God, I gotta get out of this place. I was going to try and get out one way or another. In due time they started coming out with these seasonal jobs—cannery workers and sugar-beet workers, and so forth. I began to do those just to get out of camp life. But it didn't do anything for me. There was a lot of stoop labor. Then I began to organize the Boy Scouts and community activities for the kids. In camp this was my major concern, to keep the kids busy.

In camp I was not my own person. You had four walls around you. You could do only so much work and come home. Then they would have dances and that sort of thing, but your heart really wasn't in it. You knew it was just a facade, the whole thing. I told my parents, I said, "I'll try to get out in some form. When I get out, I'll be able to call for the family." But I was only twenty-one years old. I was trying to divert my mind, but it was frustrating all the way through. Because all during this time I kept asking myself, why am I here? How can I get out? Then I applied for different scholarships, but my grades were not competitive enough.

Then we began to hear rumors that they were going to create a Japanese combat team. Along comes Lee Tracy, a movie actor, and he starts talking about volunteers. My brother and I really talked it over and decided perhaps this is our chance to go. We didn't know it, but we both went down to volunteer. My brother said, "I'm the older one, so I'm going first." I said, "Okay, I'll stay behind but I don't think that's right. I should go and you should stay." He took his physical and he flunked because he had a heart murmur. The minute I found out that he was rejected, man, I was there. When I volunteered I said that I wanted to leave camp and go to New York. I had the money and had a friend I could stay with. They cleared me to leave camp and I think that delay saved my life because if I had gone in then I would have been right in the middle of Bruyeres Campaign.

I joined because I always felt very strongly about patriotism; I felt that this was my country. I didn't know any other country.

When war broke out with Japan, I was ready to fight the enemy, and I had no qualms about whether it was Japanese or German or whatever. This was my country and I wanted to defend it. It was that simple. But when I was getting this treatment, I was a little confused. I thought, wait a minute, here I want to defend my country and they lock me up. Why? Then I said, well, the opportunity has got to present itself. I've got to get out of here. And I've got to demonstrate in one form or another that I am what I am. That opportunity came, and when it came, man, I was right in there. I mean there was no second guessing.

I was a loyal American and I wanted to prove that the Japanese Americans were real Americans, just like anybody else. And this is what a lot of my friends didn't understand. When this yes-yes, no-no business took place, I was disappointed in some of them who went no-no. It took me a number of years, but I suddenly realized that a no-no answer was all part of the democratic process, that somebody else had his choice and I had my choice. We had some problems in camp because some people wanted to go as a block and say no-no. We had a considerable amount of discussion on that, because we have our own individual rights and we can express ourselves any way we want to.

There was democracy going on right in camp, in spite of the enclosure. But there were friends fighting against friends, there were brothers fighting against brothers, and it was terrible. And people asked, "Why do you want to volunteer?" I just said, "I don't understand what the argument is. Our country is being attacked and I want to defend it. It's that simple." They looked at me and said, "You must have holes in your head." Maybe it was because of my early childhood; being among Caucasians, I never thought myself different; even today I don't feel any different. When issues come up, I don't look at myself as a Japanese; I just look at myself as a person that wants to say what he wants to say.

But the thing is, I think, for the Niseis there was a strange thing going on. You know, when we joined the Army and when we went through basic, none of us really said anything about why we joined or anything else. We knew we had a job to do. But we never even talked about what we had to do. We were going to do the best that we knew how. We never sat back and said, Here we are—the old rah-rah business. None of that happened. It seemed like all of us knew exactly why we were there and why we were going to give it our best shot. No one ever came around and told me such and such, and this is what you are going to do, and so forth.

I always felt that I'd come back, and I always felt that when I came back I was not going to lead the same life I led before. I felt very strongly about that. It's a strange thing, but I've never felt pessimistic about things. I knew what I wanted and I knew what I was going after. My entire life I have always been goal-oriented. I'd pick out a target and away I'd go. When I attained that one, I'd set another one, and I'd just keep doing this because I like challenges. If I'm in a cut-and-dried kind of operation, I'm not very happy.

Anyway, there was a real closeness in the 442nd. We kind of felt like brothers. We really looked after each other. There was an unspoken trust between us that was evident constantly. I noticed a big difference when I left the 442nd and went with another group. In the 442nd we were like brothers under the skin, so to speak, and I knew all the fellows from San Francisco and from the Bay Area. I guess it was an extension of our life, from before camp. And it was also a good mix of Hawaiian boys and mainland boys.

What really made the 442nd a good fighting unit was that the education of most of the boys in it was above average—way above average. That was number one. Number two, they had a strong sense of pride, very strong.

And all of us were scared, no question about it. None of us felt like heroes, but we didn't want to bring shame upon our families. So we didn't want to show that we were scared, but, man, I was scared with the best of them. But then you knew you had to do a job, even though your stomach is tied up in knots and your skin is just prickly. You sense everything, all your senses are operating. When we went into combat, it was that way. Once you got into the heat of battle, it was just like you were playing football or basketball. You're doing all the things naturally, but you're fighting for your life. They would point out our objectives, and we would be going toward our objectives. It was really amazing, some of those kids—God, they were gutsy guys.

I think the Japanese culture really came into play, all the things that we were taught as kids—honesty, integrity, honor. And *haji*, "not bringing shame on the family." Your upbringing and culture are there and they are not something you talk about. But it was very noticeable among all the boys, because when we were in combat, we were looking after each other constantly, and we would worry about each other. We knew that we were not going to be left out there if anybody ever got hit; somebody would come after us. We had the buddy system. And you talk about guts. I mean some of these guys, wow, I take my hat off to them. You see a situation that's almost impossible, and you see this guy going up there, all alone. You just feel naked. All you have is just an army shirt which is paper thin—no bulletproof vest, no nothing, no protection at all. The guys were out there crawling around, trying to knock out machine-gun nests or other strong points. When I saw that, I wondered if I could do the same thing. But when my time came, I was out there, right along with the rest of them, scared stiff, but still doing my job.

It was teamwork, and we felt secure with each other. My war was only fifty feet in front of me and fifty feet to the right and fifty feet to the left. That was about it. So like any other GI, I really didn't know what the 422nd accomplished until after the war. But from what I saw, really, I was amazed. You can call it superhuman effort, some of those guys were really rugged individuals. The medics especially I take my hat off to. Under fire, they were out there taking care of the wounded.

A lot of people think that the 442nd was used merely as cannon fodder. I don't think so, because I've been in the Army for twenty years, and I retired as a major. You generally try to use your best troops as a spearhead to accomplish an objective, and the 442nd was good—I mean they were damn good. But as a GI I didn't know one way or the other. Once I was commissioned, I saw things completely different—you would take your best troops and use them, and this is exactly what had happened. The 442nd was spearheading most of the attacks because they were damn good, and our casualty rates were high because we were spearheading attacks. This is where the cannon-fodder talk started, but I don't think we were really used as cannon fodder. They wanted to use us effectively, which was demonstrated in our final push when the Gothic Line fell in thirty-four minutes and we accomplished the impossible. We started climbing the hills silently at ten at night. By five the next morning, we were in position to attack. The Germans didn't even expect us. We came up right behind them.

That was the campaign where the Allies tried to break the Gothic Line for six months with three divisions—forty thousand men. Meantime, our combat team had roughly five thousand because we had some extra companies. We had our engineering company, our artillery battalion, and certain things that were a little different from the makeup of a normal regiment. But let's see, I Company climbed the cliff, and there was K Company and F Company and G Company. Generally there's about 250 in each company. The 100th Infantry Battalion had gone in on the left flank; the 3rd Battalion was climbing one hill; and the 2nd Battalion was climbing another hill. I would say that roughly half the regiment was moving.

It took thirty-six minutes to take the objective, but it took us almost ten hours to climb that mountain at night. The Allied units couldn't break through, but we had some good tactical officers in our regiment. They sent out patrols and started checking the area out. Then they came up with this plan and then had some Italian partisans show us this trail of how to get up there. We followed those trails and got up there.

I would do the whole 442nd thing over again, because of the general thinking of a lot of my friends—they all have this American show-me attitude—and I demonstrated to them where I come from. Even today I find that I'm leading the way showing what I can do, and it makes them sick because my work ethic is so different from theirs. I'm constantly working toward an objective, and it surprises them that even today I have this drive in spite of the treatment I got.

So in the 442nd, a lot of us felt that this was our only chance to demonstrate our loyalty; we would never get a second chance— this was it. We saw the treatment that we were getting and we wanted there to be no question about what we were and where we were going. At least that's the way I felt: give me a chance, at least, to show what I can do or can't do.

There were other things I learned in the Army, because before, I guess I didn't know any better. Maybe my world was so small that I didn't know what the other world was like. Once I got a taste of the other world, I said, this is for me. I said I will never go back to the world I came from. I will never ever let my kids be domestic help. Never. I said I'll never teach them to be subservient to anybody. That was that.

But I didn't know enough about the government in 1942. I had to trust something really. My Hakujin friends told me, "There's some good people out there; don't be bitter." The strange part was I was never bitter. I was angry and there is regret, but I never really felt bitter. Maybe it was because somehow when I joined the Army for the first time, I was getting an opportunity to do something about it. What little I could do really.

HARRY UENO

Manzanar

I am a Kibei and was born in a Hawaiian company camp on April 14, 1907. I had two brothers, one five years older, one five years younger. After awhile our family moved to another place in Hawaii, a bigger camp there, called New House. And there's a lot of Japanese, Okinawan, and some Korean there, too. Those days some Japanese is married but most of the Okinawan is bachelor. A few years later I saw one Okinawan get married, but the rest was all bachelors, about fifty of them. And Korean, same thing, all bachelors.

My father finally get out from a plantation camp. He leased a place, about ten acres; then he leased more land to plant the sugar-cane. That was about 1913. I stayed there till 1915. Then one day my uncle want to go back and get married, so my father decide to send me back to Japan with him. So I met my uncle in Maui and I went back to Japan. That was August 1915, summer vacation in Japan at that time. And I stayed there until 1923, for a little less than eight years. I went back to my father's hometown, about twelve miles south of Hiroshima City, where I finished the seventh grade in the Japanese school and lived with my aunt who lived in Fukuoka.

In the meantime, my father came back to Japan with a younger brother and my mother. My older brother went to Milwaukee after he finished high school in Hawaii. He wanted to continue school in America. When families separate when you are young, there's always problems there. All Kibei had the same problem, some kind of wall between them and their father and mother. When you needed them they weren't there, and nobody can replace the father and mother, because your grandfather or grandmother take care of you, but still you have the difference. So I decide that maybe I get out the house. Meantime, some family relative came from Tokyo, and he told me, why don't you come to Tokyo? Well, I thought, maybe.

Then I went to Tokyo. That was in 1922, early summer. I went to the private school there for a while. We had room and board at the private school and I delivered the newspaper. On a contract with the newspaper, they said they'd pay me so much, so I continued school. But in reality, they never paid anything. All they give us was food and shelter but nothing paid up. So I had to commute to the school in Shosendensha, that's in the outskirts of Tokyo. They had an electric train just like Chicago has.

Delivering newspapers is very hard in Japan. They had so many papers. They had about fourteen different kinds; you carry every one of them. About four o'clock in the morning you start off. Then you go to school. Then you come back. Then you have to deliver the evening papers. And weekends you have to solicit the customers and the collection, everything. It takes your full time. I stayed there six months, but that's all I could last, because nothing came in to pay for tuition or books or anything, so I gave up. I was still fifteen.

Then I went back home to Hiroshima. Some of my friends were already in high school, and I couldn't stay around home, so I got to figure to do something. So finally I decided to come to the United States. I came alone. And that was May 20, 1923. When I came, my brother was in Milwaukee, Wisconsin, so no way to communicate with him, because I forgot all about English. I only went to third grade in the United States, that's all—not even finish the third grade. He used to write Japanese but he forgot all about it, because in Milwaukee, there's not a single Japanese there, and only one Chinese restaurant. That's what he told me when I met him. He came to the mainland in 1919.

So I started working in lumber mill in Washington. Less than three months later that big earthquake hit Tokyo. The lumber mill was very busy. I was working six days a week, ten hours a day. In the early 1920s in Washington, there were about five or six sawmills that hired Japanese. It was a pretty good job in there, clean job, not like a farm. And pay was pretty good compared with domestic or farm work. I used to get about $80 a month plus overtime. I worked Saturday overtime and two hours extra every day. I make about $120 or $130 a month in those days; I was twenty-three years old. That's good wages. I even donate for the earthquake out there in Tokyo. The whole camp pitch in. There's about 125 Japanese. They send about $3,000. That's a lot of money for those days, because, like myself, I think I donate a little over a week's wages.

I didn't get a chance to continue school because I got nobody here. So I work in that sawmill for three years. In 1926 I decide to visit my brother in Milwaukee. So I took a train, Northern Pacific, I think. I went out there. I remember the address, 666 Jefferson Street. I never forget that. I met him and he seems to be completely different. We were separated from 1915 to 1926, so that's eleven years lost. And even when I met him, there's no communication between us, because I couldn't speak English, he couldn't speak Japanese. So it's kind of difficult.

He said there's hardly no jobs now—it's 1926. Chicago was the largest industrial city in the United States; the Depression hit there first. We decided Milwaukee got nothing there, nothing. So we go to Chicago and look for the job and I got nothing. You look at the ads, for instance, warehouse helper. We got up there seven or eight o'clock in the morning; you see more than two blocks of people lined up for one job. When I looked at that—hopeless. Only one warehouse job, already that much Depression. So I loaf around for six months out there and finally decide to come back to California. And I had a cousin who came from Hawaii, working in Stockton for awhile, so I visit him. I did a little tractor work, but that's awfully dirty job. Pay not so good as sawmill. So I went back to Seattle. Then, I stayed there for another year or two and then come back to California, again to Stockton.

A lot of Hawaiians was in Stockton. One reason is that baseball was very popular in those days. Stockton, all around, they had baseball teams. And most of the players came from Hawaii. And another thing, Stockton had a lot of Issei. They can lease the land they want to farm, so they ask the Hawaiian Nisei to loan their name to lease the land with. A lot of farmers out there, Japanese farmers, they haven't got enough money to buy the land, but they could lease the place and farm. So a lot of Hawaiians gave their name and they probably got fifty cents or a dollar an acre to lend the name.

I farmed a little while, but Stockton is awful dirty place and I get sick drinking water all day that come from river. They strain it with sand and everything, but still was a lot of typhoid fever. Then I lived in San Francisco for awhile, a couple of years. I done all kind of jobs—work in bookstore, work in transport, in hotel. All odd kind of jobs.

Finally I move down to L.A. in late 1929. Los Angeles had lot of jobs because Japanese run about 60 percent of wholesale produce market. Then I don't know how many hundred retail outlets are in L.A. All fruit stands is run by Japanese. I started working on retail store. It's pretty good type customer out there. It's sort of the kind of upper middle class like Norman Chandler of the L.A. *Times.* His wife is shopping there and all the rich people trading. And then soon the supermarkets start opening, so they knock off the small ones. So they have to cut down the people working there. Then a lot of competition. This fellow who run the butcher shop —his name is Mankers, he's Dutch descendant—he want to open the store in Beverly Hills. So he asked me if I could run the market for him. That's more challenge. I start going to the wholesale market, buy all the vegetable and fruit, then manage the place, and then get off early. I hire about three or four Japanese that work for him for a couple of years. I save up a little bit, even though I have three children come one after another. I was married in 1930. First son born in 1931, the second one born the following year, and the youngest one born in 1937.

Then I start my own store. I decide to buy the little market and run it by myself. I pay about $500 for the business, but these Italian fellows, they sold me the store and only one quarter block away one of them opened a bigger one. He didn't say anything about he was going to open that. He sold me the business, then he took all the customers he had before, see. So, in other words, I had a hard time. I lost about $1000, and that's a lot of money. Because I had to buy the fruit stand and have everything built for me. A fellow named Mr. Okamoto, a Japanese name, used to go around and build fruit stands. It cost me $350 or $400 to build that thing. Then I have to close up that place there because no longer could I continue business.

Then, next thing, I have some Jewish people looking for fruit-stand man in their store, not to work for them but to run it by myself. Their trade is mostly by telephone. Almost all trade by telephone, because that's all Beverly Hills in Hollywood. All the Jewish trade. Most were producers and directors of the movies and writers of the movies. We were there for . . . let's see . . . up to almost the end of 1937. But you see, those movie people are very difficult to accommodate. One time they buy a hell of a lot of stuff, then they go on vacation, and the whole thing is shot to hell. And they want something not in market, stuff like, this time of year they want asparagus, in January or February they want it. Nobody has it. The only way you could get this stuff is from Hawaii. They ship that produce from Hawaii. Very expensive. No other people could afford it. And today you could buy a lot of things in frozen markets, but in those days the only vegetables are all fresh; that's the only thing you could sell them because no way to keep them. In those days they didn't have refrigerators, only icebox.

At beginning, business was good. End of the day, the fellow who run the market pay me whatever I charge them. They carry the charge. They had a lot of good customers over there. Jewish people accommodate the Jewish people there; they want Kosher meat, everything Kosher. I remember the good customers; chairman of Twentieth-Century Fox. He used to live in Sunset Boulevard. And Darryl Zanuck, president of Twentieth-Century often came, too. David Selznick. All rich people. Warner Brothers in Santa Monica. Norma Shearer, and even Douglas Fairbanks, they bought stuff from me for awhile. He was married to the Lady Ashley. He divorced Mary Pickford. I remember one guy's name, cowboy, he's the first cowboy star. He died soon in an auto accident, Tom Mix. Yeah, he was customer, too. I was at this market about two and a half years. Then the business is getting poor, so I finally quit and started working in a Jewish market on Western and Sunset. I take care of the fruit stand. Not a big place, but all Jewish people there. It was pretty good. They treat me very good.

When the war broke out, Issei were rounded up by the FBI. I never met him but there was a Dr. Honda; he used to live in I think Gardena. He was a veteran of the Japanese Army, and he was a doctor. So he was taken in by the FBI, and he die in jail while they interrogate him. The reason I bring that up is that a friend of mine who lived in the back of my house, he told me on the day

Dr. Honda die that he had a friend who went over and verified his corpse because the FBI want somebody from the family to come over and verify him in the morgue. Instead of family going, his friend was related to Honda's family, so he went there. He looked at it, he opened up the cover, sheet, he saw that both hands are tied up with wire or something. He saw that and thought that doctor must have been tortured, and he told my friend back here.

Next hour two FBI came over. I want talk to you. They took me out to the FBI headquarters. Then FBI man said, where you hear that? Oh, last Sunday I went to the pool hall and while I was around somebody was talking. I don't want to mention my friend because he's Issei. So if I mention his name he's got no chance whatsoever. They'd take him away. He had a family and three children, too. I was held for more than an hour, but I never mention his name. They said, well, you go back and next off day you go to pool hall and find out who was talking such a rumor. I said, okay. I went back and I don't do nothing. I didn't say nothing.

About two or three weeks later they came over and pick me up again. What'd you find out? they said. Well, I couldn't find out who was talking there. Maybe they hear through the radio or something such a rumor. I think I picked some sore point of the FBI. They must know something, they don't want nobody to know that.

There's another lady used to take care of the oil tanker used to come in quite often to the L.A. harbor. Japanese naval oil tanker. She feel sorry for those navy men out there because all they get was twenty-seven or twenty-eight cents in Japanese money, so that all they could do is to buy a pack of cigarettes or something. When they come into L.A. they got no chance to make a trip through the city or anything. So I think what she did was she called volunteers and then they help those people to just make it through, they give them lunch and send them back. She didn't do anything else. But a lot of people pitched in and maybe give fifty cents, a dollar, so she could do this. Poor thing, they were looking for anybody that sympathizes in the past like that. So I hear she been a suicide, hang herself in the jail.

In Manzanar altogether about nine or ten times they questioned me. Every time they call me in and they ask me, who do you think is going to win the war? That's a foolish question. I don't pay attention to those kind of things. I got no respect for some of those guys.

We went into camp by the bus. Some people went in by the

train, the same day. We reach there at almost six o'clock. Still long daylight. They assigned us to the room and all that process took about three hours. About nine o'clock that evening finally they give us a room. I had two other families in the room all together. Two other families: one a bachelor and another family is a stepmother and a son. They were all grown-up people. The only privacy you have is pull the rope and they put the sheet down, that's the only way.

They had four different directors, Merritt was the last one. I didn't know him too much. He just came in prior to the incident, you know. Meantime, Campbell, Ned Campbell, he was always running the camp because other directors in and out. He was transferred from the Army. So he was actually controlling the policy of the camp, running the camp.

The first month I was cutting the sagebrush and clearing the land for the additional buildings. That was one month. Then they decide to open the mess hall; I applied for a job there. Of course, they had that blood test. Some people reject it, some people accepted. I got the job in the mess hall as cook's help. So I picked early morning job about five o'clock up to early afternoon. Sometime in September the troubles started. They used to supply us with oranges and cookies for children and the aged people—I think for children six and under.

All of a sudden nothing coming. It's wartime so I figure maybe some materials short. But I see my neighbor's bag full of orange and some cookies she bought in the canteen. The same thing happen with other things. So I thought, that's kind of funny. I went over to the canteen and see it. The same thing we used to get in the kitchen. I went over to Block 16 because I used to go eat in there for three months, so I knew Kanda—he's the manager of Block 16. I talked to him.

At that time we didn't organize the mess hall, yet. I just worked in there. "Why don't you raise the question in the block managers' meeting?" I asked him, "because things that people are buying we used to get for nothing." I told him, they're supposed to be supplied to us. But he said, no, no, he don't want to antagonize the administration, so he backed down. So I went over and see Tateishi. He said okay. He raised the question in block managers' meeting, and I think Campbell was going to investigate and let the block managers know. A week later they put in the papers that by mistake, truckload of those things went into the canteen. Unless you bring up the subject, they don't want to tell the people. They know already they made the mistake long time ago. As long as the people keep quiet they just want to cover it up. But Tateishi raised the question; they have to have an answer for that. So finally they admit they made the mistake.

You know, one of the Kibei reported to the FBI and WRA about the Kibei meeting. I never met him until that time. A friend of mine lived in the same block and worked in the mess hall. His name was Tsuji, and he said we should go see that other Kibei, because he made that report to the WRA about a Kibei meeting where Joe Kurihara, Tateishi, and some others made a speech. Tusji said, this Kibei translated to English everything from the meeting, like Joe Kurihara's speech and Tateishi's speech, and reported it to the FBI.

So we went over to see that Kibei, about nine or ten of us. He opened the door and invite three or four people in the house. (I didn't go to that Kibei meeting, so I just more like an observer.) Tsuji or somebody told him, you reported Kibei meeting to the WRA, but you were wrong. You said you had three witnesses, but two of them never speak Japanese; they can't understand Japanese. And another witness, you said he never been in Kibei meeting, so how the heck can you use those three people for your witnesses? That Kibei guy said, "That was my mistake." Then he say he going to retract that statement, and he did. About three or four days later, he put in the camp paper that he made the mistake, and he retract. When they talked to him, nobody threatened him or tried to make things bad for him. Maybe he felt kind of threatened because the way he reacted against a lot of people in the camp.

So that was the beginning of the real conflict that started in camp. That's the very beginning. When we went to camp on May 15, most of the administration jobs, desk jobs, good jobs are all taken by early comers. The first one went on March 20. For most of the Kibeis, only thing left is cleanup jobs or mess hall jobs. And not only that, most of the Nisei try to control the camp. For example, any kind of meeting, they want to conduct in English, no Japanese; that eliminate a lot of Issei, too. Later on they try to bring out those work codes and Fair Play Committee, all those things. But the Nisei already selected representatives—the people going to head all the divisions. Even Tayama chose his own wife as one of the heads of the committee. If you want to be democratic, why not ask everybody? Let them choose who to represent them. But no, they want to dictate to the people, you know. That's one thing.

Another thing is, in the summer the camp let all the citizens go out on furlough for the work. In the fall, harvest time, they stop all the Kibeis from going out for jobs—only the Nisei could go out. Naturally the Kibei need a job so they were stuck in the mess hall or something like that.

There were a lot of problems. Like with cooking utensils: they give us only so much and never enough for the people to feed on. We request the additional pie pan or cooking utensils or knife, but we don't get them. They search our bags, everything, and take them away—like kitchen knives that people have in the camp for cooking, even sugar. I had ten-pound bag of sugar they took away, and maybe about two months later they brought it back. But they took everything. If you ask for knife supplied to the mess hall, they say, no, it's wartime; we can't get those things. But some people give them money from their own pocket to buy things for them, and they get them right away, see. But the kitchen knives we bought for the mess halls were the same ones they took from us.

So there's funny things going on there. A lot of complaints nobody ever hears. The only way we figure is to organize—make them hear the people's voice; then they have to listen. That's why we organize, not to get more pay or better working conditions or anything, nothing like that. We don't complain. We willing to do the best we can for the people.

The only thing we want is our right to receive things like food, especially meat and sugar. Sugar is the easiest thing those who kept the record could steal, so that's why we use sugar as an example. But people addicted to sugar, so they could feel the shortage of sugar more than anything else. Meat, they could get by, because they use a lot of vegetables. But we know that meat is short because they send in the one-quarter steers once a week, three and a half pound a person a week, the meat was. But after a while they cut down the meat to three pound or something like that. In beginning we used to get tenderloin steak with rib, so we used that for the children. But months later we open the mess hall, and no more showing up. We know somebody's taking it away.

They know they doing us short for sugar, but they never mention it till we pin them down. So everybody complain, but only way to prove it is to see the records. So I went over to Block 21 and to mess halls where I knew people. They keep the records. Sugar is easy to skim. It come in fifty-pound bags. Every month they give us less and less, first one ounce short each time, then more and more. Japanese they don't care for too much coffee unless they put the sugar in. We put a quarter spoon of sugar in it; nobody want to drink it without sugar. Then we went into a Caucasian mess hall, and they have a bowl of sugar, two bowls of sugar, on each table, and they have a big cake with frosting always available in snack time. I could see. They offer me the cake too, but I don't eat. They take it from same warehouse. Those people that eat in there, they got ration coupons, too, but they not going to use them.

The sugar, that's what started the big trouble at Manzanar. Because they try to hide this thing from the people. That's what the problem is. If they came out and told us why the sugar is short, all right. They might say ration board doesn't send enough sugar or so-and-so do this or that. If they explain to the people, the people understand the situation, and they won't complain. But they tell us instead, hospital use lot of sugar. I went over to hospital, and they kept records, and they're not getting an ounce more than we do.

So several camp policemen told me there are two to three hundred pounds of sugar sacks in back of Campbell's car. He went outside the camp almost every night. So everytime that Hakujin went out he was taking stuff in his trunk—two or three hundred pounds of sugar sacks. Everybody knows something sinister is going on. Sugar is black market, just like meat—any price they ask for it they can get. Administration never admit that.

In October everything is so much short that people just complain. People don't go direct to administration, but they complain to the people who work in the mess hall. They blame them. We get the pressure from people, so we have to go after the administration. Finally the people formed a committee to investigate why the sugar is short. They don't need that if the administration is honest. They formed a block managers committee. But the block managers' reaction is slow. They don't hustle around to find out, because every day in the mess hall shortages are felt, so every day you have to react fast.

The administration one day explained to the block managers that they use a lot of sugar in making the soy sauce and miso. The very next day I went over to the soy sauce factory. Miso don't use sugar. I met the production manager—his name is Nakamura—and asked him how much sugar he received. He said they brought in three 100-pound sacks. But of that he said he used only 225 pounds. Three sacks doesn't mean too much for the whole camp, because there's so many thousand pounds missing. By this time, I had two guys in the administration tailing me all the time.

Anyway, sugar was 6,100 pounds short in October. The administration admit that. They say they make up for that in November. In other words, they going give out that much more in November. Then I went over and investigated. They know I did that. On my way home I met Kaku and we both went in the warehouse and check how much reserve they have.

We were checking when a Hakujin came over and asked what we are doing there? He tear up what we had recorded. Somebody reported that we went to the warehouse and checked. So they keep close watch on us. Finally they know we found out how much difference there was so they couldn't hide it. They admit it in the paper. They tell the people they going to make it up in November. November is only nine days away. They got no way to get 6,100 pounds extra sugar. But every time we complain they give us ounces, a little more, instead of six ounces they give us seven ounces or something like that.

We heard that the same thing was happening at Tule Lake, prior to the strike there. They used to have hog farm and chicken farm, and they slaughter the hog outside the camp, but under camp control. The guy taking charge in slaughter house is Caucasian. One day he had an accident. He had his own car for going out of the camp, and if it wasn't for the accident, they never would have found out. He had a trunkful of hog meat in there. That's the way they do it. They charge that the Nihonjin kill so many hogs and so many pounds, and charge to Japanese in camp. Meantime, he's all the time taking out a trunkful of meat to the black market outside.

Same thing in Manzanar with the sugar. If you keep quiet, they keep doing it. In the meantime, a lot of people complain, but they don't have guts enough to go after them. So good thing we have backing of so many people to go after them. Finally they have to admit that, because if it wasn't for getting the evidence and going after them, they never going to admit that.

The problem started on December 4. The FBI came in, and I

met the FBI. They came to take two Nisei away from the camp. Two Nisei! Naturally the people know that time they are stool pigeons. And I saw those Nisei report that the Issei is pro-Japan. We were trying to have public debate with administration. Joe Kurihara and myself and Tsuji and the others, a public debate in camp. And we challenged Tayama and Slocum and Ko Ariyoshi and others. Ariyoshi came around to my mess hall once in a while, so I asked him, "How about debating?" He went back to ask the others, but they say no. At first he said maybe that's a good idea but then he withdrew. That's why the debate never took place in Manzanar.

We wanted to talk—both sides—whatever they had in mind, bring it out and debate on it. Who's right, who's wrong. After all, we all Japanese in there, all Japanese. On one side, you take Joe Kurihara—he went overseas to France to fight for the United States. Joe was a citizen, natural-born American. And he volunteered and he showed his loyalty to the United States. Everything he showed. And yet the government don't recognize that. So to him, what more he could do? Volunteered and don't show any results. Why should he repeat again?

So, for a lot of these Nisei or Kibei the feeling was the JACL was not asking us to represent us; they took for granted that they represent us. But they were just a minority. And even with the JACL, Issei still got taken away like that—behind barbed wire. A lot of Isseis get upset because they got a farm just like older Niseis, and that's hardship for family there. Anybody met some kind of disasters, injury, or family problem, or something like that, everybody feels kind of hurt because Japanese is small community. If any Japanese commit a crime, we felt kind of guilty toward the other society. That's the way we feel—close.

And we feel sorry that a lot of Issei met with family tragedy. Before evacuation, there were very few find jobs outside the Japanese community. You can't get the job in a Hakujin factory or anything. You could almost say there were no jobs there. So we owe our living to the Issei. Most the jobs is given to us by Isseis. They create jobs for us.

So, for all those mixed-up feelings, in camp, anybody stool pigeon, we felt doubly angered for the action they're doing, see—turning against their own people.

Anyway, about the riot at camp. At nine o'clock two jeeps full of policemen and Assistant Chief of Police Williams knock at my door and say, "We want to talk to you." "You don't have to bring a half dozen policemen," I said. "All you have to do is send one man out and I would go right down. I got no place to run away to." So I was in bed, and I changed my clothes and went down to the police station. Then they asked me where I was earlier, and I told them I went over to Block 15 and saw a PTA (Parent-Teacher Association) movie or something, because I belong to the PTA in Block 22. Then I came back about eight o'clock and got into bed, because I have to get up at five o'clock in the morning. So they questioned me; Williams questioned me for about ten minutes or so. Then Guilky, the chief of police, came over and questioned me. Then after that, for two or three hour we didn't say nothing. We just sit down and talk about the camp in general.

Then close to midnight Guilky came in with handcuffs and put the handcuffs on me. Then Campbell drove his car in front of police station and tell me to ride in back, and chief of police ride beside me, and they took me out to the Independence jail. I didn't know where they was going to take me, just out of camp, I thought. So I turn to the right and tell the chief of police, "Will you tell my family where you going to take me? I don't know where you going to take me, but tell me where I going to be." Then Campbell said, "No, where we are going to take you nobody knows." He was pretty angry at me. Then I told them, "Well, maybe I won't come back to the camp for a long time, like you said. But someday, for what you doing to the Japanese people, you might be going into a bigger jail." He was mad as hell.

Independence is only six miles away. It was close to one o'clock. The sheriff took everything and put it in a bag and show me the bed where I was bunking. So I slept, and in the morning, they have about half a dozen Caucasian in there. They were surprised to see me, a Japanese, in the jail. They was nice, though; they said, "Come on, let's have coffee." We got coffee and toast. Then about half past three, the sheriff call me. So I went out and saw cars waiting. And Chief of Police Guilky is there. He opened the front door of car. "We're going back," he said. I was surprised. No handcuffs, no nothing. I ride with him in the front. Then on the way home he told me, "I'm going to take you back to the camp." So we reached the camp. He introduced me to Merritt, the camp director —the first time I saw him. Also Captain Hall, that MP commander, was there. We shook hands. And Merritt told me, "Right now, the negotiating committee is negotiating, so you wait in the jail and wait for the final results." So then I met the negotiating committee, altogether five people, and they told me the same things. I wait in jail. I don't know what made the administration change so fast.

I went inside the jail. The jail is just like an ordinary barracks; they have the two big windows in back and front. They have about a half dozen boys in there. They told me what happened the night before. Then a lot of people came in, and they said they'd be back at night. At five o'clock I ate supper. Then close to six o'clock, a lot of people come in, and we shake hands. Nobody carry any stick or any rock or anything.

A little after nine o'clock, people were singing the Japanese Navy marching song; I admit that, they were singing it. The window was open, and the wind was blowing about thirty-five miles an hour. December 6 is pretty cold in Manzanar. I notice the MPs put on the gas masks. They carried them, and then they came behind the police station and they start putting them on. Meantime, Captain Hall was walking toward the sentry box at the entranceway to Manzanar. The lights were on so we could see. I could see three people. I guessed it was Captain Hall, Merritt, and Guilky, because the committee was waiting for Merritt to come in and talk with them.

In meantime the committee promised there would be no big gathering, but it was not their fault the people followed the committee. Joe Kurihara, Tateishi, Suzukawa, and Yamaguchi, and one more were on the committee. There's five people. I told them, "They putting on gas masks so you better back off. They might want to throw that tear gas." So people start moving a little bit. Then, as soon as the MPs put the gas masks on, they started throwing the canister from way beyond the police station. That smoke just covered the whole area; people were running away. I couldn't see the movement because my view was from in front of the police station. But the campsite was all filled up with people beyond the administration building. A sergeant taking charge in front was yelling, "Remember Pearl Harbor, hold your line." I could see some of the young MPs kind of shaking, scared because the crowd so big there. They throw the tear gas, and the whole area is covered. And the same time, before the gas is cleared, they start shooting.

Nobody give the order, they just start shooting. I don't think the sergeant give the order; he was shooting, too. I heard about a half dozen shots. Then when the gas is a little bit clear, I notice one man is lying facedown, flat, facing toward the camp. Three people came out from the police station and tried to carry him in, but you know when men is completely gone, they're heavy. So I jump out the window to help them carry him inside the police station where they have a table just like we had in the mess hall. We lay him down there. He's bleeding, but he's shot close range so bullet must have penetrated from the back . . . yeah, everyone being shot in the back. They never mention in any document anybody get injured from the back. All they say is operated on stomach or operated on leg, that's all they say. The way I see and hear it, everyone's injured from the back.

Joe Kanagawa said, "I think that's Ito; I don't know for sure." Ito I think was barely eighteen, and he came from Pasadena. We lay him back, and then Captain Hall came running, carrying a ceremonial sword, that long one. He carried that and he's wearing long boots and he's running. "Who fired that shot?" he yelled out. The sergeant said, "I fired two shots." The one close to the police station said he fired three shots. And another one Captain Hall pointed to, said he shot one shot. So altogether six shots were fired right there. Many MPs had guns. I couldn't see how many exactly. But they were all barricaded in; they had sandbags, and way over yonder they had a machine gun set up because I could hear when they started shooting, dot-dot-dot-dot. I couldn't see, but I could hear. That's when somebody rammed the truck—put the gear in and put weight on the pedal and let it run toward the administration building. In the FBI report, they said they tried to break the jail and release me, but hell no, that wasn't what happened. They aimed the truck at the administration building. So as soon as the soldiers saw that truck they started shooting with the machine gun. I know who did that, the man is dead but he told me what he did, you know.

No Nihonjins I could see carried any sticks or weapons or anything. The crowd were all kinds—women, young people, Nisei, Kibei, all of them. After we dragged that man in, I went back into the jail to wait. After midnight, I think, the MP came over and took me and the five on the negotiating committee and two others and put us in an army truck. The MPs sat on a bench, and we sat on the floor. There was a bunch of ice in there, and I had to sit on top of it. And they had small tommy guns, a half dozen or so. They took us to Bishop, the sheriff. He was very nice because his son-in-law used to be chief of police in Manzanar. He gave us all kind of information about what they said on the radio, what the news said. I even got the newspapers when he got them. Then after we were there about three days, around December 9, close to midnight the MP came over in the same truck and load us on again. I thought they were going to take me back to the camp, but instead of going to camp, they passed it and went to the jail in the town of Lone Pine.

There was about eight people already there in an awfully narrow place, and they only had four bunkers for sixteen people to sleep in. You could hardly walk around. And one light hanging from the ceiling and the ceiling was pretty high—about ten or twelve feet, and one small light in the corner there. They had an oil stove but no oil in it. They didn't feed us for almost twenty-four hours. Mr. Arataka had diabetes and he needed insulin every day. They didn't give it to him for two, three, days, and finally WRA sent a man to check him out. That's when we complain. We only have one cup for sixteen people to drink the coffee. We had no oil to burn; it was cold out there.

I had a cold already. I caught the cold because I sat on top of the ice in the truck. I expected some kind of hardship, but not like what happened to Mr. Arataka; he need insulin. After a couple of days at Lone Pine, people in camp started sending us their food. You'd be surprised what beautiful food they sent us. Especially during Christmas and New Years. The food was not from the regular supply department but private stuff they cooked and brought over—sushi and everything.

We were in that jail from December 9 to January 9. About two or three days before we were moved, Morton from the WRA came over. He said, "You write down why you have been detained in here." Instead of them telling us why we were detained, they said, "You write it down." We said, "You write it down. It doesn't make sense. If we be charged for something we did, then explain why." But they want us to admit we did something wrong. Several of us never wrote anything; we just turn in the white paper. Then about three days later, they came over and said, "Write anything. As soon as we send to Washington you'll be released sooner to the other camp instead of going to jail." I didn't write anything.

Around that time they formed a second committee at Manzanar —Odamoto and Murakami. They came over and visited us. They said, "Write anything, they're going to send to Washington and you'll be released to the open space."

On January 9, in the morning, they bring a little slip to us signed by Dillon Meyer. It say they would transfer us to the other camp and get us a speedy hearing. We got that little piece of paper. Then we went up to the bus. There's three people from the Independence jail; they was on that bus too. We got onto the bus and went to the train depot. There was a pullman and dining car connected together. We rode in the pullman car. I don't know how many, but there was a bunch of MPs in there. Because the shades were down, you don't know how many cars were on that train or anything. You can't see nothing. You can't walk around; you have to just sit in there in the middle of the pullman.

We didn't know which way the train is moving. Then that evening about eight or nine o'clock, the train finally stopped for quite a while and I could hear the foot noise, walking on the platform. A lot of people movement, and I just peeked through the shade so I could see the sign "Salt." Must be in Salt Lake, I thought. That night about nine o'clock, a porter came over and fixed the beds. We have to stand up on the side and wait for him. I asked the porter, "Could you get me a pencil and paper and a envelope? I want to write a letter to the family." He didn't say nothing but he show with the eye where he going to put them. So after he fix the bed—MPs going to sleep in the bottom bunk; we sleep in the upper bunk—we wrote a letter to the camp. And I don't send it to my family because I know they not going to receive it. I send it to some other friends. We're in Salt Lake City now. Next morning when the porter comes I leave him a dollar; all I had was a dollar. He mailed the letter. That black porter, he really take chance because even the bathrooms, they wouldn't let us shut the door. The MP was standing right there.

We ended up in Moab. We stayed together, most of the group. For a while MPs were controlling everything. They had a sentry on the front of the barracks so nobody came in or out. We were cooped up in one building. If you wanted to go to the bathroom, you had to tell the MP; he had to come with us. That is isolated place, Moab, thirty miles away from a small mining town, dinky old town. We were way out nowhere. All around, nothing but sagebrush, not even trees. About seven or eight old Citizen's Conservation Corps (CCC) camp buildings left standing there. No place to go.

MPs cooked for us, and every day at lunchtime we line up, and they had an MP guarding us at both ends. We marched to the mess hall and ate. First two or three weeks, no mail came in, and you can't write nobody. We were completely shut off from outside. Then after that every bit of mail is opened up, I mean, it came in with a seal. Then we protest, "We put the three-cent stamp on them, and you got no right to open up our mail, not with a stamp on it." "Well," they said, "next time don't put the stamp on it." And then they say not to seal the letter because they going to open it up anyway. So everything's opened.

Only visitor was from naval intelligence. He was a commander or something. Then the FBI came over from Salt Lake City. The FBI agent called me in, and he interviewed me for half an hour or so. He asked me if I be given a good job would I go out and work? I said, "No, there is no job. I like to stay in the camp," because he probably give me the same question as Campbell did. Before the incident, Campbell called me in one time to the office. He tried to tell me, why don't you quit making trouble and go outside? He said, "I have a friend in the outside and he's a millionaire and he's willing to give you a job. If your wife want to work, he give her a job, too." The FBI from L.A. came over and investigated, and they tried to harass me. I told the FBI, "You investigate the wrong person; you have to look into it! They shorten our food and everything," and I point to the administration building. "They are the problem, not me."

About a week or so later, the FBI from Washington came over because sugar was ration food. Sugar and meat and all those things were under federal regulations. So FBI came, and they investigate. First they called me in and said, "You said the administration cheating you of food, that's a very serious charge. If your statement's wrong you could be in serious trouble." That's what they told me. I said, "I know, but I'm right. You better investigate them instead of me." So, they went over and for two or three hours they question Campbell. I didn't hear nothing from them after that, so they must have found something.

I don't think we could have stopped evacuation, because Japanese population was so small and powerless in politics. There was no base for anybody to support them. Like today we have some ground and political power, that's different, somebody could speak with a little more authority. Those days we were nothing but farmers and salesmen, and market workers and fishermen. We got no power, nothing. So despite the fact we didn't like it, I guess we had no chance against the government. Japanese people don't like to demonstrate like other races. Japanese never demonstrate against anything with force or anything. Like the word we use, *shikataganai*, "can't be helped." We don't like it but we can't help it.

I think instead of cooperate, we should have just stood our ground. Maybe we don't be recognized as loyal to the United States if we didn't volunteer. But instead of begging for their mercy, I think best we just keep quiet, wait till the war end. That's the way I think that most of us feel. We don't have to yell at the government, but at the same time we don't have to beg for their mercy. I think it was the wrong decision at the beginning of evacuation when the JACL said they would ask our people to cooperate and not resist. But Japanese don't resist. Maybe Yasui tested the case, but very few of us would resist. He was a single man. If I was single man I might do what he did. But if you have a family, you have to think for your family, too. I don't think we would resist, but still we don't say we cooperate. No, we don't.

I think government in those days wouldn't negotiate with the Issei organizations, like the Japanese American Association. The only Japanese organization they recognize or listen to is the JACL. They looked at them as leader of the Japanese; they negotiated with them. But JACL made mistake.

When the war broke out, the United States tried to unite the people to fight against the Axis powers. Roosevelt said several times in his Fireside Chats that American blood will never be shed on European soil. He said that. But then he had to do contrary to what he promised. So he needed some kind of excuse to unite the people. I think it was mid-January in 1942 when they started shooting at midnight. Antiaircraft exploded in the sky above Long Beach, California, for about fifteen minutes. But all we could see was light, nothing flying. But Army blame the Navy, Navy blame the Army. After everything, nothing happen.

Next thing we know, we hear that Japanese subs torpedo the lumber ship in Oregon. That was close to end of January. Then about ten days later they tell us that it was not the torpedo but the rough ocean. It was during the wintertime, and ship was carrying too much lumber, and it flooded and then it sank. But the people like to see the headline, "Jap Sub Sunk Lumber Ship," and "Coastal Traffic Is Menaced by Jap Sub." Then several other ships report near-miss by torpedo. They see the big wave coming; they see the torpedo, they see the ghost there.

In that way the government made propaganda, hatred propaganda. And in the Philippines, the same thing. The government was desperately trying to unite the people to fight against the Axis. They mold the hatred toward Japan and maybe toward us too; the people start hating us more. It's kind of difficult to go outside tide of public opinion, and none of the papers sympathized with the Japanese American. They didn't care, they didn't give a damn, guilty or not guilty. Americans they see Westerns: one Indian did something wrong, they hate all Indians, all tribes. They willing to kill whole tribes. Same thing, same mentality here. Japanese have very low crime and never try to show themselves superior to others. And most of us had been in United States for so long, we didn't have too much contact with Japan, and none of us was willing to take arms against the United States. No sabotage or potential fifth columns, but sabotage is what government did, what they did to the whole Constitution. They had the chance to use us to help the war cause.

I think people like me spoke up more because of the place we grow up, the environment. When I was going to school in Hawaii, they were half Caucasian and half Japanese. In other words, we equal to the Caucasian population. So we don't feel inferior. Every time we had an argument or fight, we fight equal.

But even in Japan, when you go back to your family you are outsider for awhile, but after awhile you are equal. Because same race, you don't feel any different; they treat you equal. But in this country, prior to war, people grew up always under pressure—you inferior, you second-rate citizen, and so on. They didn't say so openly, but you felt that thing—every day, pressure. You work in a store; if they have any disagreement, they say you so-and-so Jap, right away. And if you insult a Caucasian, next thing, they call the police right away. Even if you're right, you have to apologize or else you be in jail. That's the way they are. In other words, a Kibei's sense of pride or dignity was different from the Nisei; the Kibei don't feel the same kind of pressure that made the Nisei feel inferior to Caucasians. Too bad in this country, before the war, the people bring so much pressure. Unconsciously I think that a lot of Nisei felt that pressure. They can't resist pressure.

My children told me I could sue the government individually. But like most Kibei I was kind of hesitant. But if you keep quiet and just stay behind, then this thing could occur again. Different government and there may be a similar situation come up and it start again. They give an excuse. The only way is we go after the government so they can't repeat the same thing, the same mistake. So only way is to sue the government or get the government to pay enough compensation, so we could have some Issei home or something. We could start off by making past generation be a little comfortable in later years. That's why I join the suing thing.

We were detained without any hearing or nothing, just because we were Japanese. If we were Caucasian, they never can do that. They probably would have a hearing and the public wouldn't accept that; but just because we were Japanese descendants, they could do anything they want. A lot of these people were ignorant. Even today I see once in a while in the paper they say: pay Japanese reparation. That's ridiculous. It doesn't pay back for a lost son. They don't know what is right or wrong. They should teach the people what the Constitution means. Lots of people don't know. They think they know, but they don't know.

Take a man like Campbell or any director in the camp. They be nothing but bosses of Indian reservations. Most of them came from there, and you know how the Indians are. Once a month the government gives them sugar, coffee; most of the reservations they are just welfare cases. So whoever take charge of reservation is just like a boss, a dictator. So these people come in the camp and snap their finger and think all of a sudden ten thousand people say Yes sir. People like Campbell talk just like they talking to somebody who's nothing, a slave or something. Sometimes I pounded the table and argued with Campbell. The whole office looked at me, like who the hell is this guy. They were doing sinister things, so they tried to hide them. So they were weak on their side. I wasn't afraid to talk with them.

Many of our friends is gone. This year Tateishi is gone. Before that, Tsuji gone. The government never come out with the real truth, and they got no excuses. All they could do is to say people were troublemakers, Axis sympathizers. Not many persons know what happened in camp. All they know is there was a riot. All they know is Axis sympathizer make celebration for Pearl Harbor Day. That's all they know. That's all the government tells them. They never tell the truth. The people even in the camp, they never tell the truth, they were just plain ignorant out there. They never find the truth.

FRED FUJIKAWA

Jerome

I was born in San Francisco in 1910, and I lived there until I was seven years old when I moved down to San Pedro. I've lived in Southern California practically all my life except for the time I spent in camp. I went to San Pedro High School, and then I went to UCLA for a couple of years, from 1927 to 1929. Then my family moved out to Westwood in 1929 and I had no way of going from there to UCLA. So I went up to Berkeley for one year, and after three years I got into Medical School—Creighton University in Omaha. I finished there in 1934 and then interned at the L.A. County General Hospital for two years. I opened my office in Terminal Island in August of 1936. So at the time the war broke out, I had been practicing there a little over five years. I was married in May of 1941. Until I was married I had just a room across the street from my office where I stayed. But after we were married in 1941, we had a house on Seaside Avenue in Terminal Island.

On December 7, 1941, I went to the hospital and made rounds and then came back to my office. It must have been around 10:30 A.M. or so, our time, which would be 8:30 A.M. Hawaii time, and I was puttering around in the back in my treatment room. A friend of mine, Harvey Takeuchi, was reading the Sunday paper in my waiting room and listening to the radio. All of a sudden he came tearing into where I was working and told me, "Dear Fred, come out here and listen to this radio broadcast." So I came out and somebody was describing the events that were occurring at Pearl Harbor at that time—all the airplanes dive-bombing, the battleships and so forth—so it must have been sometime after the onset of the strike because certainly the reporters had to be notified and they had to go out to that area. But we listened to it for five or ten minutes, and then suddenly it was blocked out.

My reaction was total disbelief. After things sank in I became concerned about what was going to happen to us—the family, my parents, who were Issei, me and my wife. That was my one concern, what's going to happen to us? I worked at the office until I finished, and then I went home. That day we had some visitors; there was one girl visiting my wife from Sacramento and another friend, Lily Okura. They were visiting on the island, and they couldn't get off, because just as soon as the war started, within a matter of minutes, they closed off the bridge and the ferry. Those were the only means of access or egress from Terminal Island, the ferryboat and the bridge on Fourth Avenue. The only other way to get off would be to take a railroad bridge at the eastern end of the island, but they just blocked it off and they wouldn't let anyone go out or come in.

I tried to get our friends off the island by taking them down to the immigration station. It was evening already, and I took them down there, and they knew me because I used to go on the Japanese ships that came in to see the sick people on board and so forth. One fellow I knew there—I forget his name, he was a Japanese fellow—grabbed me and he asked me to come this way, so I did. The next thing I knew I was pushed up against the wall, and they had a long pole with a number on it. They pushed that against my chest and took my picture, two views, and then I told them, "Wait a minute, all I'm trying to do is a favor for my friends, trying to get them off the island, get permission." They said, "Oh, we know that, Doc, we know that, but come with me anyway." And the next thing I knew they were fingerprinting me; so they had my prints and they had my picture with a number on it. At that time I was in a hallway, and an elevator was going up and it stopped. The door opened and it was just filled with Japanese fishermen. They looked at me and they all said, "Oh, the doctor is here too." So they thought I was going to go with them too. I don't know where they went from there. I had one heck of a time trying to get those girls off the island.

They had two shipyards. I think one was Todd Shipyard and the other was Kaiser. Kaiser was building Liberty ships already at that time. And then the naval base was fairly new, but it was there and they were building it up. They also had an airfield there, Reeves Field, and we noticed that they had these P38 fighter planes on the airfield.

We had about three thousand people of Japanese parentage in an area I would estimate as about half a square mile, and they had housing there owned by the cannery. Right after the war broke out, the FBI came in and started rounding up all these fishermen, people with fishing licenses, and all of the so-called enemy aliens. I'm pretty sure that all the fishermen had fishing licenses, commercial fishing licenses, and I'm sure they were all picked up. The island was overrun by soldiers. And the jeeps, they had three men in the jeeps, the driver, the shotgun, and the guy in the back with a machine gun. And you know, after the war started people would stand around and talk about it, wondering what was going to happen. If there was a group of more than two or four people, they'd disperse them or take them in.

On the morning of the twenty-fourth, I think it was, at two in the morning, we were awakened by gunshots. So we got up and we went outside and we saw that there were antiaircraft batteries all around our house in Terminal Island, all around that area. And then we looked up in the sky and they had searchlight beams going up to something way up high, and they were shooting at it. Later on it was proven to be a weather balloon. The next morning they issued the notice to move, to evacuate Terminal Island within forty-eight hours.

When that forty-eight-hour notice to evacuate became known, I immediately called up Beacon's Storage Company and asked them to send down a big van to evacuate my office and my home and my parents' home, and I stayed up all night dismantling all my equipment, my X-ray machine.

Right away, all of these junk dealers came into town and oh, it was terrible. These poor women whose husbands were rounded up by the FBI; they were all fairly young and they had small children and no one to help them, and they had to somehow make ready to leave the island in forty-eight hours. And here come these junk dealers, these opportunists. This was in December, so a lot of the families had already bought their Christmas presents, like new phonographs or radios, refrigerators—and they had no men around the house. These guys would come in and offer ten or fifteen dollars and because they had to leave, they'd sell. My mother had some furniture that she didn't want to take and some things that she wanted to take but couldn't, like some of the articles that I had made in wood shop, and she wasn't about to sell them to those guys. And so she made a fire and burned everything up, kitchen table and chairs and so forth. It was a pretty sad situation.

Our neighbors right in the back were the Shigekawas, who were married right after we were. Mrs. Shigekawa had one of the pharmacies in Terminal Island, the Ishi Pharmacy, and she had quite an experience there, because she couldn't empty out her store. She just locked it up hoping to come back in a day or two to clean it out. When she did go back a day or two later, she told me that the place was completely ransacked and, you know, nothing left. A lot of those people who had businesses in Terminal Island suffered tremendous losses.

The Japanese American Medical Association of Los Angeles included about thirty-two doctors of Japanese ancestry. Most of them at that time were Issei doctors; Nisei doctors were at a minimum, but we had a meeting at the Japanese hospital, and the Public Health Service doctor came and asked us if we would volunteer our services to go into the camps and take care of our people. We asked him about pay and he told us that yeah, we would be paid a fair salary. And so we thought that we would probably get Public Health Service equipment, but we just got sixteen dollars salary. And anyway, I volunteered to go to Santa Anita.

The hospital at Santa Anita looked like a shed which I understand was used for saddling the horses. They converted that into a hospital, and right in the middle of that shed was a sort of small tower—I think there was a clock on it—that was the operating room. We had a clinic at one end, and we had patients at the other end. We had obstetrics and we had surgery too, general surgery, and any complicated cases we transferred to the general hospital. We had the general hospital to back us up so we were pretty confident. However, there were only six of us taking care of some eighteen thousand inmates there.

We had to inoculate everybody there with three shots of typhoid, then paratyphoid, and two shots of DPT, which is diphtheria, whooping cough and tetanus. We vaccinated them for smallpox, and a lot of them got very sick, especially with the typhoid shots— they got fever and then diarrhea. The people would line up to get into the toilet, and I saw some patients faint waiting in line, with cramps. It was terrible, that was the worst thing that I saw in camp. The other was the so-called riots, where they labeled somebody an "inu" or a spy and went chasing after him; that happened at Santa Anita too.

THERESA TAKAYOSHI

Minidoka

I was born in New York City. My father was Japanese and my mother was Irish. When I was two years old, we moved back to Seattle because my father had contracted tuberculosis. He had a brother here and felt that if he came out here to his brother's, he'd get well. He didn't, and he died. And then my mother remarried, a Japanese. I can remember so well the indignities that she suffered. For instance, when she'd go out to rent a house, everybody was anxious to rent it to her until she had to say, "Will you rent to Japanese?" Because they couldn't always tell what we were, my sister and I. And they would say no. So then she'd kind of walk shamefully away, you know.

And what happened was that it had a psychological effect on her, because towards the end of the evacuation, during the time we were away, she completely denied any Japanese affiliation. She changed her name and after my stepfather was evacuated, she began to pose as a widow. And she changed her name back to a very Irish name, one not even like her maiden name.

My two brothers did not have to leave. We're Catholic, and my mother talked to the bishop and he pled her case saying that be-cause my brothers were minors they shouldn't be taken away from their mother. I'm half Japanese, and my brothers are half Japanese, but I had to leave.

When my brothers got permission to stay, my mother told me

to go and talk to this person at the command post. So I went and talked to this lieutenant, who happened to be Italian. And he said, "Well, I'll write all this information down and send it to the Presidio in California, but I'm not real sure how it's going to come out."

The verdict came back that I could stay, but my children had to leave. They were two and six at the time. Well, I wasn't going to let them and my husband go without me. My husband really wanted me to stay because he felt that I'd be better off here, keeping the store and so forth. And he kept thinking that it was only going to be a few months until he'd be out. But we all went to Puyallup, to Camp Harmony. One Sunday my mother came out to visit us. Not knowing the rules and regulations, she started to hand me a box of pastry through the fence, and the soldier on guard just practically turned his gun on her and said that he had to inspect everything. He inspected it and finally he let us have it. But let me say that because I married a Japanese American man, my two children were three-fourths Japanese. Now according to Army regulations, if you had one-sixteenth Japanese blood, despite age or whatever, you had to go to camp. My mother, who was full-blooded Irish, married a Japanese and later married another Japanese. So you might consider me half Nisei, but I consider myself full-blooded Nisei.

A lot of people have asked me how come I'm so Japanese, since my mother didn't speak Japanese, or cook Japanese. We were raised strictly American. Well, there was an incident when I was in the eighth grade. I was thirteen years old, and we went to a parochial school. There were two of us, another girl who was full-blooded Japanese. As we were graduating from the eighth grade, there was this round of parties. I think every girl in the class gave a party, but we were not invited to any of them. And at thirteen years old, that hurt. So I just kind of turned my back on the Caucasian population and started dating Japanese boys when I was old enough to date. So I am very Japanese in my thinking. Among my Caucasian friends at that time I was considered Japanese even though, if I were out, like on a streetcar or something, people would look at me and say, "What nationality are you?" They could never figure out whether I was Mexican or Spanish or whatever. I know I look very Caucasian.

I was twenty-four just before evacuation, making me twenty-three and a half at the time of Pearl Harbor. Before it was attacked, my husband and I had decided to have a family picture taken because we didn't have one with the children. We had gone to this studio not too far from the house, and then we came home to open our ice cream parlor. On the way people were just running out into the street saying, "The Japs have bombed Pearl Harbor!" Well, my heart just sank because my sister had just moved out to Hawaii. We kept the radio on all day. We had to go to a birthday party that afternoon at my in-laws', and everybody there had long faces wondering what we were going to do, what was going to happen to us. I remember it very well.

My husband and I owned an ice cream parlor where we made our own ice cream. We'd had the store for two years, and as business got better and better, we put in sandwiches and soup. We had a soup kitchen, I made chili and, you know, we had a lot. Our business was good.

After Pearl Harbor some people started to stay away from our business. However, most of my neighbors stuck with us. They gave me a surprise party in April, just neighbors around the store. This was April of 1942. They gave me so many things that I could use in camp, like heavy pants and heavy nightgowns and things like that. By April, obviously the word was out officially that the evacuation was going to take place. But my husband and I hung on until the last, thinking that the government was going to say it couldn't handle all those people.

We sold the store for a thousand dollars the day before we left. We had done an inventory, and the contents of the store were worth ten thousand. Our machines alone were worth eight thousand—that's what we paid for them. And we sold the whole store for a thousand dollars. By the time my husband went into the service, I think we had two hundred dollars left. Just enough to buy little odds and ends we needed.

Anyway, we had put an ad in the paper, and it ran for weeks and weeks. The way the paper wrote it up was: "Ice creamery, library, lunches, residential spot, sacrifice, evacuee." And then they had our address. Well, we had people coming in droves offering us a hundred dollars, two hundred dollars. And finally this man offered us a thousand dollars. We put him on hold for a couple of days, but we took it the day before we left. And my husband had to hurry to get it to the bank. The store continued to operate because I had my brothers check on it; it was open for about three months and then he went under and just closed the doors.

Evacuation took place on May 9, 1942. There was a beauty shop right next to our store, and in front of it, a young fellow bought our car for twenty-five dollars. It was a 1940 Oldsmobile, not very old. Well, he bought it for twenty-five dollars. He then drove us down to Dearborn and Seventh, where there was a big bunch of people and luggage all over. The Army had told us that all we could take was what we could carry. You can't expect a two-year-old and a six-year-old to carry very much, and we followed the rules to the letter. Then I remember getting so angry because some of those people had bicycles and everything, you know, and they had maybe six or eight things and packages. My mother came and my two brothers and some of my friends. I can remember getting on the bus, and at that time they hadn't told us about visitation or anything. I can remember thinking I would never see my mother or my brothers again.

We went to Puyallup, or Camp Harmony, which had once been a fairgrounds. When we got there, I got sick to my stomach. I really did. I don't ever remember anything having an impact on me like that. Because the first thing they did was give all the men these great big sacks, and they told them to go to the back of the camp and fill them full of straw for mattresses. Then we got these canvas army cots; and the boards on the floor had maybe about a half an inch of space between them. So eventually the grass grew up between them. Then there was not a full partition between our compartment and the people next door. So you could hear everything that went on, because I think the roof was sort of pointed and the partition ran straight across. I can still picture it. We had a door on each side, but it was very small quarters, very small.

I was a mother with little kids, but I just didn't know. Because at that time nothing had been announced about relocation centers. And so I kept thinking that this was just a temporary thing, until August. Then they announced that we were going to have to leave. Meanwhile, I had some really bad experiences because of misdiagnoses by some doctors. Once I was quarantined under the grandstand with my youngest child who had a big lump sticking out. The doctor kept saying it was mumps. My older son had had the mumps so I knew what to expect. This thing turned red; mumps don't turn red. So anyway I was under the grandstand, and it was so damp and I couldn't leave that place and nobody could come and see me. My little boy and I stayed there for six weeks. Finally my cousin who was a registered nurse came to see me. And I told her to go and get Dr. so-and-so and bring him in here and show him this child has not got the mumps. It's something else because it hasn't gone away in six weeks. And so she did, and he came. At first he said, Well, that's Dr. so-and-so's patient; I'm not really supposed to see him. Then he said, "No, he hasn't got the mumps, he's got a swollen lymph gland." He let me out. I got to go back across the street.

Well, that was one incident. And then my older son got very, very ill, and I was afraid to call a doctor because I didn't have any confidence in them anymore. He was vomiting and I didn't know what was the matter with him or what to do. Finally the ambulance came with my cousin and the doctor. My cousin told the doctor, "I know my cousin, she doesn't get excited over nothing." So he came over, and the minute he walked in he started sniffing and said, "Acidosis, this child has food poisoning. I want him to go to Tacoma immediately to a hospital so they can pump his stomach and we can have evidence because there's been a lot of people saying they had food poisoning, but you don't know because of no evidence." So at two o'clock in the morning, this Army car came with a big black man who was supposed to be some kind of security person and my cousin, and we rode to the hospital.

I'll never forget that hospital; I've never had the guts to go back and look it up in Tacoma. We climbed stairs; I'll bet we climbed a hundred stairs to get up to the night door. When we got there, the nurse came rushing out with a wheelchair. She got my son in it and turned around. When I started in after her she said, "You can't come in. You're supposed to be in the prison camp." That's the way she put it.

Then the next morning, back in camp, my husband, who is kind of a hothead anyway, wanted to call the hospital to see how our son was. We weren't sure, at that point, what had happened to him. And the guard, for some reason or other, took it on himself to not allow us to use the phone. So we went and got the Red Cross contacts, Min Masuda and Sam Hokari. They asked to use the phone, and the guard refused to let them use it. So then my husband, Min, and Sam threatened him and told him that if he put down that gun and came inside, they'd show him. In the meantime, the Army guards were right across the street and a lieutenant saw what was going on, and he came over and he asked us what was going on. We told him. He relieved that guard immediately and he handed us the phone.

We were told that our son was going to be released that afternoon. So again, we drove over to Tacoma and this time they did let my husband and me in. And when we did, here's this little six-year-old kid; he was lying on his side and just crying, but silently, you couldn't hear him. I asked him what was the matter and he just threw his arms around me and held on to me. And he said, "Oh, take me back to camp. They were going to let me die last night." I said, "What are you talking about?" And he said, "Well, the nurse said, 'Let this little Jap die, don't even go near him.'" And to this day he remembers that. He's forty-five years old now, but he still remembers that.

When we got to Minidoka, there was no barracks for us, no barracks for us to live in. They were still building them, but my sister-in-law was already living in Block 6. So the soldiers ordered us into the rec hall where there were bachelors and families and everything. And my husband said, "I'm not going to have my family live here." He said, "What do we do for privacy?" The soldier said, "Well, just hang a blanket across between the two families." And my husband said no. And he got a little hot then, too. So finally his brother, seeing how upset he was getting, said that we could move in with him, right across the road. They had the end barracks, which was only supposed to be for two or three people, and they had a little girl. So we put seven beds in there. In order to make the beds, we had to pull one out, way out, halfway out the door, to make up the other six and then make that one up and slide it back in. It was like we were all sleeping on one big bed. This lasted a couple of months. And then, finally, we were put in the barracks in Block 12.

Minidoka was just so dusty, so dusty, and so cold in the wintertime. None of us from Seattle had clothes that were warm enough for that climate. The dust storms that would just come up without notice were just terrible. And I felt that the family situation was deteriorating. I was young and I had these two little children, but I was alone with them most of the time because my husband worked in the cost accounting department in the camp. I think he got sixteen dollars for skilled labor. I worked in the mess hall and got twelve. There were lots of times when he would be playing cards—they played a lot of gin rummy in camp—he'd be playing several blocks away at mealtime, so he'd just go straight to the mess hall. And I had to take the kids myself, even though I worked in the mess hall.

But there were funny incidents too. I remember one time I had gone and got two buckets of water to give my kids a bath in a big washtub. And after it was over, I took the wash pail out and I was just dumping it over the side of the porch when this windstorm came, and it backed up the water and the dust all over me. I was a mess. I marched right over to the laundry room where I saw my husband talking with some fellows and I said, "I don't know about you, but I'm leaving here tomorrow." He said, "Good-bye." But I just don't know, you have to look at the humor of it sometimes; otherwise I think we would have all gone crazy.

About evacuation, I was very young then and I was very quiet but believe me, they'd never do it to me now. See, I never thought of myself as anything but an American. And right after Pearl Harbor there was talk of shipping us all to Japan. And I had told my husband, "They'll never get me over there, I'll jump boat." I still consider myself a very good American. I never miss a vote, and I work for certain political candidates. But I certainly look at the whole experience like I think any other American would look at it if it happened to them.

Obviously, at Minidoka we couldn't get out. We had to apply for a pass, and then after so many days they might grant it. In short, we were not free. I definitely felt like a prisoner because there was no other way of getting out; you had to apply for this pass. And then it might or might not be granted. There were times when they put a freeze on passes.

From the time I left Seattle, I was in Minidoka eighteen months. My husband had volunteered for the 442nd, and in fact, he had been one of the ones that had gone around kind of recruiting for the 442nd. And I can still remember how I thought it was good at the time. But it was a put-up-or-shut-up situation. These poor guys were told to either put up or shut up.

Of course that's when the loyalty oath thing came up. Almost immediately after my husband left, Mr. Schafer, who was the assistant camp administrator, sent for me. He told me that he did not want me to stay in camp. I asked him why, and he said, "Well, because I don't want you to stagnate." He felt that some of the people were just going to rot away. And he felt that I had too much spirit.

He wrote a letter to the Presidio asking whether I could come and live with my mother, because all the Japanese girls that were married to Caucasians were by then out of camp. And here I was not even, you know, full Japanese. They turned me down again. I packed up, and he asked me where I wanted to go and I said, "I'll go to Omaha. I have a sister-in-law now living there." No job, nothing, but I had the two kids. Meantime, my husband got an early discharge out of the service because he had a medical problem. We got to Omaha in October, and he joined us the following January. My husband had volunteered because he felt very strongly that if he volunteered, I might be able to take the kids and go back to my mother. That is absolutely what he thought.

But going to Omaha was scary. We had a one-way ticket, and I left with my sister-in-law's sister and her six-week-old baby. On the way we stopped in this little town of Shoshone, Idaho. Neither one of us had ever traveled on a train; we had no idea what to expect. As it turned out we became separated, and I was on a troop train with just one of my sons. Those soldiers were so nice to me. The train was packed. One soldier, when my little boy fell asleep on my lap, got up and let me have his seat to put my little boy on. But they weren't that way in Shoshone; the people were very belligerent in that town. The soldiers, though, were so nice. They had box lunches that they offered to share with me and my little boy. There wasn't one that was nasty. Really ironic, isn't it? And all of them were white.

Anyway, the doctors at Camp Shelby (where the 442nd received basic training) had told my husband that he needed some kind of easy job because he had worked hard all his life. They suggested he go back into accounting. But the pay scale in Omaha was so low for a CPA; they were starting at twenty-five dollars a week. So my husband's brother sent a telegram from Indianapolis that said: "Come at once, job waiting." And we went. There was no job waiting, but eventually everything worked out well.

How did I recover from all of it? I think the biggest help was not coming back to Seattle right away. During the twenty-five years we spent in Indiana we met many, many nice people. They were all Caucasians and they all accepted us as if we were just one of them. And not one of them knew about the evacuation, not one. When I would tell them about it, they were aghast. I think because we lived out there for that long, had almost no contact with Japanese people and were more or less accepted, the bitterness kind of went away.

I'm half Irish. None of my children married Japanese girls or boys. I even have an adopted Caucasian child, my youngest. I've tried to teach them to be very tolerant, because I can remember when I was a child, it was so hard. In those days, about the only Caucasian women that married Japanese were prostitutes. I know my mother used to just really come apart sometimes when somebody would get very nosy and ask where and how she met her husband. So I mean she suffered a great deal during that period. I realized after I grew up some of the painful things that she had to go through. I was kind of precocious and I can remember hearing things, little digs. Maybe that's part of why I turned my back on Caucasians.

But I never felt any prejudice from the Japanese. As kids they all knew what I was. I mean I didn't hide it from anybody. I have friends who say I'm more Japanese than they are. This may be true because I accept the Japanese culture and I'm trying to learn to speak Japanese now. I always taught my kids about being Japanese, even after the two older ones went to camp. I never played down the fact that they were Japanese.

In Indianapolis, I enrolled my son in a parochial school, and this priest who was very Irish—his name was Sweeney—came out to the playground to check on the kids. He was quite protective of us. He came out and looked things over and called Tom over and said, "Don't let any of these big Irish bullies get tough with you." And Tom said, "Oh, Father, I can take care of myself. I'm half Irish too." But in Indianapolis they made a fuss if you were black. The population was one-third black.

I remember my husband used to say, you know, I worry about these guys who are always condemning the blacks because I wonder what they're saying about me behind my back. He said, usually if you're prejudiced towards one group, you're prejudiced towards the others. But the people in Indianapolis could be very nice too.

YOSHIYE TOGASAKI

Manzanar

I was born January 30, 1904, in San Francisco at the site where the Geary Theater is now. My father had a store there, and we lived upstairs. I was the fifth of eight children. There were two boys and two girls ahead of me. My sister, Mitsu, and I were sent to Japan to be with my maternal grandmother in Tokyo because my grandmother was all alone and five kids were a little too much for my mother to handle at that point. We stayed there for five years, until my grandmother died, and then we spent six months with my paternal grandparents in the country, in Ibaraki-ken. When we returned to the United States in 1910, I was six years old and was immediately placed in school because it was almost the end of the school year.

I entered Hearst Grammar School the next fall. My famliy moved from 15 Church Street in San Francisco, which was part of the temporary postearthquake quarter, to 1721 Post Street, where the Peace Center is now. My father started his business there, first the retail grocery business, and then around late 1917 or so, he moved downtown and went into the wholesale import-export business—Japanese foodstuffs and ceramics. Also, he'd take fliers on things like silk, but basically it was tea and canned goods or dry goods—*setomono* ("dishware"), as they used to say. During World War I, he was importing onions by the thousands of sacks because they were needed over here for some reason.

Anyway, I finished Lowell High in December, 1921. Then I went to UC, but I was out of school for about two years because of illness. I graduated in 1929. I left in 1931 to go to medical school, Johns Hopkins in Baltimore, and I finished there in 1935.

I could have been the first Japanese woman to graduate from Hopkins. Apparently they got a gift from five Quaker women, with a stipulation that women be admitted as well as men. If they did not admit women, they would have to return the money with compound interest. So, they've never returned the money and women have always been admitted there. On the other hand, there was considerable difficulty. The professors didn't want women; they made snide remarks, or they completely disregarded us. But women were admitted and that was that.

I went to Los Angeles for my internship and then accepted a residency in communicable diseases. I started an office in September of 1941 in Los Angeles on Vermont Avenue. December of that year was Pearl Harbor. The JACL was asking for young women volunteers to go up to the first camp at Manzanar. They wanted secretaries for the office and they wanted them ahead of time. You can imagine, mamas were not going to release their innocent daughters just because somebody said they needed them. So, the JACL frantically looked around for somebody who could be sort of a chaperon for these girls, about ten of them. Finally one of the nurses and I went ahead.

We established the medical unit quickly because we knew we were going to need it. In two or three weeks, the convoys started coming in with huge numbers of people, hundreds maybe even a thousand. The maximum number of people expected at Manzanar was ten thousand.

It is pretty arid and dry on that east slope of the Sierra, so you know how the wind was and the dust when they started digging and building. The dust and the wind bothered a lot of people because the dust was very fine. All the cracks . . . there was no point in sweeping out anything. It was difficult setting up a medical unit, because most of the doctors were accustomed to private practice and handling individual persons. They weren't accustomed to thinking in terms of community needs; and although I had not practiced, I had handled communicable diseases. I had public health experience behind me. Two years after graduation I worked for the city of Berkeley as a bacteriologist in the public health department. That experience served me well when I went to Manzanar.

I knew that we were going to have problems with tuberculosis, and I also knew that we would have problems with typhoid because a lot of people had already had typhoid in their youth out in the country or back in Japan. They were still carriers. So these were two illnesses I felt were preventable, and this could be done in part by vaccination. Tuberculosis required careful diagnosis and isolation. Preventing disease also meant that the people who worked in the kitchen and handled food had to be very careful, and dishwashing had to be done properly. I think the kitchen staff were all mad at me because I insisted that dishes should be sterilized after meals. They were able to make these wooden slatted things that allowed them to dip the dishes and take them out so that they didn't burn their hands. They didn't like it. But Manzanar did not have the kind of food epidemics that some of the camps had.

At first the military had absolute power. They sent a naval captain to supervise the medical program, and he was very nice. He wanted very much to be helpful, but when you're a naval captain and a surgeon, you really don't understand all the needs of babies and mothers and the general population of the elderly. The administration, for example, was holding back this order for baby formula; it was a powdered formula. I requested it because I didn't want to be bothered with a whole lot of formula made in a great big vat and then have that infected. I told them that with this powder you only put as much as you need in boiling water and use it all right away. Anyway, we finally set up a system of boiling the bottles and preparing formula.

The women did not even have a place to boil water in their rooms. If they brought an electric plate along, they were fortunate, but not everybody had simple things like that. From April on, the weather got warm, and whooping cough was cropping up. So were scarlet fever and measles, and in those days we didn't have antibiotics. We didn't have any vaccine for measles either. The population had not been immunized, so we were getting some awfully sick children. And you try to take care of kids in a barracks with no running water and only one electric bulb above you.

Well, the nurses were very good in instructing the parents, and parents were devoted and they were very cooperative. They weren't fighting the doctors and nurses, which is something you might find when parents are emotionally upset. They were very good even with the hot weather and the wind coming up in the morning, coming down in the evening, and all that sand blowing. You felt so sorry for those little kids, you know. But fortunately, no child died. As for the elderly, they probably had a lot more kidney infections because we didn't have medicine for them, or they might have tuberculosis.

But the elderly really were not isolated. They had companionship; they could talk to each other. They would sit, play go, and they'd do all these things. Being uprooted would be a hardship and some of the comforts of home were not there, but at least they had companionship with their age group and they could meet together.

I think that the evacuation was tragic. It was inexcusable in the sense that it really didn't need to happen. It's the same old story: when power whips up hysteria, power generally gets what it wants, and they got it. Like your yellow press. The Hearst papers, like the San Francisco *Chronicle*, the San Francisco *Examiner*, the Los Angeles *Times*; and the McClatchy papers like the Sacramento *Bee*. These papers were really wild. The organizations like your American Legion and your Grange, boy, they weren't quiet. They were constantly whipping up anti-Japanese feeling. You have to remember that even before the war was declared, in 1941 and 1940, there had been actual attempts at hangings.

I am a doctor. I understand that a lot of people who had much more tragic experiences than I did were not in a position to cope with things because of their background. And I understand why they can really be mad and feel resentful. But I don't understand those who say things like, if it hadn't been for the JACL we would never have been in camp. That's nonsense, but they still believe it. To this day. Well, my response to them is, What would you have done? How would you have stopped it? I don't see that there was anything that could have stopped the evacuation from happening.

The Quakers were great, though. A Quaker doctor came to me and said, "Togi, if there's anything we can do, let me know. We are going out to Terminal Island all the time, trying to find out what we can do to help them, but if you hear of any individual families that need help, let us know." On the other hand, the president of the Council of Churches of the State of California said to me the filthiest darn things, things like, You're just a traitor, and How do I know how to trust you? I don't know you from anything—you're

Japanese, so you're not trustworthy. And there were a lot of dirty cusswords in between. Unfortunately, I went to him to ask him to speak on behalf of the employees down at City Hall so that they would not be fired. I said I'd already been fired because I was not a civil service employee. I was an appointed person, and I was also part-time. But a lot of the others, working mostly in the lower jobs, were having such a hard time. But I got nowhere with him or with the health officer of the city of Los Angeles.

But the Quakers were always very steadfast. You could always depend upon them; you knew which way they were going. Also, the Catholic Mission fathers and sisters came in with the evacuees; they were committed too. And then some Episcopals and Unitarians came to help very early too.

FRANK CHUMAN

Manzanar

I was born April 29, 1917, in the town of Montecito outside of Santa Barbara, California. My father was the caretaker of a very large estate, for a wealthy family who would come to Montecito every year as a summer resort area. When I was three, my father felt there was no future for us in Montecito, so we came down to Los Angeles in about 1920. He was a gardener there in those days. In 1927, I believe it was, he purchased a dry cleaning business in Los Angeles and worked there with Mother helping him. Los Angeles was the place where I lived while I was getting all my education.

On December 7, my sister and I had just come back home after attending the morning worship service at St. Mary's Episcopal Church. All of us sat down to lunch—my father, my mother, my sister and myself—when there was a radio announcement that Pearl Harbor had been bombed and that we were at war with Japan. I was tremendously shocked, and my immediate reaction was that Japan had done a very foolish thing. This was my very first objective, cold reaction to Japan's bombing of Pearl Harbor. My parents' reactions were a little different. Their reaction was, Now that we are at war and we are of Japanese ancestry, we don't know what's going to happen to us; and in order to protect ourselves we should dispose of everything that has to do with any affiliations or associations with Japan.

There were certain awards that my father had gotten when he was with the Kagoshima *Kenji-Kai* ("prefecture association")— Kagoshima is where he came from. There were many letters, and pictures from Japan of members of my father's and mother's families. They pretty much destroyed all of that. I believe my father took them in the backyard, put these papers into an incinerator, and burned them. They kept very carefully all of the documents that pertained personally to themselves in Japan, for example, their Japanese scholastic records and graduation certificates. The graduation certificates and report cards of my sister, brother and myself. Everything that pertained to America, and especially pertained to themselves as a family originating in Japan or us as sons and daughters they were able to keep. It didn't amount to very much, maybe a little box full of documents. But they were able to take that with them when they went up to Manzanar. The only earthly material possessions that they saved were their own family records and ours. Nothing else.

As family heirlooms my father had two swords he had brought from Japan when he came to America in 1906. Of course, since I was very small, I never really knew he had those swords until I was about fourteen or fifteen. Then he showed me these two swords. One was a rather large sword, maybe five feet long, the other one was about two and a half feet. As I remember now, the outside scabbards of the swords, were a deep maroon color, ceramic in texture, with little flowers. They were ornamental swords, not for combat, decorated all over with petaled flowers. The hand parts of them were woven with some very fancy twine and then they had very fancy sword guards, with handguards on them. My father said to me then that he wanted to give those swords to me because I was the oldest son. My sister was older than I was, but I was the oldest son; I had a younger brother, George.

When the war broke out on December 7, my father and I took out these swords, which he had placed in a closed drawer, and we then went outside into the backyard. My father proceeded to separate the component parts of the sword. He removed the steel handguard and left the bare, naked steel sword blade itself. He did that with both the swords while I watched him. He then thrust the naked blades of both of the swords deep into the ground, not flat, down into the ground as deep as they would go and covered them so that they couldn't be seen from the surface. Then he threw away the scabbards.

I thought to myself, how stupid of Japan to go to war with the United States. I felt that my relationship with Japan as a nation, as a people, maybe even emotionally, would end with the outbreak of the war. This, of course, was very naïve thinking, but that's the way I thought. And the symbolic act of dismantling the sword and burying it sort of severed any emotional feeling I had at that time for Japan. It's almost like trying to bury a very unpleasant thought: you get it out of your sight and then it's out of your mind. Of course, there was another practical consideration, I think, on the part of my father. I never suggested to my father that he destroy the swords, but I'm sure that he was also thinking of the practical side: any swords, cameras, radios, pistols, rifles, were considered contraband. I believe from the news reports that if he was found in possession of Japanese swords he might have been considered suspect or something. I think this shook him up.

All my father and mother had were these swords, but I'm sure that other families had things as precious or more so in terms of not only intrinsic value, but also of actual monetary value. I'm sure that a lot of families had beautiful cloisonné vases or ceramic objects, paintings. I'm sure that they had hand scrolls, for instance, *kakemonos* ("wall scrolls"). I'm sure that there were just hundreds and thousands of Japanese families that brought these things from Japan, and I'm sure that in the panic that followed many families destroyed those things. Even today, I still have a sort of ache in my heart, because I would be very proud to display those swords in my home.

While there were a lot of things in the newspapers and on the radio during that period of time from December 7 to March, when I went to Manzanar, I was not really the object, personally, or directly, of any anti-Japanese feelings. Maybe a lot of people did get the full brunt of the anti-Japanese hostility, but I didn't. In the first place, I was attending school and I was also working forty hours a week in the Los Angeles County Probation Department, and I kept the job with the county until the Board of Supervisors gave an order to all department heads in the county department similar to those given in the city and state and federal governments to discharge all Japanese Americans. But even in the probation department I didn't really get anti-Japanese venom directed toward me. I knew most of the people in the probation department, I knew the students, being a student myself at USC Law School, and I wasn't often around the house or the business where my father was operating, so I really didn't get the impact of that.

When the order came from the Board of Supervisors to the acting chief probation officer to discharge me, I being the only Japanese American in the department, the officer called me into his office and said, "Frank, I do not have any legal cause nor any personal cause to terminate you, to fire you." He said, "I'm supposed to fire you. I'm not going to do that. But I have to let you go. You can't work here anymore. I will give you a leave of absence." So, I got a leave of absence. The leave of absence remained in effect all the way through evacuation.

So I didn't get the full brunt of the anti-Japanese hostility which was a hell of a good thing, because when I went to Manzanar there was a delayed reaction for me. What the hell am I doing in camp? I thought. While I was very busy working in the hospital, I said to myself, Why should the United States Government doubt our loyalty to the United States? We haven't done anything to justify this kind of treatment. Certainly not myself and certainly none of the others that I know of. And yet here I am in a camp of ten thousand people—men, women, and children. So I began to think to myself, because I had studied law—constitutional law and constitutional rights and due process and equal protection and all the rest of it—Jesus Christ, we've been deprived of our constitutional rights. There's been no accusations against me, and yet I'm suspect and I'm arbitrarily told to go into a camp. It's completely in violation of my rights. And I began to get goddamned upset. I thought, what the hell is the government doing, to put us away like this and incarcerate us and consider us disloyal and think that we're going to sabotage the United States' war efforts or anything else? What is it with the United States Government that has brought this to pass? And I really got angry and very, very upset at the United States Government for doing this kind of thing to not only me, but all Japanese Americans. I really got upset.

The Army recruiting team came into Manzanar around the early part of 1943. We had a big meeting in this mess hall of all persons eligible for military duty with two white soldiers and a person of Japanese ancestry, and this guy was trying to persuade us all to volunteer for the Army, and I'm not too sure whether I got up and spoke back to him or whether I said it in my own mind, but I said, "Why should we fight for the United States Government as soldiers, when the United States Government distrusts us? Why do they now want us to serve when they consider us to be disloyal? Why do they want us to serve when they have taken us out of our homes and schools and businesses, and now they want us to become loyal to the United States? It doesn't make sense, and so far as I'm concerned I'm not going to do anything to go into the United States Army until the United States Government does something to remedy this unjust situation." I cannot remember whether I stood up and said it or whether I felt it.

In any event, that's the way it was. In the latter part of 1943, this questionnaire came out sponsored by the WRA, and in that questionnaire it had something like "request for relocation" as well as the questionnaire. It was in two parts. And there were these questions 27 and 28, "Are you willing to foreswear any allegiance to any foreign potentate and say that you are loyal to the United States?" and, "Are you willing to bear arms for the United States?" The first answer that I gave to both questions was no. I was so goddamned mad at that questionnaire. It was insulting, impugning without any evidence, just from the top down that there was something that made us Japanese Americans suspect in loyalty, allegiance, that we wouldn't fight for the government and saying now you're going to fight. They don't have to push it down my throat—are you willing to bear arms to defend the United States? That's so goddamned obvious that I would do that that it just really made me angry.

So out of a feeling of anger and disappointment in the United States Government's attitude towards us and their unwarranted suspicion, and the way they treated us to make us all get out of our homes without any real basis for it made me so goddamned angry that for the record I wanted the government to know that I was angry. So I said, "No-no, just shove it up your ass." It was completely impulsive. I was pretty hotheaded back in those days. But pretty damn hotheaded towards things which involved injustice, things which I considered to be not fair. You know, on those kind of issues I have a tendency to get very hot and indignant.

I did not remain a no-no, because all of a sudden I thought to myself, after I had said that, I regretted it, because it wasn't my true feelings. There was no way that I could hate the United States Government, but I was goddamned angry at them for doing things like that about us. I got to thinking to myself that maybe I should do something about changing it and get the record straight as to what my real feelings were. I knew the project director, Ralph Merritt, and I was very close to him, because as administrator of the hospital I had to go down and see him about many, many things—the procurement of medical supplies and trying to take care of the sick and so forth. At least I had considerable personal contact with him.

So I went to Ralph Merritt and I said to him, "You know I regret that I gave the answers no-no." And he said, "Yeah, I think so." He said, "I don't think you really meant that, but you've already said it and put it on the record. It's been filed back in Washington with the WRA." I said, "Well, is there some way I can erase those answers?" He said, "God, that's tough. That is very, very difficult." But he said, "I'll tell you what, I'm in Washington many, many times as project director of Manzanar and I will do everything I can to see if I can get those answers changed for you. But I can't promise, because they were ordered by the military although it's on WRA paper."

So over a period of three or four months, he'd go to Washington and then he would call me in and he'd say, "I went to see such and such who was an officer in the United States Army." And he said, "The officer who has your answers is absolutely adamant about not doing anything about it. You knew what you were doing and when you answered that way, that became your answer." The officer said, "I have no sympathy with Chuman. He knows what the hell he's supposed to say and if he didn't say it, too bad." So Merritt said to me, "The first overture to try to erase the record has not been successful, but I'll try again through somebody else."

I found out later that he had gone almost to the top of the military hierarchy that had anything to do with the WRA questionnaire which really went out to all Japanese American persons of military age. That's what it was for, it was really a draft questionnaire, which later was used for men and women in the relocation camps as a general loyalty questionnaire. I know that Ralph Merritt took this matter about me as a personal crusade. Ralph Merritt gathered together all my background. He checked my background, he checked my school, my church, my Boy Scouts, my community activities up to that time; he checked with different persons who were my character references from the prewar days which we all had to list; and I know that he checked with the camp officials, he checked with people on the hospital staff who were Caucasians. He did a hell of a lot of work on that.

I didn't know that all of our mail was monitored. I was writing to a lot of people. Goddamnit, they were monitoring that. These people would write to me and I would write to them. If I had said anything that was hotheaded or anti-American, I was dead. But that didn't happen, I didn't write in that vein. So he had gathered all these papers together and next time he was in Washington he persuaded somebody who was high up that Frank Chuman was born in the United States, that he had never been to Japan, that from ages seven to eleven he was growing up at a grammar school; then junior high, high school, and so forth; that he was varsity debator and he was on the track team, he was captain; he was Boy's Senior Board at L.A. High School; UCLA; he was YMCA; Bruin Club, Boy Scouts, Eagle Scout; and all the rest of that stuff. While he was at Manzanar he was working diligently in the hospital, and he had said nothing derogatory about the United States Government.

Ralph Merritt said, "When I go to Washington the next time, write me a letter why you think you ought to have your answers changed." I did write that letter and wrote that, out of disgust for the United States Government's policy towards us, I thought it was unjust, I thought it was unfair, and so forth. He persuaded the powers that be that Chuman had just said that out of impulse and out of anger and disappointment rather than out of maliciousness and out of real feelings of hostility. So they changed me back to yes-yes.

The American Friends Service Committee in Philadelphia established the National Student Relocation Council. Many people were in it. I remember some of their names, Tom Emlen and Betty Emlen, a recently married young couple who had both graduated from Haverford College in Pennsylvania. I know that there were several others from other schools, but the only direct contact I had was with Betty and Tom Emlen. So I wrote to the National Student Relocation Council and said, "I'm interested in continuing law school if I can. I have no money. Can you help me?" Within a couple of weeks while the Emlens were on their regular circuit to different relocation camps, they came in to see me, and I told them what my plight was. I had to interrupt law school right in the middle of a semester and lose my credits because of it. I had no money and could not return to USC. I didn't know any other law schools outside of California. So they said, "Fine, we'll try to do something for you." And they made all kinds of efforts to find a suitable law school for me. They reported back to me that they had found a Valparaiso Law School in Indiana, Drake University, Boston College in Boston, and the University of Michigan among others. I said I would like to enter the University of Michigan Law School at Ann Arbor. So the Emlens were the ones who arranged for the transcripts, dormitory housing, and so forth.

The dean of the University of Michigan Law School wrote to me saying they were happy to accept me for the fall 1943 semester. Following that letter, about a week later, came this letter from the president of the university, saying, "I understand that you've been accepted into the Law School at the University of Michigan. I regret to say that you cannot enter the University of Michigan Law School because it is the policy of the University that no Japanese Americans are accepted into any department of the University, professional or undergraduate, because we are involved in sensitive war defense work." So that pulled the rug from under that. To go to Boston College Law School, which had already accepted me, required at that time, a clearance to enter the Eastern Defense Command. I did not have that clearance. It would probably never come or it would probably take months and months and I would be out as far as trying to attend beginning with the fall semester of 1943.

So among the schools in the Midwest and not within the Eastern Defense Command was the University of Toledo, which was found for me by Betty and Tom Emlen. I consulted with Ralph Merritt, who suggested that I go to the Midwest, and enter the University of Toledo. "After that," Ralph Merritt said, "there is nobody, not even military authorities that can prevent a United States citizen from going into the Eastern Defense Command without the clearance." He said, "You're free to travel throughout the United States. The idea is to get out of Manzanar with your clearance. There's nothing to prevent you from going out of camp because I'm the one that will allow you to go out and go to the Midwest. After that you're free to go into any college along the Eastern Defense Command. Nobody can stop you constitutionally or legally." So that's what I did, I went to the University of Toledo.

Before I left Manzanar for Toledo, I talked about continuing school with my parents—that I wanted to leave, that I didn't know what my future was, that I at least wanted to finish law school instead of going out to find work.

My father dug way underneath the cot where he slept. He pulled out a sack, a fabric sack, I can't remember exactly, but it was kind of a deep stocking sack, and he dug way in there and he pulled out of that sack $150, and he gave it to me. He said, "This is all I have left from the evacuation. We lost our dry cleaning business, equipment, big heavy equipment, and dryer, all kinds of things, furniture and household properties. All we've got is $150." But he said, "You take it. You need it. There's no more money. We don't have any more money. We cannot help you anymore on money; but we want you to finish your school if that's what you want. Don't worry about us, we're here in camp."

There had been some turmoil while we were at Manzanar. On December 7, 1942, a riot broke out. As a matter of fact there were two riots that were going on at the same time. I was in my offices at about seven that night when it happened. One of the riots took place in the northern part of the camp, mess hall 24 or something like that, where a lot of the primarily pro-Japanese, anti-JACL elements were having a meeting where they were denouncing the JACLers for either informing on some of the Japanese or for being too much in favor of the United States Government. I don't know whether it was by coincidence that it was on the first anniversary of Pearl Harbor or not, but anyway it was December 7, 1942. So this group were getting all heated up and excited, and they were all saying, "Well, let's go out and kill these guys." Apparently the anti-JACL elements dispersed and were scouring the camp looking for these people (JACLers) really with the intention of either killing them or doing them great harm.

In the meantime, at the opposite end of the camp, at the guard entrance, a group of persons had congregated because one of the evacuees who was working in the warehouse had accused the warehouse supervisor, a Caucasian, of diverting sugar from the delivery supplies for the camp evacuees and selling it on the black market. I know that the Japanese American was then summarily removed from the camp and put into a temporary jail in Lone Pine. When word got around that this Japanese American was arrested, some of the residents who knew of it gathered at the gate to lodge a protest at the administration building. The evacuees demanded that this person in jail be returned to the camp because he had done no wrong. As I understand it there were several hundred who had gathered at the gate beside the building. The evacuees were getting very riotous; they were saying a lot of bad things about the government, about the camp administration, and against this Caucasian warehouse supervisor, and they were getting very heated emotionally about the unfair arrest of this evacuee.

The project director then ordered the military police to come and restore some order at the entrance. The story I got, although it was told by many people with different versions, depending upon where they were at the time, is that the military police were lined up facing the crowd. The evacuees were coming closer and closer to the military police. The military police had shotguns. The information I had was that there were three military guards there. They ordered the crowd to disperse. Suddenly, as some of the crowd were turning around to leave, there was a shot or a sound as if a shot had been fired. Later I was told that a light bulb had been thrown by an evacuee towards the military guard, and it shattered on the pavement, which was asphalt, causing a shotlike sound. Anyway, the military police were pretty goddamned scared; I'm sure they had been instilled with a lot of anti-Japanese feelings anyway, and so while some of the crowd were trying to leave on orders of the military, other evacuees were sort of approaching the military police. When this noise that sounded like a shot was heard, the military police panicked. They thought that they were being shot at, and as a result they fired their shotguns into the crowd. The result was two dead and nine injured.

It was seven at night; it was dark, about dusk. A telephone call came in to me at my office in the hospital saying that a riot had taken place and that a lot of people were dead or injured; the voice on the phone said he didn't know how many. I immediately told the ambulance drivers who were on duty at the hospital to go down to the place to pick up these injured people.

I sent runners around to get the hospital doctors, nurses, and orderlies who were off duty, plus the warehouse staff to come to the hospital at once because I didn't know the nature and extent of the injuries. The ambulances went out to the entrance to the camp, and they brought the injured and, as we later discovered, some of the dead back to the hospital.

At the same time the riot at the northern part of the camp, around Block 24 which was across the firebreak across from the hospital, was in full progress. The rioters were searching for Tokutaro Slocum and Joe Masaoka and Fred Tayama and some others. There were a lot of people who were being sought out by the rioters. There was turmoil going on all over the camp.

As the ambulance was bringing up the injured and the dead from the entranceway, the military police followed the first two ambulances and came up to the hospital entrance. I was there, and I was only allowing the hospital personnel to come in, although the crowd from the entrance were sort of belligerent toward me. They were saying, "Let us in, let us in," like they were going to beat me up. But I stood on the steps and said, "No, nobody can come in except those who work in the hospital." They respected this, and they quieted down. The injured were lined up along the corridors inside the hospital.

The doctors came and looked at the ones lying on the stretchers in the corridors. Two were dead. The nine who were wounded were immediately brought into the surgical room, examined, and operated on as necessary. The Board of Inquiry from the Army headquarters in San Francisco came down and tried to whitewash the military police shooting incident. They tried to get the evacuee doctors and nurses and all the other witnesses to say that the evacuees who died or were injured were threatening or were in the process of attacking the military police and, therefore, it was justified for the military police to fire upon the evacuees. However, the medical examination, the records, and the trajectory of the bullets showed that the victims had been either shot in the side or in the back. Dr. Goto, who was chief of the medical staff and was the chief surgeon at that time, conducted the surgery and was asked to change his testimony and records to show that the bullets fired by the military police came from the front. He refused to do that, and I know specifically that as a result, his services were terminated the following day as chief of the medical staff. He was sent out of the hospital to some other relocation center.

The government didn't give us a chance. The government just

automatically said, You're part of the enemy. We consider you disloyal. We think you're going to commit sabotage. We know you're going to commit espionage because of your bloodline.

I can never justify this evacuation based upon law. It was clearly unconstitutional, regardless of the Yasui, the Hirabayashi, and the Korematsu cases; to me it was a flagrant disregard of individual rights, personal rights, constitutional rights, and it was a violation of due process. They never gave us a chance to show that we could still take our place in society, although at that time I think it would have been a very great travail for us to be in that kind of a society.

I believe that under all the circumstances, even if it were not the military policy, the Japanese and the Japanese Americans would have been evacuated anyway eventually. I think this because there were the politicians, plus economic interests, plus in some parts of the community, the anti-Japanese feeling was so strong.

I have no remaining anger towards the government for what they did. I believe I understand it. I have no lingering, festering animosity that makes me sour towards America. It's funny that I say so. I not only understand, but I can forgive the U.S. government for what they did. And despite all the hardships—and there's no way you can get away from all that—I understand that, and I think I can forgive the U.S. government for the tremendous miscalculation of us as a people in the society.

Am I left with a sense of betrayal? Yes, in this sense: the government did not really protect basic human rights, nor the basic legal procedural and substantive protective rights of individuals. Yes, I think in that sense the government, from President Roosevelt down through the secretary of war, the military commanders, and the politicians—the total forces for the evacuation—engaged, even if not intentionally, in a tremendous conspiratorial activity of maligning persons of Japanese ancestry. From that standpoint, the government and its proponents of the evacuation trampled upon our rights and definitely violated our rights, human as well as constitutional rights.

CHIYE TOMIHIRO

Minidoka

I was born in Portland, Oregon, in December of 1924. There was only three of us. My father was in business, my mother was a housewife, and I was going to school when the war started.

My father was involved in real estate. He had an interest in a lumber mill in Canada, and he had hopyards. Various things. He had a hotel building. He was also an attorney. He graduated from the University of Oregon Law School, but because he wasn't a citizen he couldn't practice law. So he spent a great deal of his time helping people, especially the Issei, with their legal problems, and he was very much respected in the community.

In 1940 things were getting a little better, especially the hotel business. It was a big hotel. It was a half a block, the property; and my father owned the building, and there were stores in it. We were having a pretty tough time until about 1940.

During the evacuation an attorney friend of my father's kind of ran the business for him. Evacuation came and the attorney agreed to keep the business going for a while, but after the war started and we were in camp for some time, things got to a point where there were still mortgage payments and then the man just didn't feel that he wanted to continue to handle it, so he felt it was best if we sold it. It was sold for practically nothing.

My father was arrested on December 7 during the FBI roundup. My mother and I were not home that evening. We went to some kind of a social affair at a church, and when we came home, they had ransacked the apartment, taken a lot of things, and left the door open, unlocked. Then we learned that my father had been taken away. We had a night clerk who told us that he had been taken away by the FBI. You know, it's really silly, the reactions you have. At the time we thought it was because he spoke English well and because he was quite prominent in the community, that they probably needed him for some interpreting or some darn thing like that. Never, you know, realizing that he was going to be interned. They stuck him in the Multnomah County jail, and I went down to see him the next day. Then they brought him back one day to pick up some things, and he said, don't worry, don't worry, but we didn't see him after that until we went to visit him in Santa Fe, New Mexico, where he was interned.

To me, the saddest thing that happened was when my father came out of internment, after being idle for four years. He had to resettle in Chicago, and he didn't have any money. No capital. No nothing, and even with his education. As you can imagine, a sixty-year-old man trying to get a white collar job—there was nothing available for him. My father kept looking for work, and he couldn't find anything. Finally he decided he would try opening some kind of an office and do bookkeeping services and try to sell real estate and things like that. He never was able to get back on his feet in the real sense of the word. I think that after having gone through the whole trauma of the Depression, and then, just when he was getting back on his feet, to have this second setback, I think that was just too much.

Going to camp was difficult for me socially because I was attending a school where there were so few Nisei. There were six or seven Nisei in the entire school, and although I did have some Nisei friends, it was such a change for me to suddenly be in this camp environment where everybody was Japanese, and it was kind of an awkward situation for me. I had a hard time making some real good friends. It took me a while. I felt like a little bit of an outcast for a while.

When I think about the evacuation now, it makes me very sad, more than anything else in the world. I think the feeling of being betrayed is probably the thing that really bothers me most of all, because I remember how we tried to be so patriotic, and we were so trusting. And we used to argue with our parents all the time because we'd say, "Oh, we're American citizens. Uncle Sam's going to take care of us, don't worry." This kind of thing. We always felt this way.

We were so damn naïve. I don't think any of us ever believed it would happen to us, and I think even as we were being hauled away we didn't believe it was happening to us. Just like the Jews being led to slaughter. I think that we were just like in a trance. Well, of course, we were awfully young, most of us. What could we do? We didn't know which way to turn. After all we were taught in the history books that our rights were going to be protected and all this other stuff. And I think that that feeling of having been betrayed is the thing that really makes me the saddest of anything.

We trusted so much in this country and, you know, it's like having a father who is a criminal or something, and you don't really want to believe that he is. See, you really don't want to think that, and so you just kind of push it out of your mind. It's very hard I think for younger people to realize this intense feeling that we had about loyalties to this country. And so we had this feeling of being betrayed. And to this day I really don't trust this country.

BEN TAKESHITA

Tule Lake

I was born in Alameda, California, in 1930. When I was four, our whole family moved across the bay to San Mateo, where my father became a gardener. That's where I went to grade school, and then I went into camp. I was eleven when evacuation came. After camp I started in eighth grade, two years behind, and then I went to San Mateo High. I went to San Mateo College after the Korean War, and I finally graduated from Berkeley in 1958.

In school, even before the war, a lot of us Japanese used to play handball together; we were a clique. And the reason we were in cliques is because we didn't feel that welcome with the whites. When Pearl Harbor was struck we tried to stick together because we didn't know what to do; we felt that in groups we would be stronger. In our classes, though, we didn't have those cliques. It was only on lunch breaks or before school. In classes I didn't feel any discrimination. In fact, a Filipino schoolmate of mine after the war started would bring pictures of the Japanese planes being shot down and say, "Hey, howja like this?" And I would say, "Oh, that's great!" But you know, I felt kind of as if he was testing me out to see what my loyalty was. It was those subtle things that I felt uncomfortable about.

Anyway, I considered myself American, definitely. I didn't know Japan. It's true when I was four years old, my parents took us to

Japan for about six months and left my two oldest brothers there. I have some memories of that, almost like a dream. But other than that I didn't know how to speak Japanese except to my parents in broken Japanese. We were going to Japanese school after our regular classes, but that was more because we had to, and I didn't personally feel I was part of Japan. The real exposure developed when my two brothers came back in 1939. After that we weren't supposed to talk back to the older persons, and we had to obey, and this kind of a strict thing started to come into my life.

After Pearl Harbor there were a lot of rumors flying about—that we might be sent away. Also there were blackouts, and curfews, and we had to turn in our radios that we were listening to. I remember thinking, Gee, what's going to happen to us next? But beyond that, I don't remember much. Anyway, our family was big, and we were poor—father, mother, and eight brothers and sisters. So we couldn't really afford to buy defense stamps to show that we were Americans. I had again a guilty feeling in making the effort to buy them rather than candy to prove that I was American and was for America and not for Japan. That kind of thing I certainly remember.

I also remember the day that we had to leave our house and walk to this assembly point in San Mateo and then get on the bus to go to Tanforan which was that racetrack. I remember those posters, all of a sudden on every telephone pole. The posters made us again feel guilty and that we better again stick closer together. We were just fearful. And the same question occurred to us, What's going to happen to us? But in our family, anyway, we didn't discuss this with our parents. We didn't ask them anything. We just assumed that they would take care of us and do things. I don't recall much discussion at the family table, for example, about these things.

We were told by our parents to wear as much as we could so we could take more with us—several shirts and jackets. I was eleven, so I had to carry more things. I'm about in the middle. I have a younger brother, two years younger than I, and a younger sister, four years younger than I, and the youngest, who was then just a baby. I remember carrying things and walking down the street to the assembly point and I remember seeing our neighbors, the Hakujin and Portugese, peeking out of their curtains. They were friends we used to go to school with, and yet they were not coming out and saying, "Gee, I'm sorry you're leaving," "Wish you luck," "Come back," or whatever. They were afraid of being accused of being Jap lovers. Anyway, I felt like an outcast walking down that street. We had a strong feeling of shame. We felt we were going to be taken away as if we did something wrong.

From Tanforan, we went to Topaz, and I remember going on this train and knowing that train could only go south because we were on the peninsula, and from San Francisco you could only go that way. I remember asking the MP when we got on the train if, when we came to San Mateo, we could open the shade and look? And he said, no, definitely no. I remember him watching to make sure that I didn't open the shades. It was still daylight, but the shades were drawn so it was dark, and we really didn't know where we were going. I remember consciously counting the bells, you know, the railroad crossings, trying to figure out if this was San Mateo and wondering about when we would get back to there and trying to listen for every little thing that might help me identify it. I remember that feeling vividly, and I remember that it was a long train trip, the first in my life. After that I don't recall anything until Topaz.

At Topaz, the first thing you noticed was the fine cementlike dust. You stepped down and swhoof, swhoof, swhoof; It was like walking on fine cement. The barracks were just built out in this desert, and there was no rain.

Topaz felt like a prison. There was this one older man, an Issei, who went too close to the fence, and the guards shot him. In those days many of the older people picked seashells and they would break them to use for their artistic work, making flowers or whatever. So this man got too close to the fence one day while he was picking shells and was shot in the back as he reached down to pick a shell off the ground near the fence. And so, because of this kind of incident, we knew that it was definitely a prison and that we'd better not venture too close to the fences.

I was at Topaz until September of 1943. From there we went to Tule Lake. We were sent there because my two older brothers had gone to Japan for an education from 1934 to 1939. I found out recently that while they were in Japan, they were discriminated against because they were Americans. The authorities tried to force them to join the Japanese Army, but they refused to. So they were very much aware that they were American citizens by the time we got into Topaz.

When the no-no yes-yes questionnaire came out, my oldest brother, who was about nineteen, thought it was absurd for people to answer those questions yes-yes and volunteer for the U.S. Army when our citizenship meant nothing. He was one of those who went to mess halls and talked to groups trying to convince them to answer no-no. I remember he was taken by the FBI to be questioned, but he always returned. He had become the leader in our house; my father was not that much of a leader by then. He also tried to convince my other brother, who really wanted to stay in America, and be a scholar and be educated, to vote no-no. But I remember the infighting going on between them. He finally convinced my second brother to go no-no. I remember my parents saying that they were voting no-no because we wanted to stay together as a family as long as possible. At that point I was thirteen and didn't know what the issues were except that if you answered no-no, you were going to be considered disloyal. As a no-no family we had to be moved to Tule Lake, and we went together by train and arrived September 1943.

Compared to Topaz, there was a lot of grass at Tule. And being in California, you felt you were close to home. My brothers, within a month, started a Japanese-language school, and being a brother I started attending immediately, beginning in October 1943. Come January or February of 1944, when the American school started, most of us wanted to go to the English classes and go to Japanese school only after school or something. But my brother decided that we wouldn't go to English school, and we would go to Japanese school full-time, because their feeling was that eventually we were going to be sent to Japan, and we better learn Japanese, otherwise we'd never make it.

So they exposed us to Japanese culture and Japanese education, as they understood it. Kibeis taught us and used methods like making you sit on the floor for an hour, and if you moved you got hit on the head. This kind of thing. They were definitely serious. So when the English classes started and we wanted to go, my older brother, who already knew Japanese and didn't have to learn it, was the only one who went to American school. He was going to high school then; the rest of us had to go to Japanese-language school. I guess that was the first time I resented my oldest brother who forced us to do something we didn't want. To me English was my language. Yet their purpose was to teach us Japanese and forget English. You know enough English, they told us, now you have to learn Japanese. We had no choice, we knew who the boss was and we just went along and went to Japanese school. All day we were in Japanese school. We were learning the language and being hit. The school forbade speaking any English; you had to speak only Japanese even at home. So when we came home and our friends who weren't going to the Japanese school came over and we started talking English with them, the teachers next door would hear and the next day come around and say, "You spoke English." So we would be made examples of, and we would definitely be hit harder—with the ends of those cot beds. We soon learned to speak Japanese.

At our school the boys had to cut their hair, you know, bozu, and the girls had to wear pigtails. And Tule Lake started *wasshoi-wasshoi* ("an exercise chant") running for exercise. About the summer of 1944, there were these *seinendans* ("young men's groups") beginning to form, and every morning in groups, they would do wasshoi-wasshoi. That to us was a very political thing—pro-Japan. That's understandable, considering they committed themselves to no-no, but when those movements started we didn't continue the wasshoi-wasshoi. We stopped it. We were allowed to let our hair grow a little bit, not as long as it is now, but at least crew-cut style, and we got away from the nationalistic things. But in school we learned Japanese ethics, *shushin* ("moral teachings") and about *oyakoko* ("filial obligation to one's parents") and soroban (a Japanese abacus). We learned *chi-li*, which is geography, and then we had history. We went through the whole educational thing in our schools. And to this day I feel I know a lot about Japan because of that education, because it was very rigid and we had to learn.

At Tule Lake there were food riots, because there was not enough food. And this guy next door to us got shot. He was a driver named Okamura. He was a big guy, but so gentle. He used to play with us kids, and he was always fun. But he was big. Evidently the MPs got scared when he started coming towards them to ask them what they wanted because they stopped his truck. He was the driver. He got out and went towards the guard because he wanted to know why he was being stopped. He was stopped at the gate for some reason and one of the guards who had a rifle went to the back of the truck, which was halfway through the gate. The cab of the truck was inside the gate, and the guard went to the back of the truck and Okamura got out and the guard told him to come to the back. Apparently it was the way Okamura walked toward him that made the guard feel that he was being threatened. The guard shot him from about five feet away and killed him. The guard was charged with misuse of military property and fined fifty cents for the bullet. There was a court-martial, but he wasn't convicted of anything.

There was tension because of this type of thing. From time to time they had raids and came into our barracks and looked for things. My oldest brother, the teacher who advocated the no-no thing, was questioned a lot about what kind of activities were going on in camp. He was really a teacher and he hadn't gotten himself involved in the politics of the camp, but they questioned him about that, because having *undokai* ("sports tournament") was militaristic or nationalistic as far as the camp authorities were concerned. After about two or three days of questioning, they got to a point where they said, "Okay, we're going to take you out." And it was obvious that he was going before a firing squad with MPs ready with rifles.

He was asked if he wanted a cigarette; he said no. . . . You want a blindfold? . . . No. They said, "Stand up here," and they went as far as saying, "Ready, aim, fire," and pulling the trigger, but the rifles had no bullets. They just went click, and when I heard that four or five years ago I really got mad. To think that they would go through all that. My brother talks as if there was nothing to it. But I really got mad listening to it, because the torture that he must have gone through, and the MPs allowing it to happen. I mean it's like the German camps. Torturing the people for the sake of trying to get them to break down or something. At the time, we didn't know what happened. I guess he talked about it to my parents, but we were not privy to that.

Anyway, you constantly heard about these riots, these beatings, these factions, and so you never knew where you were. We were told just to concentrate on our Japanese. And that's what we did. It got to the point after about two years that when friends would come to talk to me, I couldn't speak to them in English. It would just come out in Japanese, and they couldn't understand me.

Eight of us left camp in October 1945 to go back to San Mateo.

My oldest brother decided to go back to Japan. The second brother decided to graduate from high school before he left camp, but he was definitely not going to go to Japan, so my oldest brother was the only one who did. He felt the obligation to go back. I didn't understand that at the time, but I had a lot of resentment for him, because he not only forced us to go to Japanese school, but sometime in mid-1945, when he had a dispute with the other teacher, he forced us to quit the school. Now we got used to that school and had made friends, but he forced us to go to another school. My older sisters and my younger brother and I resented that a lot. I feel that because he taught us Japanese and so on, he felt that he had to go back. You know, he didn't want to lose face, and he just didn't want to stay in America. My second older brother only wanted to study, study, study; so he didn't want to go back to Japan. He wanted to stay in the United States. His mind was made up, and he was old enough that the older brother couldn't influence him anymore. My oldest brother left for Japan in early 1946, a few months after we had already been out.

My oldest brother was in Japan until 1960. He wanted to come back. He got married over there, and I saw him there during the Korean War. I'd visit him on weekends and my resentment was beginning to soften. When I started with the Department of Employment my brother asked if I would sponsor him and his wife and his two boys to come back to the United States. That's when I had to really decide whether I wanted to do this after all the things he had done to us. But I decided, well, yeah, I guess I should. Looking around at my other brothers and sisters, I felt that I was the only one who really had a steady job at that point. I guess I was the only one who could sponsor him. Both my older brothers had renounced their citizenship, and they got it back through the Wayne Collins class action suit to restore American citizenship for the renunciants.

When I got back to San Mateo, I should have been a high-school sophomore, but because I had gone to Japanese-language school I was two years behind. I didn't want to go back to my old school because of the shame, because I was two years behind. And so I ended up going to this school that I considered to be our rival before the war, and I went into the eighth grade there. Then the year after that I started high school. That's when I really started feeling very bitter about this whole experience. I was bitter towards my brother for making us two years behind; my former classmates were all in high school, and here I was, still in grade school.

So when I got into high school, I made sure that they weren't going to mistake me for an enemy again. I made sure that I joined the A Capella Choir, which no Japanese American participated in. I joined the band. I joined the Junior Statesmen. This was while I was going to school, so I had to budget my time. I had to really get back after school to do some chores at the place where I worked, but I tried to tie everything in by having lunch meetings. The A Capella Choir started half an hour before school, so I would go to the school early enough to participate in that, and from the very beginning I got involved in these activities and encouraged others to participate and not stay in cliques, and to mingle with the rest of the students. But at lunchtime they would stick together. I would always make sure to greet them, but I would eat with the other people, the Hakujins, and try to assimilate. That was how I spent my full four years. My family was Buddhist, but I didn't want to go to a Buddhist church, because it was too Japanesey. I mingled with Hakujins and made a point of doing that.

WILSON MAKABE

442nd Regimental Combat Team, Italy

I was born in Loomis, Placer County, California, about a hundred miles west of Reno, on January 11, 1919. My father's name was Shinzo Makabe, and my mother's name was Nao, originally Tejima, or Teshima. My father came to this country in 1897, and my mother came in 1903. I had three brothers and four sisters. I am the seventh of eight with one younger sister.

Before the war we had over a hundred acres, a fruit farm that was cleared and in production. We had mostly plums, peaches, and pears, with grapevines planted between the trees. And then we had about thirty acres of straight vineyard. And we were rather proud that we had the finest grapes in the country. The orchard wasn't as big or as productive as some of the others, because some of the trees were fairly old. The grape varieties were planted in such a way that the earliest grape harvest would begin around the first of June, and we would continue to harvest right on through until November.

My mother passed away in 1930, when I was eleven. But by then, my two oldest sisters were married. My oldest living sister is Grace, seventy years old, and she became the acting mother. With her energy, she worked right along with the fellows—an amazing person—and then in the evenings, she would do the housework. And even my younger sister, who was only nine when my mother passed away, she'd help with the housework and the yardwork too.

December 7 was quite a shock. We were working the back, at the end of the ranch, which is almost a mile from the house. We went in for lunch. (We were all working on Sunday, because in those days in farming you worked seven days a week. And because we were in school during the week, we had to work on the weekends.) Our oldest sister, Hide, was there. She was married, and her husband was sort of disabled. So she was staying at the house. And we had this cottage right next to the main house where they lived. She came in to tell us that the Japanese bombed Pearl Harbor.

It was hard for us to believe. But shortly after that, while we were eating, a car pulled up and people got out and identified themselves as being from the FBI. They started talking to us and my father. Then we went into the house. And that's when one of the most amazing things happened: a person who had never been in our house before knew just where to go to look for things. He pulled out correspondence that my father had from Japan. Some old papers from way back, twenty, thirty years before. So, he gathered some things up and he said, "You come with me," and he took my father. My father never had a chance to pack his clothing, or his suitcase, or anything. He went in the car, and that's the last we saw of him until he joined the family in Tule Lake.

When the rest of the family was evacuated, my family and I went to a place called Arboga, a camp just being built in the desert, outside of Marysville, in the Sacramento Valley. It was the end of May, and it was hot and dusty. I can remember the tar-paper barracks and the community toilets with bathrooms. We had to help to construct the kitchen facilities and got paid only four dollars or so per month. But I signed up for whatever was available. I ended up as a fireman, and then, when they had an appeal for sugar-beet thinners, I took that on.

There were about thirty people, a few of them Kibei, who had worked on farms earlier as migrant workers. They were used to doing some of that work, and they made out pretty good. That stoop labor was the hardest work I ever did in my life. We were on a farm outside of Twin Falls, Idaho, staying in a labor camp about two miles outside the city. And then, when the beet thinning was over, two of us went to work on another farm, where they raised cattle, oats, barley, and vegetables too.

One day I went with the owner of the big ranch to Twin Falls to buy some fruit. He went every year to this orchard and bought peaches. I looked at the trees there, and I thought, oh, that's sad! They never pruned the young peach trees, about eight years old. The fruit was so small. In the apple orchard, you couldn't even see the sun because the branches were so thick, and the fruit was so small. Anyway, I told him we used to raise fruit; we pruned heavily and we thinned and we had huge, beautiful fruit. I never thought anymore about it and went back to the other ranch. A week or so later, the fellow called and asked the owner where I worked if I could go to work for him. He offered me a job and said his mother was just placed in a nursing home in Twin Falls. He was a county commissioner, named Kenyon Green, who had a big, old, family ranch house, but he himself had built a more modern house on the same property, maybe a quarter of a mile or so away. So, this family house was vacant. He offered me the house if I would stay and work for him year-round and farm the way we farmed in California. He said he would go to Tule Lake and bring the family over.

Well, it took a few weeks to get the paperwork done, and by then my father had rejoined the others in Tule Lake. So, I think it was the early part of December, 1942, that Green took his car, drove to Twin Falls, picked up my two sisters, my brother, and my father, and what luggage they could load on the car.

When we were living and working in Idaho, I heard about the organization of the 442nd. That was the latter part of February, 1943. I tried the local draft board, but they didn't even know about it, so I took a bus to Salt Lake City and signed up for the 442nd there. They said, "Go home and we'll let you know when to report." So on June 6 I was notified to report to Fort Douglas, Utah, where I was sworn in. Then I went to basic training at Camp Shelby, Mississippi. But, before I got there, I was given a ten-day pass, plus travel time. I was able to go to Loomis to visit the farm.

I walked from where I got off the train—it was only a short walk —to the fruit house where the manager had his office. While I was in his office, some people—and the worst part of it was that some of them were people I knew and grew up with—joined a bunch of rabble-rousers and wanted to make a riot. So, the manager of the fruit house, Charles Day, told me that we had better leave and took me out to the offices of the justice of the peace. He asked me where I wanted to go. I said, "Oh, whatever might be the safest route, and then I'll call the MPs as escorts." It took about half an hour before the MPs came down in a staff car. They took me out to the farm and then later took me out to Auburn, where I could catch the bus to Tule Lake. I decided I would go up there. I had plans to spend several days in Loomis, to see how the fruit was doing and so on, but instead I left after maybe a couple of hours. I was run out of town, yes.

I remember one girl, a Spanish girl, I never knew her name. She tried to argue with those others telling them that I was in uniform and that I was a soldier, that I was a good citizen and grew up there. Yet some of those people were prominent people, active people, big basketball players who were deferred because they worked on farms.

I got up to Tule Lake and I was able to get a ride from the community up to the camp. They wanted to see my pass and travel orders. And armed MP checked me in at the gate. You could see the guard towers, the barbed-wire fence. Oh, what a depressing scene. To be an American soldier and having to be frisked. Anyway, I spent only one night in Tule Lake. I remember waiting in line with the families. I had two sisters up there. The older sister had four children living in one room; by the time you get six cots in there, you don't have room for anything else. Then my other sister had three children, and I stayed there right on the floor on a blanket and waited in line for dinner. Everybody had to wait in line for the community toilets and the showers. It was sad. When I visited with some of the kids I grew up with, some of them asked me how it was "outside"; others called me a damn fool for volunteering and said, "All you're going to be is cannon fodder," something you've probably heard before.

Anyway, I just didn't feel like staying any longer, and here I had the extra ten days, but in fact I spent a couple more days in Idaho and then I reported to Camp Shelby for basic. We went from Camp Shelby to Newport News, Virginia. We shipped out in old Liberty ships—thirty days on the ocean in that big armada— and then we landed in Anzio, Italy. We didn't know right up to the day before where we were going to go or what our destination was. I was with the 442nd, I Company, 3rd battalion, a rifleman.

I saw only about thirty days of combat before I got wounded. I was in northern Italy, up as far as the Arno River across from

Pisa. We could see the enemy with our binoculars. We could see the Leaning Tower; the Germans were actually using it as an observation post, but we couldn't lob any shells there.

I really don't know what happened. The last thing I remember was somebody said, "Look out!" I was out for about ten days. When I came to and opened my eyes, someone was working on me in the battalion aid station, a blackout tent. They had flashlights and were working on me. I had both legs in casts. When they saw me open my eyes they gave me a shot and knocked me out again. Next time I woke up I was in a hospital fifteen miles back, the field station. This was in June of 1944, and that tent could be mighty hot, even when they had the flaps up. I remember when I first opened my eyes, there was a black fellow in the cot next to me; he was groaning, and when things quieted down, the nurse came and pulled a blanket over him and took him away. I saw others that were rushed right back to the general hospitals farther back. For ten days I had both legs in a cast, a body cast up to my armpits, and then they got me back to the general hospital near Rome, flying me during the night.

The first morning the nurse came to take my temperature which was pretty high, I guess. He dashed out of the room, and the chief nurse came over and said, "What are you complaining about?" I said, "I'm not complaining." She said, "There are other sick people." I said, "I didn't say a thing." The nurse said she would be back with the doctor. This was early in the morning, before seven o'clock, even before we got breakfast. I remember the doctor came, took one look at my foot, said, "Get him up to surgery." Gangrene had started up on my right leg; my toes were already turning black. I don't know how long I was in surgery, but it was about midnight when I finally came to.

The chief nurse was still on duty and beside my bed. I remember that night somehow because she said, "I'm sorry. I didn't realize your condition and the circumstances." And she said, "We will have to take your leg off." I was so weak I couldn't lift my head, but I said, "No, I can still feel that leg; it's still there." Then I said, "How about my back?" I remember when they lifted me off that bed they put me on a litter to take me to surgery. Maggots! That bed was crawling with big white maggots about an inch long. I said, "God." At that time I didn't realize they *put* the maggots in there to eat the dead flesh up on my back, because when they took the body cast off I had a lot of dead flesh that was inside the cast. But I remember asking that nurse, "How about my back?" I was still groggy. She said, "The back is all right, but we have to take the leg off."

They didn't expect me to leave the field hospital, let alone the general hospital. I spent over four months in that general hospital in Rome. They never thought I'd ever make it. First several months there, every time I opened my eyes, seemed like a chaplain was sitting there by my bed. He came to see me when they finally gave me my orders that I would be heading home. First they put me back into a body cast. I had several shattered fractures in my left leg. So they moved me to Naples, kept me there for ten days. Then a big general hospital where they kept me for about two weeks, and then they flew me to Casablanca for another two weeks. Eventually they flew me home by way of the Azores, Bermuda, and Miami, Florida. I landed in the States on December 23, 1944. And boy, was I happy when I got back on U.S. soil!

One of the first things they offered me was a free telephone call to any place in the country. So I called my brother, George, in Idaho. That's when I learned that someone had set fire to our house in Loomis. Apparently it was within hours after the radio announcement that the Japanese people could leave the camps and return to their homes on the West Coast. When he told me that . . . oh, you can't describe the feeling. I remember the pain and the hurt, the suffering in the hospitals in Italy—that was nothing compared to this. I cried for the first time. All that time in the hospital I don't remember shedding a tear, but I cried that night. You wonder if it was worth going through all that.

It wasn't much of a house but my dad had built the thing, with some of the other people helping. In those days everybody helped each other. It was a big house where all of us grew up, and I remember a big dining room that fed all of the help at one time, so that we would have as many as twenty or more people sitting around. We had some valuable things that had been brought from Japan that were stored in one section of the house. Everything was probably ransacked very early, but we had silk screens. And I remember we had a beautiful Bengal tiger all hand stitched. We had put all those things into what in those days were called parlors. We boarded up the house; we put our valuables in there—pictures, gorgeous things we couldn't carry into camp. We put all that into this room, and hoped that it would be there when we got back.

Anyway, in Miami we were taken to the Orange Bowl game, and were really treated nicely. I remember a retired general saw me. He was a classmate of my original battalion commander at West Point. He said, "You know, it would be a privilege to be able to push you around and take you wherever you want to go." For several days he did just that. He would take me out to any of the places or any place around the hospital that I wanted to see. I still hear from him, General Harris.

Until I arrived in Florida, my cast was sort of smelly, and I had lost weight until I was about sixty pounds, cast and all. They sent me to Brigham City, Bushnell General Hospital. When I first arrived in Miami, they gave us three choices: first was Letterman General Hospital, second was Walter Reed—because I had heard that that was an outstanding hospital—and third was Bushnell, because my family was in Idaho at the time. So the next day, the first thing, I was on my way to a hospital in Atlantic City, and then to Bushnell in Brigham City, Utah. There were quite a few Nisei there. I remember an officer, Bill Oshiro, who was a leg amputee, but he was able to get some of the other fellows to push my bed. I was in a frame and in traction. They pushed my bed outside when the girls from Salt Lake City came with all the Japanese food. They had entertainment and everything for us.

The doctors did surgery on my leg. I was there about five months. After surgery, fifty days after surgery, in checking my leg, I said, "My bone's sticking out the side of my leg. The doctor said, "Nah, that's only hard tissue." So he just let it go. Later on, after about a month, they had X rays taken. The commanding officer, I remember, a Colonel Myers, a former orthopedic surgeon, looked at the X rays and he said, "Who the hell did that surgery? We're going to have to break that again and straighten that out. There's a right-angle fracture." My bone was actually sticking out. He said, "If we try to fit him with an artificial leg and he's going to have to try to walk, he's going to . . ." There was no way it would heal right. So they rebroke that leg, reset it, and later on they transferred me to Walter Reed.

I remember ambulatory about the first of December, 1946, about two and a half years after I got hurt. I had the long brace on my left leg, artificial leg on my right—nothing like latest things today.

I could barely walk, it was painful, but I made up my mind that I was going to walk. The doctor said I would never walk again. I just made up my mind that I wasn't going to have to live in a wheelchair. Well, I stayed there long enough.

I tried to get into American University; they had this special training session for service losses, and I thought maybe I'd try to go into that field of work and get my degree there. But I couldn't get around well enough to actually attend the classes yet—it was only a few days after I started walking—so I got a little apartment in Washington so I could go back for therapy at Walter Reed. Then in March, 1947, I heard that my dad had had a stroke, and I flew back and visited the place. At that time my brothers and sisters had come back from Idaho, they had moved into the cabin that we had.

How did we get home and how was it? We bought a used hospital bed, and the furniture was very minimal. I asked my sister, Grace, if she could remember about their coming back to California. She said it felt like the old forty-niners. Our savings, what we'd earned in Idaho, everything was gone. We bought an old used Chevy, we rented a trailer, we put our few things in it and drove back. Coming over the mountains we had troubles. An old recap tire blew out. When we got back we saw this one cabin, just two rooms, where my dad and my sister stayed. Then I went back, and I saw the remains of our big house—the concrete foundations, the half-burned birch trees, what was left—standing there.

My older sister never did get married. She took care of my dad. My older sister stayed and helped my brother George and my dad to renew the farm. My father would grasp a grapevine where the tops had died—the roots were good; the suckers would come up. Digging down with a shovel, getting down to the root head, crown, cutting the trunk, and putting new buds into that. And covering it up to the top. That was hard work. One day after lunch he lay down and then he couldn't get up. We didn't know why. We went out to work and thought we'd let him rest. That evening we found that he was completely paralyzed.

He was in the hospital about three months. We just couldn't put him in the county hospital—pride and all. We just worked extra hard and borrowed a few extra dollars and tried to get back on our feet. He lived for maybe three years, completely paralyzed. He was a big, strong person. He weighed about 160 pounds. He was a sumo champion and was undefeated in northern California. I couldn't do any outside work, so I started taking care of my father before he died. This is about March 1947. My sister got out and worked on the farm, pruning, thinning, outside. I learned to cook pretty good, and I did that until the fall of 1947, when I could start junior college in Auburn. It became impossible to operate the farm as one unit, so we divided up the property into so many acres each to those of us still living.

We took a beating. My oldest brother was in the Army for two years before they had started the foreclosure. We had about a $1,200 mortgage on fifteen acres in his name—the best vineyard on the property. But he didn't know about that mortgage being foreclosed until he came back in 1946, after five years in the service. He came back and found he didn't have the property he'd heard about. There was a law on the books that Congress had passed called the Soldiers and Sailors Relief Act that said it was illegal to foreclose. The law was commonly called The Moratorium. But by the time he got back he didn't have any money, and he had a young family. Because of the sentiment in Placer County, it would have been impossible for us to get a favorable judgment even if he did try to recover some of that property. You know, that piece of property changed hands several times. We had a chance to buy it back for about $45,000, but we couldn't accept the idea that we had to buy our own property that was legally ours to begin with— the family ranch. It sold for $800,000 because it's right off that freeway. Just figure what the whole ranch would have been worth in today's market.

When I first sold part of my property, the fellow who wanted to buy wanted to put in an over-the-freeway restaurant. He had the forms drawn up and everything. This fellow came up and I said I didn't want to sell it for the price he was offering. He had the nerve to say, "Don't you think you owe the community of Loomis an obligation to get that project going?" I didn't sit back, I said, "You said the wrong thing. I served in the Army. I went through hell. I've suffered these disabilities all these years, and I got run out of this town by bastards like you that didn't even go into the service, who got deferred because they wanted to stay out. And you say *I* owe the community! I think the community owes me a lot." I said, "I don't feel a *bit* of obligation to community."

I said, "I want a certain price, and that price has just gone up."

A little later on I sold part of it for not much, but that restaurant never did materialize. Just the idea that somebody would say something like that! I could walk down the street and hold my head high.

One of the fellows had a service station, and when I first came back, I went into this station. I knew the family. The fellow's father was one of the old settlers in Loomis and knew my father well. When he saw me at the service station getting out, struggling to get out of the car, to fill it with gas, he came out. After I was all through he said, "I'd like to talk to you." I said, "Hop in." He traveled with me down the road from the station. He said, "Y'know I was one bastard. I had signs on my service station saying 'No Jap trade wanted.'" He said, "Now, when I see you come back like that, I feel so small." And he was crying. That was one of my experiences when I came back.

ABOUT THE AUTHOR

JOHN TATEISHI was born in Los Angeles in 1939. At age three he was evacuated with his family to the Manzanar internment camp, where he remained until 1945. He attended high school in Los Angeles and then spent two years in the Army. He studied English literature at the University of California at Berkeley, and did his graduate work in literature at the University of California, Davis. From 1967 to 1970 he taught literature at a college associated with the University of London, England, and from 1970 to 1981 at the City College of San Francisco. In 1976 he became involved in the Japanese American Citizens League's redress movement and, at the national convention in 1978, was appointed chairman of the National Redress Committee. He now serves as the National Redress Director of the JACL.

Mr. Tateishi lives in Marin County, California, with his wife Carol and his children, Stephen and Sarah.